NEW CENTURY BIBLE COMMENTARY

General Editors

RONALD E. CLEMENTS
(Old Testament)

MATTHEW BLACK
(New Testament)

Ecclesiastes

NEW CENTURY BIBLE COMMENTARY

Based on the Revised Standard Version

Ecclesiastes

R. N. Whybray

WM. B. EERDMANS PUBL. CO., GRAND RAPIDS

MARSHALL, MORGAN & SCOTT PUBL. LTD., LONDON

First published 1989 by Marshall Morgan & Scott, England

Printed in the United States of America
for
Wm. B. Eerdmans Publishing Company
255 Jefferson Ave. S.E., Grand Rapids, MI 49503
and
Marshall Morgan & Scott
Middlesex House, 34-42 Cleveland Street, London W1P 5FB, UK
Marshall Morgan & Scott ISBN 0-551-01853-4

Library of Congress Cataloging-in-Publication Data

Whybray, R.N. (Roger Norman)
Ecclesiastes : based on the Revised Standard Version.

(New century Bible commentary)
Includes index.
1. Bible. O.T. Ecclesiastes—Commentaries. I. Bible.
O.T. Ecclesiastes. English. Revised Standard. 1989.
II. Title. III. Series.
BS1475.3.W45 1989 223'.8077 88-33511
Eerdmans ISBN 0-8028-0406-3

CONTENTS

PREFACE

Scholarly interest in Ecclesiastes has greatly increased in recent years. It has given rise – in addition to numerous articles in the learned journals – to three new commentaries apart from my own, all of which have appeared since I began my task: those of J. A. Loader, J. L. Crenshaw (both listed in my bibliography) and G. Ogden. The last of these, published by the JSOT Press, Sheffield in 1987, appeared when my work was already completed, though its author's approach to the book had already been indicated by a number of articles published in *Vetus Testamentum* and elsewhere. Professor Crenshaw's commentary was kindly made available to me by the publishers in advance of its publication, and I have been able to consult it with profit from the outset, although I have refrained from making overt reference to it. Each of these three scholars has made a valuable contribution to the study of Ecclesiastes. The present-day student of the book is well served.

R. N. Whybray
May 1988

ABBREVIATIONS

BIBLICAL

OLD TESTAMENT (*OT*)

Gen.	Jg.	1 Chr.	Ps.	Lam.	Ob.	Hag.
Exod.	Ru.	2 Chr.	Prov.	Ezek.	Jon.	Zech.
Lev.	1 Sam.	Ezr.	Ec.	Dan.	Mic.	Mal.
Num.	2 Sam.	Neh.	Ca.	Hos.	Nah.	
Dt.	1 Kg.	Est.	Isa.	Jl	Hab.	
Jos.	2 Kg.	Job	Jer.	Am.	Zeph.	

APOCRYPHA (*Apoc.*)

1 Esd.	Tob.	Ad.Est.	Sir.	S 3 Ch.	Bel	1 Mac.
2 Esd.	Jdt.	Wis.	Bar.	Sus.	Man.	2 Mac.
			Ep. Jer.			

NEW TESTAMENT (*NT*)

Mt.	Ac.	Gal.	1 Th.	Tit.	1 Pet.	3 Jn
Mk	Rom.	Eph.	2 Th.	Phm.	2 Pet.	Jude
Lk.	1 C.	Phil.	1 Tim.	Heb.	1 Jn	Rev.
Jn	2 C.	Col.	2 Tim.	Jas	2 Jn	

GENERAL

AB	*The Anchor Bible*, Garden City, N.Y.
AJBI	*Annual of the Japanese Biblical Institute*
AJSL	*American Journal of Semitic Languages and Literatures*
Alt.	*Altertum*
ANET	*Ancient Near Eastern Texts Relating to the Old Testament*, ed. J. B. Pritchard, Princeton, 1969[3]
AOAT	*Alter Orient und Altes Testament*, Kevelaer
ATD	*Das Alte Testament Deutsch*, Göttingen
BASOR	*Bulletin of the American Schools of Oriental Research*

BAT	*Die Botschaft des Alten Testaments*, Stuttgart
BCAT	*Biblischer Commentar über das Alte Testament*, Leipzig
BDB	*Hebrew and English Lexicon of the Old Testament*, ed. F. Brown, S. R. Driver and C. A. Briggs, Oxford, 1907
BETL	*Bibliotheca Ephemeridum Theologicarum Lovaniensium*, Louvain
BHS	*Biblia Hebraica Stuttgartensia*, ed. K. Elliger and W. Rudolph, Stuttgart, 1977
Bib.	*Biblica*
BKAT	*Biblischer Kommentar, Altes Testament*, Neukirchen
BT	*The Bible Translator*
BTB	*Biblical Theology Bulletin*
BWANT	*Beiträge zur Wissenschaft vom Alten und Neuen Testament*, Stuttgart
BZ	*Biblische Zeitschrift*
BZAW	*Beihefte zur Zeitschrift für die Alttestamentliche Wissenschaft*, Berlin
CB	*Cambridge Bible for Schools and Colleges*, Cambridge
CBC	*Cambridge Bible Commentary on the New English Bible*, Cambridge
CBQ	*Catholic Biblical Quarterly*
CenB	*Century Bible*, Edinburgh
CJT	*Canadian Journal of Theology*
Conc.	*Concilium*
CTM	*Concordia Theological Monthly*
DSB	*The Daily Study Bible*, Edinburgh and Philadelphia
EB	*Études Bibliques*, Paris
ET	English translation
ETL	*Ephemerides Theologicae Lovanienses*, Louvain
ExB	*The Expositor's Bible*, London
Exp.	*The Expositor*
ExpT	*Expository Times*
FOTL	*The Forms of the Old Testament Literature*, Grand Rapids
GK	*Gesenius' Hebrew Grammar*, ed. E. Kautsch, revised by A. E. Cowley, Oxford, 1910
HAT	*Handbuch zum Alten Testament*, Tübingen
Heb.	Hebrew
HKAT	*Handkommentar zum Alten Testament*, Göttingen
HSAT	*Die Heilige Schrift des Alten Testaments*, Bonn
HUCA	*Hebrew Union College Annual*
IB	*The Interpreter's Bible*, New York

ICC	*International Critical Commentary*, Edinburgh
Int.	*Interpretation*
JBL	*Journal of Biblical Literature*
JBR	*Journal of Bible and Religion*
JJS	*Journal of Jewish Studies*
JNES	*Journal of Near Eastern Studies*
JNSL	*Journal of Northwest Semitic Languages*
JQR	*Jewish Quarterly Review*
JSOT	*Journal for the Study of the Old Testament*
JSS	*Journal of Semitic Studies*
JTS	*Journal of Theological Studies*
KAT	*Kommentar zum Alten Testament*, Leipzig
KBL	*Lexicon in Veteris Testamenti Libros*, ed. L. Koehler and W. Baumgartner
KHC	*Kurzer Hand-Commentar zum Alten Testament*, Tübingen
KHS	*Kleinkommentar zur Heiligen Schrift*, Düsseldorf
LB	*Lire la Bible*, Paris
LBBC	*Layman's Bible Book Commentary*, Nashville
LBC	*Layman's Bible Commentaries*, London
LD	*Lectio Divina*, Paris
LXX	The Septuagint
MS(S)	manuscript(s)
MT	*The Masoretic Text*
NEB	*The New English Bible*
NEchtB	*Die Neue Echter Bibel*, Würzburg
NF	Neue Folge
NS	New Series, nouvelle série
OLZ	*Orientalische Literaturzeitung*
OS	*Oudtestamentische Studiën*, Leiden
OTL	*Old Testament Library*, London and Philadelphia
OTM	*Old Testament Message*, Dublin
PEQ	*Palestine Exploration Quarterly*
Pesh.	*The Peshitta*
POT	*De Prediking van het Oude Testament*, Nijkerk
RB	*Revue Biblique*
RHPR	*Revue d'Histoire et de Philosophie Religieuses*
RSV	*Revised Standard Version*
SAT	*Die Schriften des Alten Testaments*, Göttingen
SB	*La Sainte Bible*, ed. L. Pirot, Paris
SBJ	*La Sainte Bible de Jérusalem*, Paris
SBL	Society of Biblical Literature
SBT	*Studies in Biblical Theology*, London
ScrB	*Scripture Bulletin*

SDB	*Supplément au Dictionnaire de la Bible*
SJT	*Scottish Journal of Theology*
SKK	*Stuttgarter Kleiner Kommentar*, Stuttgart
SR	*Studies in Religion/Sciences Religieuses*
StBibTh	*Studia Biblica et Theologica*, Pasadena
Targ.	Targum
TBC	*Torch Bible Commentaries*, London
TDOT	*Theological Dictionary of the Old Testament*, ed. G. J. Botterweck and H. Ringgren, Grand Rapids, 1974–
Theodot.	Theodotion
ThStKr	*Theologische Studien und Kritiken*
TOTC	*Tyndale Old Testament Commentaries*, London
TR	*Theologische Rundschau*
TTZ	*Trierer Theologische Zeitschrift*
TV	*Theologia Viatorum*
TZ	*Theologische Zeitschrift*, Basel
UF	*Ugarit-Forschungen*
Vet. Lat.	*Vetus Latina*
VS	*Verbum Salutis*, Paris
VT	*Vetus Testamentum*
VT Suppl	*Supplements to Vetus Testamentum*, Leiden
Vulg.	The Vulgate
WTJ	*Westminster Theological Journal*, Philadelphia
ZAW	*Zeitschrift für die Alttestamentliche Wissenschaft*
ZDMG	*Zeitschrift der Deutschen Morgenländischen Gesellschaft*
ZDPV	*Zeitschrift des Deutschen Palästina-Vereins*
ZThK	*Zeitschrift für Theologie und Kirche*

SELECT BIBLIOGRAPHY

COMMENTARIES (*cited in the text by Author's name only*)

Allgeier, A., *Das Buch des Predigers oder Koheleth* (*HSAT*), 1925

Barton, G. A., *Ecclesiastes* (*ICC*), 1908

Barucq, A., *Ecclésiaste* (*VS*), 1968

Baum, A., *Worte des Skepsis—Lieder der Liebe. Prediger—Hohes Lied* (*SKK*), 1971

Bea, A., *Liber Ecclesiastae qui ab Hebraeis appellatur Qohelet*, Rome, 1950

Beek, M. A., *Prediger, Hooglied* (*POT*), 1984

Bergant, D., *Job, Ecclesiastes* (*OTM*), 1982

Budde, K., *Der Prediger* (*HSAT*), 1923^4

Buzy, D., *L'Ecclésiaste* (*SB*), 1946

Cox, S., *The Book of Ecclesiastes* (*ExB*), 1890

Crenshaw, J. L., *Ecclesiastes. A Commentary* (*OTL*), 1987

Davidson, R., *Ecclesiastes and Song of Solomon* (*DSB*), 1986

Delitzsch, F., *Hoheslied und Koheleth* (*BCAT*), 1875

Eaton, M. A., *Ecclesiastes. An Introduction and Commentary* (*TOTC*), 1983

Fuerst, W. J., *The Books of Ruth, Esther, Ecclesiastes, The Song of Songs, Lamentations* (*CBC*), 1975

Galling, K., *Prediger Salomo* (*HAT*), 1969^2

Ginsburg, C. D., *Coheleth, Commonly Called Ecclesiastes*, London, 1861; reprinted New York, 1970

Glasser, E., *Le procès du bonheur par Qohelet* (*LD*), 1970

Gordis, R., *Koheleth: the Man and his World. A Study of Ecclesiastes*, New York, 1968^4

Hertzberg, H. W., *Der Prediger* (*KAT*), 1963

Johnson, L. D., *Proverbs, Ecclesiastes, Song of Solomon* (*LBBC*), 1982

Jones, E., *Proverbs and Ecclesiastes* (*TBC*), 1961

Kroeber, R., *Der Prediger*, Berlin, 1963

Lamparter, H., *Der Prediger* (*BAT*), 1959^2

Lauha, A., *Kohelet* (*BKAT*), 1978

Levy, M. L., *Das Buch Qoheleth*, Leipzig, 1912

Loader, J. A., *Ecclesiastes. A Practical Commentary*, Grand Rapids, 1986

Lohfink, N., *Kohelet* (*NEchtB*), 1980

Lüthi, W., *L'Ecclésiaste a vécu sa vie. Un commentaire pour la communauté chrétienne*, Geneva, 1960
Lys, D., *L'Ecclésiaste ou Que vaut la vie? Commentaire de 1/1 à 4/3*, Paris, 1977
McNeile, A. H., *An Introduction to Ecclesiastes*, Cambridge, 1904
Martin, G. C., *Proverbs, Ecclesiastes and Song of Songs* (*CenB*), 1908
Murphy, R. E., *Wisdom Literature: Job, Proverbs, Ruth, Canticles, Ecclesiastes, Esther* (*FOTL*), 1981
Pautrel, R., *L'Ecclésiaste* (*SBJ*), 1958
Plumptre, E. H., *Ecclesiastes* (*CB*), 1907[2]
Podechard, E., *L'Ecclésiaste* (*EB*), 1912
Power, A. D., *Ecclesiastes or The Preacher*, London, 1952
Rankin, O. S., *The Book of Ecclesiastes* (*IB*), 1956
Rylaarsdam, J. C., *Proverbs, Ecclesiastes, Song of Solomon* (*LBC*), 1965
Scott, R. B. Y., *Proverbs. Ecclesiastes* (*AB*), 1965
Siegfried, C., *Prediger und Hoheslied* (*HKAT*), 1898
Steinmann, J., *Ainsi parlait Qohelet* (*LB*), 1955
Strobel, A., *Das Buch Prediger (Kohelet)* (*KHS*), 1967
Volz, P., *Hiob und Weisheit* (*SAT*), 1922[2]
Wildeboer, G., *Der Prediger* (*KHC*), 1898
Zapletal, V., *Das Buch Kohelet*, Freiburg, Switzerland, 1911[2]
Zimmerli, W., *Das Buch des Predigers Salomo* (*ATD*), 1980[3]

OTHER WORKS (*cited by Author's name only*)

Brockelmann, C., *Hebräische Syntax*, Neukirchen, 1956
Driver, S. R., *A Treatise on the Use of the Tenses in Hebrew*, Oxford, 1892[3]
Ellermeier, F., *Qohelet Teil I Abschnitt I*, Herzberg am Harz, 1967
Hengel, M., *Judaism and Hellenism*, 2 vols., London, 1974
Loretz, O., *Qohelet und der Alte Orient*, Freiburg i. B., 1964
von Rad, G., *Wisdom in Israel*, London, 1972
Schürer, E., *The History of the Jewish People in the Age of Jesus Christ (175 BC–AD 135)*, new English version revised and edited by G. Vermes, F. Millar and M. Goodman, 4 vols., Edinburgh, 1973–1987
Segal, M. H., *A Grammar of Mishnaic Hebrew*, Oxford, 1927
Whitley, C. F., *Koheleth. His Language and Thought* (*BZAW* 148), 1979

OTHER STUDIES (*cited by Author's name and year of publication*)

Albright, W. F., 'Some Canaanite-Phoenician Sources of Hebrew Wisdom' (*VT Suppl* 3), 1955, pp. 1–15

Barr, J., *Biblical Words for Time* (*SBT* 33), 1962
—' "Why?" in Biblical Hebrew', *JTS* NS 36 (1985), pp. 1–33
Barth, C., *Die Errettung vom Tode in den individuellen Klage- und Dankliedern des Alten Testaments*, Basel, 1947
Barton, G. A., 'The Text and Interpretation of Ecclesiastes 5,19', *JBL* 27 (1908), pp. 55–6
Barucq, A., 'Qohéleth (livre de l'Ecclésiaste ou de)', *SDB* IX, 1977, cols. 609–74
Bauer, H., 'Die hebräischen Eigennamen als sprachliche Erkenntnisquelle', *ZAW* 48 (1930), pp. 73–80
Baumgärtel, F., 'Die Ochsenstachel und die Nägel in Koh 12,11', *ZAW* 81 (1969), p. 98
Berlin, A., 'On the Meaning of *rb*', *JBL* 100 (1981), pp. 90–3
Bertram, G., 'Hebräischer und griechischer Qohelet', *ZAW* 64 (1952), pp. 26–49
Bickerman, E., *Four Strange Books of the Bible. Jonah/Daniel/Koheleth/Esther*, New York, 1967
Bishop, E. F. F., 'A Pessimist in Palestine', *PEQ* 100 (1968), pp. 33–41
Blau, J., 'Zum angeblichen Gebrauch von *'t* vor dem Nominativ', *VT* 4 (1954), pp. 7–19
Bottéro, J., 'L'Ecclésiaste et le problème du Mal', *La nouvelle Clio*, Brussels, 7/9 (1955–7), pp. 133–9
Braun, R., *Kohelet und die frühhellenistische Popularphilosophie* (*BZAW* 130), 1973
Bream, H. N., 'Life Without Resurrection: Two Perspectives from Qoheleth', *A Light Unto My Path. Old Testament Studies in Honor of Jacob W. Myers*, ed. H. N. Bream *et al.* (*Gettysburg Theological Studies* IV), 1974, pp. 49–65
Brenner, A., *Colour Terms in the Old Testament* (*JSOT Supplement Series* 21), 1982
Bruns, J. E., 'The Imagery of Qo 12,6a', *JBL* 84 (1965), pp. 428–30
Burkitt, F. C., 'Is Ecclesiastes a Translation?', *JTS* 23 (1921–2), pp. 22–6
Buzy, D., 'La notion du bonheur dans l'Ecclésiaste', *RB* 43 (1934), pp. 494–511
Castellino, G. R., 'Qohelet and His Wisdom', *CBQ* 30 (1968), pp. 15–28
Causse, A., 'Sagesse égyptienne et sagesse juive', *RHPR* 9 (1929), pp. 149–69
Cazelles, H., 'Conjonctions de subordination dans la langue de Qohelet', *Comptes Rendus du Groupe Linguistique d'Études Chamito-Sémitiques*, Paris, 8 (1957–60), pp. 21–2
Childs, B. S., *Memory and Tradition in Israel* (*SBT* 37), 1962

Chopineau, J., 'L'image de Qohelet dans l'exégèse contemporaine', *RHPR* 59 (1979), pp. 595–603
Condamin, A., 'Études sur l'Ecclésiaste', *RB* 8 (1899), pp. 493–509; 9 (1900), pp. 30–44, 354–77
Coppens, J., 'La structure de l'Ecclésiaste', *La Sagesse de l'Ancien Testament*, ed. M. Gilbert, *ETL* 51 (1979), pp. 288–92
Corré, A. D., 'A Reference to Epispasm in Koheleth', *VT* 4 (1954), pp. 416-8
Crenshaw, J. L., 'The Eternal Gospel (Eccl. 3, 11)', *Essays in Old Testament Ethics (J. Philip Hyatt,* in memoriam), ed. J. L. Crenshaw and J. T. Willis, New York, 1974, pp. 25–55
—'The Expression *mî yôdēa*' in the Hebrew Bible', *VT* 36 (1986), pp. 274–88
—*Old Testament Wisdom: An Introduction*, Atlanta, 1981; London, 1981
—'Questions, dictons et épreuves impossibles', *La Sagesse de l'Ancien Testament*, ed. M. Gilbert, *ETL* 51, 1979, pp. 96–111
—'The Shadow of Death in Qoheleth', *Israelite Wisdom: Theological and Literary Essays in Honor of Samuel Terrien*, ed. J. G. Gammie *et al.*, New York, 1978, pp. 205–16
Crüsemann, F., 'Die unveränderbare Welt. Überlegungen zur "Krisis der Weisheit" beim Prediger (Kohelet)', *Der Gott der kleinen Leute*, ed. W. Schottroff and W. Stegemann, Band 1, Altes Testament, Munich, 1979, pp. 80–104 (ET, 'The Unchangeable World: the "Crisis of Wisdom" ', Maryknoll, N.Y., 1984, pp. 57–77)
Dahood, M. J., 'Canaanite-Phoenician Influence in Qoheleth', *Bib.* 33 (1952), pp. 30–52, 191–221
—'Canaanite Words in Qo 10,20', *Bib.* 46 (1965), pp. 210–12
—'The Language of Qoheleth', *CBQ* 14 (1952), pp. 227–32
—'Northwest Semitic Philology and Three Biblical Texts: Koh 10, 18; 6,4; Prov. 22,8', *JNSL* 2 (1972), pp. 17–22
—'The Phoenician Background of Qoheleth', *Bib.* 47 (1966), pp. 264–82
—'Qoheleth and Northwest Semitic Philology', *Bib.* 43 (1962), pp. 349–65
—'Qoheleth and Recent Discoveries', *Bib.* 39 (1958), pp. 302–18
—'Scriptio Defectiva in Qo 4, 10a', *Bib.* 49 (1968), p. 243
—'Three Parallel Pairs in Ecclesiastes 10, 18', *JQR* 62 (1971–2), pp. 84–7
Delsman, W. C., 'Zur Sprache des Buches Koheleth', *Von Kanaan bis Kerala, Festschrift für J. P. M. van der Ploeg*, ed. W. C. Delsman *et al.* (*AOAT* 211), 1982, pp. 341–65
de Savignac, J., 'La sagesse du Qôhéléth et l'épopée de Gilgamesh',

VT 28 (1978), pp. 318–23
de Vaux, R., *Ancient Israel. Its Life and Institutions*, London, 1961 (ET)
de Waard, J., 'The Structure of Qoheleth', *Proceedings of the Eighth World Congress of Jewish Studies*, Division A, 1982, pp. 57–64
—'The Translator and Textual Criticism (with Particular Reference to Eccl 2,25)', *Bib.* 60 (1979), pp. 509–29
Driver, G. R., 'Problems and Solutions', *VT* 4 (1954), pp. 225–45
du Plessis, S. J., 'Aspects of Morphological Peculiarities of the Language of Qoheleth', *De Fructu Oris Sui. Essays in Honour of Adrianus van Selms*, ed. I. H. Eybers *et al.*, Leiden, 1971, pp. 164–80
Duesberg, H. and Fransen, I., *Les scribes inspirés*, Maredsous, 1966[2]
Ehrlich, A., *Randglossen zur hebräischen Bibel*, 7 vols., Leipzig, 1908–14
Eissfeldt, O., *The Old Testament. An Introduction*, Oxford, 1965[3] (ET)
Ellermeier, F., 'Die Entmachung der Weisheit im Denken Qohelets', *ZThK* 60 (1963), pp. 1–20
—*Das Verbum* ḫûš *in Qoh* 2,25. *Akkadisch ḫâšu(m) "sich sorgen" im Lichte neu veröffentlichter Texte (Qohelet Teil I Abschnitt II*, Einzelfrage Nr. 7), Herzberg am Harz, 1968
Fichtner, J., *Die altorientalische Weisheit in ihrer israelitisch-jüdischen Ausprägung*, Giessen, 1933
Fishbane, M., *Biblical Interpretation in Ancient Israel*, Oxford, 1985
Fohrer, G., *Introduction to the Old Testament*, London, 1970 (ET)
Forman, C. C., 'Koheleth's Use of Genesis', *JSS* 5 (1960), pp. 256–63
—'The Pessimism of Ecclesiastes', *JSS* 3 (1958), pp. 336–43
Fox, M. V., 'Frame-Narrative and Composition in the Book of Qohelet', *HUCA* 48 (1977), pp. 83–106
—'The Identification of Quotations in Biblical Literature', *ZAW* 92 (1980), pp. 416–31
—'The Meaning of *Hebel* for Qohelet', *JBL* 105 (1986), pp. 409–27
Frendo, A., 'The "Broken Construct Chain" in Qoh 10,10b', *Bib.* 62 (1981), pp. 544–5
Galling, K., 'Kohelet-Studien', *ZAW* 50 (1932), pp. 276–99
—*Die Krise der Aufklärung in Israel*, Mainz, 1952
—'Das Rätsel der Zeit im Urteil Kohelets (Koh 3,1–15)', *ZThK* 58 (1961), pp. 1–15
—'The Scepter of Wisdom. A Note on the Gold Sheath of Zendjirli and Ecclesiastes xii, 11', *BASOR* 119 (1950), pp. 15–18
—'Stand und Aufgabe der Kohelet-Forschung', *TR* NF 6 (1934), pp. 355–73

Gese, H., 'Die Krisis der Weisheit bei Koheleth', *Les Sagesses du Proche-Orient Ancien*, Paris, 1963, pp. 139–51 (ET, 'The Crisis of Wisdom in Koheleth', *Theodicy in the Old Testament*, ed. J. L. Crenshaw, Philadelphia, 1983, pp. 141–53)

Gilbert, M., 'La description de la vieillesse en Qohelet xii 1–7 est-elle allégorique?', *VT Suppl* 32, 1981, pp. 96–109

Ginsberg, H. L., 'The Quintessence of Koheleth', *Biblical and Other Studies*, ed. A. Altmann, Harvard, 1963, pp. 47–59

—'The Structure and Contents of the Book of Koheleth', *VT Suppl* 3, 1955, pp. 138–49

—*Studies in Koheleth*, New York, 1950

Good, E. M., *Irony in the Old Testament*, London, 1965

—'The Unfilled Sea: Style and Meaning in Ecclesiastes 1:2–11', *Israelite Wisdom. Theological and Literary Essays in Honor of Samuel Terrien*, ed. J. G. Gammie *et al.*, New York, 1978, pp. 59–73

Gordis, R., 'Ecclesiastes i, 17—its Text and Interpretation', *JBL* 56 (1937), pp. 323–30

—'Koheleth—Hebrew or Aramaic?', *JBL* 71 (1952), pp. 93–109

—'The Original Language of Qohelet', *JQR* 37 (1946–7), pp. 67–84

—'Quotations in Wisdom Literature', *JQR* 30 (1939–40), pp. 123–47

—'The Social Background of Wisdom Literature', *HUCA* 18 (1944), pp. 77–118

—'The Translation-Theory of Qohelet Re-examined', *JQR* 40 (1949–50), pp. 103–16

—'Was Koheleth a Phoenician?', *JBL* 74 (1955), pp. 103–14

—*The Wisdom of Ecclesiastes*, New York, 1945

—'The Wisdom of Koheleth', *Poets, Prophets and Sages*, Bloomington, 1971, pp. 325–50

Gordon, C. H., *Ugaritic Literature*, Rome, 1947

Gorssen, L., 'La cohérence de la conception de Dieu dans l'Ecclésiaste', *ETL* 46 (1970), pp. 282–324

Hertzberg, H. W., 'Palästinische Bezüge im Buche Kohelet', *ZDPV* 73 (1957), pp. 113–24

Humbert, P., 'Les adjectifs "*zâr*" et "*nokrî*" et la "femme étrangère" des proverbes bibliques', *Mélanges syriens offerts a M. René Dussaud*, I., Paris, 1939, pp. 259–66

—*Recherches sur les sources égyptiennes de la littérature sapientiale d'Israël*, Neuchâtel, 1929

Irwin, W. A., 'Eccles iii, 18', *AJSL* 56 (1939), pp. 298–9

—'Eccles. 4,13–16', *JNES* 3 (1944), pp. 255–7

—'Ecclesiastes viii, 2–9', *JNES* 4 (1945), pp. 130–1

—'A Rejoinder', *AJSL* 58 (1941), pp. 100–1

Jasper, F. N., 'Ecclesiastes: A Note for Our Time', *Int.* 31 (1967), pp. 259–73

Jastrow, M., Jr, *A Gentle Cynic*, Philadelphia, 1919

Jenni, E., 'Das Wort *'ōlām* im Alten Testament, III', *ZAW* 65, (1953), pp. 1–35

Jepsen, A., 'Warum? eine lexicalische und theologische Studie', *Das ferne und nahe Wort. Festschrift Leonhard Rost*, ed. F. Maas (*BZAW* 105), 1967, pp. 106–13

Johnston, R. K., 'Confessions of a Workaholic: A Reappraisal of Qoheleth', *CBQ* 38 (1976), pp. 14–28

Johnstone, W., ' "The Preacher" as Scientist', *SJT* 20 (1967), pp. 210–21

Jouön, P., 'L'emploi du participe et du parfait dans l'Ecclésiaste', *Bib.* 2 (1921), pp. 225–6

—'Notes philologiques sur le texte hébreu de l'Ecclésiaste', *Bib.* 11 (1930), pp. 419–25

—'Sur le nom de Qohéleth', *Bib.* 2 (1921), pp. 53–4

Kaiser, O., 'Die Sinnkrise bei Kohelet', *Der Mensch unter dem Schicksal* (*BZAW* 161), 1985, pp. 91–109

Kamenetzky, A. S., 'Das Koheleth-Rätsel', *ZAW* 29 (1909), pp. 63–9

—'Der Rätselname Koheleth', *ZAW* 34 (1914), pp. 225–8

—'Die ursprünglich beabsichtigte Aussprache des Pseudonyms *qōhelet*, *OLZ* 24 (1921), cols. 11–15

Kleinert, P., 'Sind im Buche Koheleth ausserhebräische Einflüsse anzuerkennen?', *ThStKr* 58 (1883), pp. 761–82

—'Zur religions- und kulturgeschichtlichen Stellung des Buches Koheleth', *ThStKr* 82 (1909), pp. 493–529

Klopfenstein, M. A., 'Die Skepsis des Qohelet', *TZ* 28 (1972), pp. 97–109

Knopf, C. S., 'The Optimism of Koheleth', *JBL* 49 (1930), pp. 195–9

Kroeber, R., ' "Der Prediger". Ein Werk der altjüdischen Weisheitsliteratur', *Alt.* 11 (1965), pp. 195–209

Kronholm. T., *Den verksamme Guden: Ett bidrag till Predikarens verklighetsuppfattning, speciellt hans teologi*, Lund, 1982

Labuschagne, C. J., 'The Emphasizing Particle *gam* and its Connotations', *Studia Biblica et Semitica Theodoro Christiano Vriezen . . . Dedicata*, ed. W. C. van Unnik and A. S. van der Woude, Wageningen, 1966, pp. 193–203

Lang, B., *Ist der Mensch hilflos? Zum Buch Kohelet*, Einsiedeln, 1979

Lauha, A., 'Kohelets Verhältnis zur Geschichte', *Die Botschaft und die Boten. Festschrift für Hans Walter Wolff*, ed. J. Jeremias and L. Perlitt, Neukirchen, 1981, pp. 393–401

—'Die Krise des religiösen Glaubens bei Kohelet' (*VT Suppl* 3), 1955, pp. 183–91
Levy, I., 'Rien de nouveau sous le soleil', *La nouvelle Clio*, Brussels, 5 (1953), pp. 326–8
Loader, J. A., *Polar Structures in the Book of Qohelet* (*BZAW* 152), 1979
—'Qohelet 3,2–8—A "Sonnet" in the Old Testament', *ZAW* 81 (1969), pp. 240–2
Lohfink, N., '*melek*, *šallîṭ* und *môšēl* bei Kohelet und die Abfassungszeit des Buchs', *Bib.* 62 (1981), pp. 535–43
—'War Kohelet ein Frauenfeind? Ein Versuch, die Logik und den Gegenstand von Koh 7, 23–8, 1a herauszufinden', *BETL* 51, 1979, pp. 259–87
—'Warum ist der Tor unfähig, böse zu handeln? (Koh 4,17)', *ZDMG* Suppl 5 (1983), pp. 113–20
Loretz, O., 'Altorientalische und kanaanäische Topoi im Buche Kohelet', *UF* 12 (1980), pp. 267–78
—'Zur Darbietungsform der "Ich-Erzählung" im Buche Qohelet', *CBQ* 25 (1963), pp. 46–59
Lys, D., *La chair dans l'Ancien Testament: Bâsâr*, Paris, 1967
—'L'être et le temps. Communication de Qohèlèth', *La Sagesse de l'Ancien Testament*, ed. M. Gilbert, *BETL* 51, 1979, pp. 249–58
Macdonald, D. B., *The Hebrew Literary Genius*, Princeton, 1933
—*The Hebrew Philosophical Genius*, Princeton, 1936
Macdonald, J., 'The Particle *'t* in Classical Hebrew: Some New Data on its Use with the Nominative', *VT* 14 (1964), pp. 264–75
Margoliouth, S., 'The Prologue of Ecclesiastes', *Exp.* 8 (1911), pp. 463–70
Martin-Achard, R., *De la mort à la résurrection*, Neuchâtel, 1956
Mettayer, A., 'De quel(le) mort s'agit-il?', *SR* 9 (1980), pp. 339–43
Michel, D., 'Qohelet-Probleme. Überlegungen zu Qoh 8,2–9 und 7,11–14', *TV* 15 (1979–80), pp. 81–103
Mitchell, H. G., ' "Work" in Ecclesiastes', *JBL* 32 (1913), pp. 123–38
Montgomery, J. A., 'Notes on Ecclesiastes', *JBL* 43 (1924), pp. 241–4
Müller, H.-P., 'Theonome Skepsis und Lebensfreude. Zu Koh 1,12–3,15', *BZ* 30 (1986), pp. 1–19
—'Neige der althebräischen "Weisheit". Zum Denken Qohäläts', *ZAW* 90 (1978), pp. 238–64
—'Wie sprach Qohelet von Gott?', *VT* 18 (1968), pp. 507–21
Muilenburg, J., 'A Qoheleth Scroll from Qumran', *BASOR* 135 (1954), pp. 20–8
Mulder, J. S. M., 'Qoheleth's Division and also its Main Point',

Von Kanaan bis Kerala. Festschrift für J. P. M. van der Ploeg, ed. W. C. Delsman *et al.* (*AOAT* 211), 1982, pp. 149–59

Murphy, R. E., 'A Form-Critical Consideration of Ecclesiastes VII', *SBL Seminar Papers*, 1974, vol. 1, pp. 77–85

—'Kohelet, der Skeptiker', *Conc.* 12 (1976), pp. 567–70

—'The "Pensées" of Cohelet', *CBQ* 17 (1955), pp. 304–14

—'Qohelet Interpreted: The Bearing of the Past on the Present', *VT* 32 (1982), pp. 331–7

—'Qohelet's "Quarrel" with the Fathers', *From Faith to Faith. Essays in Honor of D. G. Miller*, ed. D. Y. Hadidian, Pittsburgh, 1979, pp. 235–45

Nishimura, T., 'Un mashal de Qohelet 1,2–11', *RHPR* 59 (1979), pp. 605–15

—'Quelques refléxions sémiologiques à propos de "la crainte de Dieu" de Qohelet', *AJBI* 5 (1979), pp. 67–87

Nötscher, F., 'Zum emphatischen lamed', *VT* 3 (1953), pp. 372–80

Ogden, G. S., 'The "Better"-Proverb (*Tob*-Spruch), Rhetorical Criticism, and Qoheleth', *JBL* 96 (1977), pp. 489–505

—'Historical Allusion in Qoheleth iv 13–16?', *VT* 30 (1980), pp. 309–15

—'The Interpretation of *dōr* in Ecclesiastes 1.4', *JSOT* 34 (1986), pp. 91–2

—'The Mathematics of Wisdom: Qoheleth iv 1–12', *VT* 34 (1984), pp. 446–53

—'Qoheleth ix 1–16', *VT* 32 (1982), pp. 158–69

—'Qoheleth ix 17—x 20. Variations on the Theme of Wisdom's Strength and Vulnerability', *VT* 30 (1980), pp. 27–37

'Qoheleth xi 1–6', *VT* 33 (1983), pp. 222–30

'Qoheleth xi 7–xii 8: Qoheleth's Summons to Enjoyment and Reflection', *VT* 34 (1984), pp. 27–38

—'Qoheleth's Use of the "Nothing is Better"-Form', *JBL* 98 (1979), pp. 339–50

Osborn, N. D., 'A Guide for Balanced Living', *BT* 21 (1970), pp. 185–96

Pedersen, J., 'Scepticisme israélite', *RHPR* 10 (1930), pp. 317–70

Perdue, L. G., *Wisdom and Cult. A Critical Analysis of the Views of Cult in the Wisdom Literatures of Israel and the Ancient Near East* (*SBL Dissertation Series* 30), Missoula, 1977

Pfeiffer, E., 'Die Gottesfurcht im Buche Kohelet', *Gottes Wort und Gottes Land. Festschrift für Hans-Wilhelm Hertzberg*, ed. H. Graf Reventlow, Göttingen, 1965, pp. 133–58

Pfeiffer, R. H., 'The Peculiar Skepticism of Ecclesiastes', *JBL* 53 (1934), pp. 100–9

Podechard, E., 'La composition du livre de l'Ecclésiaste', *RB* NS

9 (1912), pp. 161–91
Polk, T., 'The Wisdom of Irony: A Study of Hebel and its Relation to Joy and the Fear of God in Ecclesiastes', *StBibTh* 6 (1976), pp. 3–17
Rainey, A. F., 'A Second Look at *Amal* in Qoheleth', *CTM* 36 (1965), p. 805
—'A Study of Ecclesiastes', *CTM* 35 (1964), pp. 148–57
Ranston, H., *Ecclesiastes and the Early Greek Wisdom Literature*, London, 1925
Reines, C. W., 'Koheleth viii, 10', *JJS* 5 (1954), pp. 86–7
—'Koheleth on Wisdom and Wealth', *JJS* 5 (1954), pp. 80–4
Reymond, P., *L'eau, sa vie et sa signification dans l'Ancien Testament* (*VT Suppl* 6), 1958
Richards, H., 'What's It All About? A New Look at the Book of Ecclesiastes', *ScrB* 6 (1975), pp. 7–11
Rostovsteff, M., *A Large Estate in Egypt in the Third Century BC. A Study in Economic History* (University of Wisconsin Studies in the Social Sciences and History 6), Madison, 1922
Roth, W. M. W., *Numerical Sayings in the Old Testament* (*VT Suppl* 13), 1965
Rousseau, F., 'Structure de Qohélet i 4–11 et plan du livre', *VT* 31 (1981), pp. 200–17
Rowley, H. H., 'The Problems of Ecclesiastes', *JQR* 42 (1951–2), pp. 87–90
Rudolph, W., *Vom Buch Kohelet* (Schriften der Gesellschaft zur Förderung des Westfalischen Wilhelms-Universität zu Münster, H. 42), 1959
Salters, R. B., 'A Note on the Exegesis of Ecclesiastes 3, 15b', *ZAW* 88 (1976), pp. 419–22
—'Notes on the History of the Interpretation of Koh 5,5', *ZAW* 90 (1978), pp. 95–101
—'Notes on the Interpretation of Qoh 6,2' *ZAW* 91 (1979), pp. 282–9
—'Qoheleth and the Canon', *ET* 86 (1974–5), pp. 339–42
—'Text and Exegesis in Koh 10,19', *ZAW* 89 (1977), pp. 423–6
Sauer, G., *Die Sprüche Agurs* (*BWANT* 84), 1963
Sawyer, J. F. A., 'The Ruined House in Ecclesiastes 12: A Reconstruction of the Original Parable', *JBL* 94 (1975), pp. 519–31
Saydon, P. P., 'Meanings and Uses of the Particle *'t*', *VT* 14 (1964), pp. 192–210
Schmid, H. H., *Wesen und Geschichte der Weisheit* (*BZAW* 101), 1966
Schmidt, J., 'Koh iv, 17', *ZAW* 58 (1940–1), pp. 279–80
Schoors, A., 'Kethibh-Qere in Ecclesiastes', *Orientalia Lovaniensia*

Analecta 13, Leuven (1982), pp. 215–22
—'Koheleth: A Perspective of Life After Death?', *ETL* 61 (1985), pp. 295–303
—'The Particle *ky*', *Remembering All the Way* (*OS* 21), 1981, pp. 240–76
—'La structure littéraire de Qohéleth', *Orientalia Lovaniensia Periodica* 13, Leuven, 1982, pp. 91–116
Schunck, K. D., 'Drei Seleukiden im Buche Kohelet?', *VT* 9 (1959), pp. 192–201
Serrano, J. J., ' "I Saw the Wicked Buried" (Eccl 8,10)', *CBQ* 16 (1954), pp. 168–70
Shank, H. C., 'Qoheleth's World and Life View as Seen in his Recurring Phrases', *WTJ* 37 (1974), pp. 57–73
Sheppard, G. T., 'The Epilogue to Qoheleth as Theological Commentary', *CBQ* 39 (1977), pp. 182–9
Smend, R., 'Essen und Trinken—ein Stück Weltlichkeit des Alten Testaments', *Beiträge zur Alttestamentliche Theologie. Festschrift für Walther Zimmerli zum 70. Geburtstag*, ed. H. Donner *et al.*, Göttingen, 1977, pp. 446–59
Smith, L. L., 'A Critical Evaluation of the Book of Ecclesiastes', *JBR* 21 (1953), pp. 100–5
Spina, F. A., 'Qoheleth and the Reformation of Wisdom', *The Quest for the Kingdom of God. Studies in Honor of George E. Mendenhall*, ed. H. B. Huffmon, Winona Lake, Indiana, 1983, pp. 267–79
Staerk, W., 'Zur Exegese von Koh 10,20 und 11,1', *ZAW* 59 (1942–3), pp. 216–18
Staples, W. E., 'The Meaning of *ḥēpeṣ* in Ecclesiastes', *JNES* 24 (1965), pp. 110–12
—' "Profit" in Ecclesiastes', *JNES* 4 (1945), pp. 87–96
—'The "Vanity" of Ecclesiastes', *JNES* 2 (1943), pp. 95–104
—'Vanity of Vanities', *CJT* 1 (1955), pp. 141–56
Stiglmaier, A., 'Weisheit und Jahweglaube im Buche Kohelet', *TTZ* 83 (1974), pp. 257–83, 339–68
Strauss, H., 'Erwägungen zur seelsorgerlichen Dimension von Kohelet 12,1–2', *ZThK* 78 (1981), pp. 267–75
Tcherikover, V., *Hellenistic Civilization and the Jews*, Philadelphia and Jerusalem, 1961[2]
Thomas, D. W., 'A Note on *bᵉmaddāʿᵃkā* in Ecclesiastes x.20', *JTS* 50 (1949), p. 177
Torrey, C. C., 'The Problem of Ecclesiastes iv 13–16', *VT* 2 (1952), pp. 175–7
—'The Question of the Original Language of Qoheleth', *JQR* 39 (1948–9), pp. 151–60
Ullendorff, E., 'The Meaning of *qhvt*, *VT* 12 (1962), p. 215

von Loewenclau, I., 'Kohelet und Sokrates—Versuch eines Vergleiches', *ZAW* 98 (1986), pp. 327–38

von Rad, G., 'Hiob 38 und die altägyptische Weisheit', *Gesammelte Studien zum Alten Testament*, Munich, 1958, pp. 262–71 (ET, *The Problem of the Hexateuch and Other Essays*, Edinburgh and London, 1966, pp. 281–91)

Waldman, N. M., 'The *dābār ra'* of Eccl 8:3', *JBL* 98 (1979), pp. 407–8

Walsh, J., 'Despair as a Theological Virtue in the Spirituality of Ecclesiastes', *BTB* 10 (1980), pp. 46–9

Wanke, G., ''*wy* und *hwy*', *ZAW* 78 (1966), pp. 215–18

Watson, W. G. E., *Classical Hebrew Poetry* (*JSOT Supplement Series* 26), Sheffield, 1984

Westermann, C., 'Der Gebrauch von *'šry* im Alten Testament', *Forschung am Alten Testament. Gesammelte Studien, Band II*, Munich, 1974, pp. 191–5

Whitley, C. F., 'Koheleth and Ugaritic Parallels', *UF* 11 (1979), pp. 811–24

Whybray, R. N., 'Conservatisme et radicalisme dans Qohelet', *Sagesse et Religion. Colloque de Strasbourg, octobre 1976*, Paris, 1979, pp. 65–81

—'The Identification and Use of Quotations in Ecclesiastes', *Congress Volume, Vienna 1980* (*VT Suppl* 32), 1981, pp. 435–51

—*The Intellectual Tradition in the Old Testament* (*BZAW* 135), Berlin, 1974

—'Qoheleth the Immoralist? (Qoh 7:16–17)', *Israelite Wisdom: Essays in Honor of Samuel Terrien*, ed. J. G. Gammie *et al.*, New York, 1978, pp. 191–204

—'Qoheleth, Preacher of Joy', *JSOT* 23 (1982), pp. 87–98

—*Two Jewish Theologies; Job and Ecclesiastes*, Hull, 1980

Wilch, J. R., *Time and Event. An Exegetical Study of the Use of* 'ēth *in the Old Testament in Comparison to Other Temporal Expressions in Clarification of the Concept of Time*, Leiden, 1969

Williams, J. G., 'What Does it Profit a Man? The Wisdom of Koheleth', *Judaism*, New York, 20 (1971), pp. 179–93

Willi-Plein, I., '*ḥn*. Ein Übersetzungsproblem. Gedanken zu Sach. xii 10', *VT* 23 (1973), pp. 90–9

Wilson, G. H., ' "The Words of the Wise": The Interest and Significance of Qohelet 12:9–14', *JBL* 103 (1984), pp. 175–92

Witzenrath, H., *Süss ist das Licht . . . Eine literaturwissenschaftliche Untersuchung zu Kohelet 11,7–12,7*, St. Ottolien, 1979

Wright, A. G., 'Additional Numerical Patterns in Qoheleth', *CBQ* 45 (1983), pp. 32–43

—' "For Everything There is a Season": The Structure and

Meaning of the Fourteen Opposites (Ecclesiastes 3,2–8)', *De la Tôrah au Messie. Mélanges Henri Cazelles*, ed. J. Doré *et al.*, Paris, 1981, pp. 321–8

—'The Riddle of the Sphinx: The Structure of the Book of Qohelet', *CBQ* 30 (1968), pp. 313–34. Reprinted in *Studies in Ancient Israelite Wisdom*, ed. J. L. Crenshaw, New York, 1976, pp. 245–66

Zimmerli, W., 'Das Buch Kohelet—Traktat oder Sentenzensammlung?', *VT* 24 (1974), pp. 221–30

—'Ort und Grenze der Weisheit im Rahmen der alttestamentlichen Theologie', *Les Sagesses du Proche-Orient Ancien*, Paris, 1963, pp. 121–37 (ET, 'The Place and Limit of the Wisdom in the Framework of the Old Testament Theology', *SJT* 17 [1964], pp. 146–58; and also in *Studies in Ancient Israelite Wisdom*, ed. J. L. Crenshaw, New York, 1976, pp. 314–26)

—'Zur Struktur der alttestamentlichen Weisheit', *ZAW* 51 (1933), pp. 177–204 (ET, 'Concerning the Structure of Old Testament Wisdom', *Studies in Ancient Israelite Wisdom*, ed. J. L. Crenshaw, New York, 1976, pp. 175–207)

Zimmermann, F., 'The Aramaic Provenance of Qohelet', *JQR* 36 (1945–6), pp. 17–45

—'Qohelet', *JQR* 52 (1962), pp. 273–8

—'The Question of Hebrew in Qohelet', *JQR* 40 (1949–50), pp. 79–102

INTRODUCTION

to

Ecclesiastes

A. TITLE AND PLACE IN THE CANON

Ecclesiastes is the title given to the book in the Latin Vulgate. It is a latinized form of the Greek *ekklēsiastēs*, the title given to it in the Septuagint as an attempt to translate the Hebrew title *qōhelet*, that is, the name—or rather the title or *nom de plume*—of the author (1:1). The subtitle 'The Preacher', found in the English translations (including *RSV*), represents an attempt to translate 'Ecclesiastes' into English (similar attempts at translation were made in other European versions).

The rendering 'preacher' is, however, wide of the mark. But 'Ecclesiastes' probably renders the meaning of *qōhelet* reasonably well. In classical Greek *ekklēsiastēs* means 'one who sits or speaks in the *ekklēsia*', that is, an assembly of local citizens. The Hebrew term *qōhelet*—which occurs only in this book—is almost certainly a participle of the verb *qhl*, 'to assemble', which is in turn related to the noun *qāhāl*, 'an assembly' (often rendered as *ekklēsia* in the Septuagint). (The view that Qoheleth was an 'assembler', in the sense of 'editor' or 'compiler' of wisdom material, is ruled out by the fact that *qhl* is never used of gathering inanimate objects but always of an assembly of people.)

qōhelet is, however, a *feminine* participle, though the fact that it is always used with masculine verbs leaves no doubt that Qoheleth was a man, not a woman. The probable explanation of this peculiarity is that Hebrew words of this type were sometimes used to denote offices or functions, and might then acquire a secondary meaning of the holder of such an office or the performer of such a function (compare titles like 'Lord Privy Seal' and 'Gold Stick in Waiting'). Such a development is suggested by certain similarly formed proper names like Hassophereth (Ezr. 2:55; Neh. 7:57) which apparently originally meant 'scribal office or function' and then secondarily a scribe or holder of the scribal office (see GK § 122r for other examples). In that case a further development has taken place, *hassōperet* becoming a personal name. Qoheleth could thus just conceivably be the personal name of the author of the book so entitled; however, the fact that the word occurs in two variant forms (twice with the article—*haqqōhelet* (see on 7:27)—and five times without it) strongly suggests that it was either a title or a nickname.

It would seem, then, that the word designates the author as a member of, and possibly as one who had some special function, such as that of convener or 'speaker', in a *qāhāl*—that is, an assembly. Unfortunately it is not known what kind of assembly this was. It may have been a religious or political assembly like the Jerusalem *gerousia*, or an academic or professional one. The only statement in the book about Qoheleth's public activity, that he 'taught the people knowledge' (12:9) gives no clue. There are several references to membership of, and speaking in, the *ekklēsia* in Ecclesiasticus, written perhaps half a century after Ecclesiastes, and in one of these (15:5) in which the original Hebrew is preserved the Hebrew term is *qāhāl*. These passages clearly refer to public activity of some importance. On the question of Qoheleth's status and profession, see below.

Ecclesiastes is placed in the third section of the Hebrew Bible, the Writings (*keṯûbîm*), after the Law and the Prophets. There it forms one of the group of books known as the (Five) Scrolls (*megillôt*) which are read in public at annual festivals, the others being Ruth, the Song of Songs, Lamentations and Esther. It has, however, occupied different positions in the Writings in earlier manuscripts and lists. In the Septuagint and Vulgate and in modern translations it stands between Proverbs and the Song of Songs as part of a group of 'Solomonic' books. In Jewish practice it constitutes the reading for the feast of Tabernacles.

The acceptance of the book into the Hebrew canon was not achieved without controversy. According to the Mishnah (*Yadaim* 3:5; *Eduyot* 5:3), its canonicity was at first disputed. Neither the arguments put forward against its acceptance nor the reasons for its eventual acceptance are there stated; but it may reasonably be conjectured that its unorthodox teaching raised doubts concerning its eligibility, while its apparent claim to have been written by Solomon, perhaps together with the fact that it does contain some unimpeachably orthodox statements, ensured its acceptance. Clearly the division of opinion about the real nature of its teaching, which has persisted to the present day, began very early.

B. HISTORICAL BACKGROUND, AUTHOR AND PLACE OF COMPOSITION

It was the traditional belief that Ecclesiastes was written by King Solomon, who reigned in the tenth century BC. This conviction was based partly on the tradition that Solomon had been an exceptionally wise man, but more specifically on the author's own statement, 'I Qoheleth was king over Israel in Jerusalem' (1:12), and on the title of the book (1:1): 'The words of Qoheleth, son of David, king in Jerusalem'. Although the name Solomon itself appears nowhere in the book, this identification seemed incontrovertible: none of David's sons other than Solomon became king of Israel. Moreover, the account which this 'king in Jerusalem' gives of his own attainments and activities—superlative wisdom accompanied by great wealth, luxurious living, and the construction of magnificent buildings and gardens (1:13–2:11; compare the account of Solomon's reign in 1 Kg. 3–11)—is not only entirely in keeping with the traditions about Solomon but would indeed not fit any other Israelite king.

Nevertheless there can be no doubt that the implicit claim to be Solomon is a fiction; and indeed, the fact that it is made only indirectly, hinting at the identification but never actually naming Solomon (contrast the direct claims made in Prov. 1:1; 10:1; 25:1 and in Ca. 1:1) may suggest that Qoheleth never intended his readers to take it seriously. In fact the fiction is dropped after chapter two and not resumed; and the subsequent references in the book to kings are clearly written from the point of view of one who was a subject rather than a ruler. The purpose of the fiction, as will be shown below, was to make in a lively and striking way the point that even the possession in the greatest possible measure of all the desirable things in life—wealth, power, wisdom—is unable to confer complete and lasting satisfaction.

The book was written many centuries after Solomon, most probably in the third century BC. The main reasons for this dating are three: the character of the Hebrew in which it is written, its mood and style of argument, and its place in the history of thought. Each of these considerations would be sufficient in itself to prove that it is one of the latest compositions in the Old Testament.

Language. Cheyne's remark that 'If Ecclesiastes belongs to the time of Solomon, the Hebrew language has no history' and Ginsburg's that 'We could as easily believe that Chaucer is the author of Rasselas as that Solomon wrote Coheleth' (p. 253), are in no way exaggerations. Qoheleth's Hebrew has all the marks of lateness. For several centuries after the time of Solomon literary Hebrew changed comparatively little: relatively late books like Chronicles and even the Hebrew parts of Daniel (the latter written in the first half of the second century BC) still retain most of the features of the earlier, classical language of the tenth to eighth centuries. The same is true of the Hebrew writings composed by members of the Qumran sect. The Hebrew of Qoheleth is quite different from these and in many respects unique. A modern student trained only in classical Hebrew, and confronted for the first time with Qoheleth, finds it at first largely incomprehensible.

How are these facts to be explained? Like other languages,

Hebrew did not develop in a purely linear way: it is not possible to arrange its literature chronologically according to a simple scheme of grammatical, verbal and other developments. If that were the case, Ecclesiastes would have to be dated later than Daniel and the Qumran sect, which is out of the question. As in the case of other literatures, some literary works are conservative, seeking to preserve earlier fashions in language, while others are innovative, heavily influenced by new fashions. Some works are purely literary in character, while others are written in a more colloquial style. Moreover, variations in dialect within the same language should not be forgotten. Nevertheless, as will be seen later, the closeness of Qoheleth's language to that of the Mishnah, which was compiled *c.* AD 200, together with the great gap which exists between its language and classical Hebrew, make it quite certain that the book was written, not at the beginning of the period of classical Hebrew (the time of Solomon), but many centuries later when the long-lived classical pattern of the language had already undergone considerable change. More will be said on this question in Section C below.

Tone and style of argument. It is immediately apparent to anyone familiar with the other books of the Old Testament that Qoheleth's style and way of arguing are unique.

That the book belongs to the category of what is known as 'wisdom literature', of which the other two principal examples in the Old Testament are the books of Job and Proverbs, is admittedly clear. The distinctiveness of these wisdom books, which have close affinities with comparable works from other parts of the ancient Near East, is that they are concerned primarily with the individual and his relationship to God, society and the world around him, and especially with the question which Qoheleth himself expressed succinctly in the phrase 'What is good for man?' (6:12; see Zimmerli, 1933). The typical literary form in which the wisdom writers attempted to answer this question in its manifold aspects is that which predominates in Prov. 10–29: the short, pithy proverb or aphorism easily recognizable by its length and dual structure. Some parts of Prov. 1–9 and the Book of Job on the other hand take the form of longer poems, although here too traditional proverbs are frequently found embedded within these poems.

Ecclesiastes also contains a quantity of proverbs of this type; but here the proverb form is used in a quite novel way. Qoheleth is no purveyor of conventional wisdom in capsule form. In passages like 2:12–17 such aphorisms (vv. 13 and 14) are cited only in order to question or at least to qualify their truth, in a wide-ranging and discursive argument. Rather than taking for granted the absolute truth of these pithy aphorisms, which by their very nature can tell at most only part of the truth (e.g. 'The wise man has eyes in his head,/ but the fool walks in darkness'), he exposes the complexity of the question of the practical use of being wise. He often speaks in his own person, revealing to the reader how he arrived at his conclusion in an argument punctuated with such phrases as 'So I turned . . .', 'Then I saw . . .', 'yet I perceived . . .', 'Then I said to myself . . .'. The distinctive character of his reasoning will be the subject of further treatment below. Here it is sufficient to point out that in order to express his ideas he was obliged to invent or develop an entirely new style of discourse. Whether he made use of conventional proverbs as his starting-point, or whether he chose to comment rather on some generally accepted truth such as the creation of the world by God—as in 3:11—the result was a new kind of literary composition. Thus, although Qoheleth clearly belongs to the same wisdom tradition which had expressed itself in aphorisms like those in the Book of Proverbs, he represents a very late stage in the history of that tradition.

From what has been said above it will be seen that the tone and presentation of the book also point to a later stage in the development of Hebrew literature. Although the author conceals his true name under the sobriquet Qoheleth, he writes entirely in his own person. One of the most obvious indications of this is that in 222 verses there are no less than 82 occurrences of the verb in the first person singular, many accompanied by the emphatic pronoun 'I'. There are, it is true, a few other passages in the Old Testament where an author—as distinct from a character in a third person narrative—speaks about himself directly, notably the so-called 'memoirs' of Ezra and of Nehemiah; but there is no other book which as a whole can be compared in this respect with Ecclesiastes (the 'I' of some of the Psalms is conventional rather than personal). The canons of ancient Near Eastern literature required that the personality as well as the name of an author should remain concealed. A change came about, however, with the impact of Greek culture on the Semitic world. Greek writers tended to proclaim their identity: many of their names, indeed, became household words in their own time as in the modern world. And it was in accordance with this custom that in the early second century BC Ben Sira, the author of Ecclesiasticus, not only spoke about himself but signed his name, as it were, to his book (50:27). Qoheleth occupies a position between the extremes. But there can be little doubt that the personal tone of both books owes something to the influence of the Greek cult of the individual which educated Jews encountered after the conquests of Alexander the Great in the late fourth century BC.

The book is also marked by a degree of abstraction which is not to be found in the earlier wisdom books. Although on occasion Qoheleth can offer practical advice in the earlier manner, he often gives the impression of having virtually withdrawn from the world, observing it dispassionately almost as a stranger (Gese, 1963). While the earlier wisdom teaching exemplified by Prov. 10–29 was addressed to the individual, it was the individual in his relationship to his social environment. There was a real concern for the well-being of the community. When Qoheleth gives his advice or makes his comments on matters of practical concern such as commerce, social justice or the inheritance of property, it is as if nothing matters except the interests of the isolated individual: for example, for him the only point of working to acquire wealth is its personal enjoyment in one's own lifetime. He ignores the idea so basic to traditional Israelite life of the importance of bequeathing one's wealth and social reputation to one's children, and laments that the fruit of one's labours will pass to 'a man who did not toil for it' (2:21) or to 'a stranger' (6:2) who may foolishly dissipate it.

This detachment from the common life is an aspect of Qoheleth's independent stance. Every commonly accepted notion must be put to the test of his personal experience of the world: nothing is to be taken for granted. In this Qoheleth has something in common with the author of Job; but he differs from him in that he entirely lacks his passionate concern, and also in that he does not restrict his observations to a limited number of topics, but sets out 'to search out by wisdom all that is done under heaven' (1:13). This determination to question everything is what gives the book its peculiar form: it is, as Zimmerli put it, a 'running dialogue' with traditional wisdom. But there is no dogmatism in Qoheleth: he has few solutions to offer, but recognizes that the task which he has set himself cannot in fact be carried out (8:17). The confident assertions of earlier wisdom are entirely foreign to him. God has not seen fit to provide answers to his questions; and 'Who knows . . .?' (2:19; 3:21; 6:12; 8:1) is his characteristic refrain.

Qoheleth is an 'intellectual' in a sense otherwise unknown to the Old Testament. In his remorseless determination to probe the nature of things he belongs to a new world of thought, though, as will be seen below, his sense of God's transcendence ('God is in heaven, and you upon earth', 5:2) is a Jewish inheritance which distinguishes him quite radically from the secular philosopher.

Qoheleth's place in the history of thought. Human thinking does not progress smoothly in a single straight line, and it is notoriously difficult to determine the date of a literary work on the basis of such a development, especially when, as is the case with Ecclesiastes, the extant works available for comparison are few and cannot themselves be precisely dated. It is probable that the wisdom books which have survived are only a fragment of a once far more extensive literature. To some extent it may be said that Ecclesiastes stands as a lonely beacon in a dark and largely uncharted literary ocean.

In fact Qoheleth's thought is by no means entirely original. For example, the pessimism which is most commonly attributed to him can to a large extent be paralleled from ancient Near Eastern literature, both Egyptian and Mesopotamian, and from Greek literature of various periods, and even from the earlier wisdom of the Old Testament itself. These parallels do not necessarily presuppose the direct influence of one author upon another, or even a continuous stream of thought from one period to another: it not infrequently happens that the same thoughts occur quite independently to different authors far removed from one another in time and place. Nevertheless developments in human thought do occur, and these can often to some extent be traced and plotted.

It is clear that Qoheleth belonged to two distinct though related traditions: as a Jew he was heir to the religious tradition of Israel, and as a wisdom teacher he had behind him an international wisdom tradition of immense antiquity, of which the wisdom tradition of Israel, with its literary deposit in the Old Testament, formed a part. In certain important respects his thought shows strong dependence on each of these traditions, and at the same time marks a significant break with them. This break is so marked that a number of scholars (e.g. Galling, 1952; Gese, 1963) have asserted that it both reflects and constitutes a 'crisis' in the history of Jewish thought, particularly with respect to Qoheleth's concept of God as hidden and remote from his creatures and to his radical questioning of the belief, common both to Israel and to the ancient Near East in general, that human beings may expect to receive in their lifetime the fate that they deserve; and also with regard to his apparently resigned acceptance of the frustrations and injustices experienced in human life.

Qoheleth is very selective in his references to the 'orthodox' theology which had established itself in Judaism in the exilic and early post-exilic periods. Nevertheless his comments on subjects congenial to him, such as the transcendence of God and the creation of the world, clearly show that he took all this for granted while at the same time putting his own individual interpretation on it. He never quotes an Old Testament text verbatim, but he often makes clear allusions to particular passages, especially to Genesis 3 and to Deuteronomy.

The above considerations all point to the Hellenistic period—from the later fourth to the early second century BC—as that during which Qoheleth lived, taught and wrote his book, rather than the earlier post-exilic period during which Palestine was under Persian hegemony. And within the Hellenistic period, the third century BC, when Palestine was ruled from Egypt by the Ptolemaic dynasty, forms the most probable background. During the immediately previous years, from the death of Alexander the Great in 323 BC to the battle of Ipsus in 301 BC which put Palestine into Ptolemaic hands, the inhabitants of Palestine had been subjected to the disastrous effects of almost continuous warfare between the Ptolemies and the Seleucids, both heirs to the larger parts of Alexander's empire. There is nothing in Ecclesiastes which suggests such a troubled time: on the contrary, he and his readers were clearly living in a time of peace and—for some—unexampled prosperity. The period following the defeat of the Ptolemies by the Seleucid king Alexander III at Paneia in 200 BC, which ended a century of uninterrupted Ptolemaic rule and brought Palestine under the domination of the Seleucids, also seems out of the question for a number of reasons. Qoheleth's work shows no signs of the increasing rift between pro- and anti-Hellenist parties in Palestine which was eventually to lead to the Jewish (Maccabaean) Revolt in 167–166 BC. In fact, his book must have been written some time before that development. It is generally agreed that it was known to Ben Sira, the author of Ecclesiasticus, which was probably composed about 190 BC. The allusions in Ecclesiasticus to Ecclesiastes, some of which take the form of direct quotations, but often put a new interpretation on Qoheleth's words (see Barton, Gordis, and Hertzberg for details), seem to presuppose a general familiarity with the latter work on the part of the readers of the former; and this means that a considerable period of time must have elapsed between the publication of the two works.

As in the earlier wisdom books, there are no direct allusions in Ecclesiastes to contemporary historical events which would provide precise clues to the date of composition, although some passages have been interpreted in this way. In particular, attempts have been made to relate three passages (4:13–16; 9:13–16; 10:16–17), which purport to relate episodes involving the activities of kings or to describe political situations, to actual political events and circumstances in the history of the Ptolemiac empire; but on the identification of these no agreement has been achieved. Sayings about kings are a commonplace of wisdom literature—there are many such sayings, for example, in Proverbs; and the admonitory tale—e.g. Prov. 7:6–27; 24:30–34—is also a familiar device in this kind of literature. Qoheleth himself employs this form elsewhere in passages where it is clearly simply a pedagogical device (the Solomonic fiction in chapters 1–2 and also 5:13–17); and there is no reason to suppose that these passages about kings are other than fictitious.

Nevertheless the book reflects a political, economic and social background which corresponds more closely with the Ptolemaic period than with any other. On the political level, although much of what Qoheleth says about kings and the importance of caution on the part of those who have personal dealings with them is derived from earlier wisdom teaching, certain features of his treatment of this subject are peculiar to him. Three terms are used to denote the political authority: *melek*, 'king', *môšēl*, literally 'ruler', and *šallîṭ* (see Lohfink, 1981). Detailed information about the structure of local government in Syria and Palestine in this period is scarce, and does not permit us to identify the precise offices denoted by these terms (see the commentary on 5:9; 8:2–4; 10:16–17, 20); but some of the references to the 'king', especially 10:20, point strongly to the Ptolemaic period, which was characterized by an oppressive and well-organized despotism.

The Ptolemaic period was one of intense economic development (see Hengel; and for greater detail, Tcherikover, 1961). The agricultural resources of the empire were exploited to the full, often on large estates (Rostovsteff, 1922). The great expansion of international trade was backed by an elaborate system of finance; and although importing and exporting and much of the means of production were controlled by the central government, there were opportunities for great fortunes to be made by entrepreneurs. Money as a means of exchange assumed an importance which it had never had before. These developments help to explain Qoheleth's preoccupation with money and profit. His comments on these topics are quite unlike the way in which wealth is referred to in earlier wisdom literature and in the Old Testament generally. Whether or not the term *yitrôn*, 'profit, advantage', which occurs ten times in this book and nowhere else in the Old Testament, was part of the commercial jargon of the day in the sense of 'net profit' made on a deal, as some scholars maintain (see on 1:3), Qoheleth by his constant use of it, especially in the question 'What profit (can one get)? (1:3; 3:9; 5:15) was, although here he was not referring to actual commercial deals, clearly appealing—and not only in the passages in which the word occurs—to the merchant or business man who asks 'What's in it for me?' His comments on the ultimately illusory value of wealth significantly refer not to hereditary wealth, regarded in earlier times as a sign of divine blessing, but to the case of the self-made man who has devoted his life to making a fortune (4:7–8; 5:10–12) or to the man who both makes and loses a fortune in business (5:13–17). He remarks elsewhere, perhaps ironically, that 'Money makes everything possible' (10:19); and 11:1–2 most probably refers to commercial enterprise and its risks: to export goods by sea is a risky business, but can bring substantial profits; however, it is advisable to spread the risk involved as widely as possible.

The social conditions reflected by Ecclesiastes perhaps point less unequivocally to the Ptolemaic period, though they correspond to it very well. More than anywhere else in the Old Testament we find here a sense of the isolation of the individual which can only be the result of a partial breakdown of the closely-knit family and community life so markedly characteristic of earlier Israelite society. Injustice and oppression of the poor—a class to which Qoheleth and his readers certainly did not belong—are noted and even deplored, but regarded as inevitable. The policies and decisions of the political authority are not to be questioned. There is no sense of any obligation laid on the individual to serve or help others. This feeling of 'every man for himself' which Qoheleth reflects so sharply probably accounts to a large extent for his questioning of the view that God gives men what they deserve in this life: that view, which had some plausibility in the old order of things, when a more closely knit social system could to some extent control the ruthlessness of the over-ambitious and at the same time mitigate the effects of personal misfortune, had lost much of its force in Qoheleth's world.

There is, then, a clear convergence of the evidence concerning the date and historical background of the book. Ecclesiastes is a work of the later post-exilic period, when the old values of Israelite society had been largely set aside as a result both of the intellectual influence of Hellenism and of the new spirit of commercial enterprise sponsored by the Ptolemies. It bears no trace of the disruptions of Jewish life caused by the constant warfare which marked life in Palestine before 300 BC. Its language marks it out as one of the latest of the Old Testament books to be written. On the other hand, it shows no sign of the party strife and growing nationalistic sentiment which characterized Jewish society in Palestine in the years preceding the outbreak of the Maccabaean Revolt in 167 BC: indeed, it was already known to Ben Sira, whose book was also clearly written before those events. The fact that a substantial fragment of the work, copied probably during the first half of the second century BC, was found at Qumran tends further to confirm a Ptolemaic date, since a considerable time must be allowed to have elapsed between its composition and its acceptance in the sacred library of the Qumran sect. It is of course not possible to date the book with precision; but a date about the middle of the third century

BC or a little later would seem to correspond best to such evidence as we possess.

The author. Qoheleth tells us a great deal about his thoughts on a variety of subjects but virtually nothing about himself. All we really know about him is that he was well-to-do if not wealthy, closely in touch with the aristocracy of wealth, and a wisdom scholar who wrote a book and who, according to the admirer who appended 12:9 to the book, 'taught the people' (though *'am*, 'people', does not necessarily mean 'the *common* people'). It is not clear in what sense, if any, he was a 'professional' teacher. Little is known about any kind of systematic education which may have existed in his time: all our information comes from later periods. It is unlikely that the Greek system of education had yet been fully established in Palestine, even in Jerusalem, which was something of a cultural backwater. In fact it is now widely agreed, after an intensive study of this subject, that there is no evidence that Qoheleth was familiar with the Greek language: no Greek word or idiom appears in his book. There may have been Jewish schools of some kind in Jerusalem in his time, though the evidence put forward for this is purely inferential. Qoheleth is nowhere described in the book as a 'scribe' (*sôpēr*), nor does this word appear in the book. He is described in 12:9 as 'wise' (*ḥākām*), but he himself always employed that word in a general sense, often simply in contrast with 'fool'.

That Qoheleth should have been well-to-do, as is indicated not only by the topics with which he deals, but also by occasional remarks like 7:21, which takes for granted the possession of slaves, is not surprising. The literary tradition in Israel as elsewhere was the preserve of a prosperous, educated class.

Two other supposed characteristics of Qoheleth are purely speculative: that he was a bachelor, and that when he wrote his book he was an old man nearing the end of his life. His remarks about women in 7:26, 28 probably do not represent his personal views, but are the commonplaces of the wisdom tradition (see the commentary), while the recommendation to 'Enjoy life with the woman whom you love' in 9:9 indicates a clear approval of married life, or at least of the company of women, as something to be enjoyed. Despite what has been said above about Qoheleth's 'isolation', there is no reason whatever to suppose that he was himself unmarried.

The idea that he was in extreme old age when he wrote the book is principally derived from his famous description of decrepitude and death in 12:1–7, but is equally unfounded. Qoheleth was an acute observer of the human condition, not an autobiographer. Such a passage is more likely to have been written by one who looked forward with apprehension to the condition which he describes than by one who had already begun to experience it. As an experienced teacher who addresses men younger than himself (11:9) he may be presumed to have been of mature years; but more than this it is impossible to say.

Place of composition. Attempts to prove that the book was written in a Jewish community outside Palestine (e.g. Volz, Dahood) have not carried conviction. The evidence for a Palestinian setting, and in particular for Jerusalem, as the home of the author is extremely strong. The references to climatic conditions such as the unpredictability of the weather, dependence on rainfall and the direction of the wind (11:4, compare 1:6) and to successions of rainstorms (12:2) do not in any way correspond to weather conditions in Egypt, but reflect those of Palestine. Nor is the almond tree (12:5), mentioned several times in the Old Testament as growing in Palestine, to be found in Egypt: in fact, almonds are mentioned in Gen. 43:11 as among the 'choice fruits of the land (of Canaan)' exported from Palestine to Egypt. Among local customs mentioned by Qoheleth we find several which are characteristic of Palestine but improbable in Egypt, such as the hewing of wood (10:9) and the use of cisterns (12:6). (See Bishop, 1968 and Hertzberg, 1957).

Equally decisive for a Palestinian locale are the references to the Temple. In 5:1–7 there can be no doubt that the 'house of God' mentioned in association with the offering of sacrifice is the Temple in Jerusalem: the somewhat unusual expression occurs elsewhere in late Old Testament texts. There is a further reference to sacrifice in 9:2. 'The holy place' in 8:10 also refers to the Temple. The way in which Qoheleth's advice in 5:1–7 is offered, without any suggestion that visits to the Temple might be unusual occurrences, makes it probable that he is addressing readers who lived in Jerusalem or within easy reach of that city.

Against this evidence the arguments that the book was written in Egypt or elsewhere are unconvincing. As has been stated, Qoheleth shows no knowledge of the Greek language as might be expected from a resident of Ptolemaic Egypt, and he evinces no more familiarity with Greek culture and thought than might be expected of an educated Jew living in any part of the Ptolemaic empire. As has been suggested above, his references to attendance at court and to having access to the ruler or 'king' make far better sense as references to local seats of government than to the imperial court at Alexandria, since it is improbable that his readers should, wherever they lived, have attained as a class the highest positions in the imperial government itself. Finally, the references in the book to maritime trade have been thought to indicate familiarity with the great seaport of Alexandria; but, as has already been remarked, maritime trade was an important feature of the economic life of Palestine in the Ptolemaic period.

Dahood was of the opinion that Qoheleth was a Jew resident in a Phoenician city. This would not preclude familiarity with Palestine and Jerusalem. But Dahood's view, which is based on a particular linguistic argument, that Qoheleth's use of Hebrew has marked Phoenician features, has not been generally accepted.

C. LANGUAGE

The peculiarities of the kind of Hebrew employed by Qoheleth are so great that some scholars—notably Burkitt (1921–2), Ginsberg (1950), Zimmermann (1945–6), Torrey (1948–9)—have maintained that the book was originally written not in Hebrew but in Aramaic: that the extant Hebrew book is a translation from Aramaic made by one who has left clear traces of his work, leaving many words untranslated and rendering peculiarly Aramaic syntax and idioms literally into Hebrew, so creating a crabbed and often opaque style. It is this process, they maintained, which has made much of the book so difficult to understand if it is read simply as Hebrew. Alternatively it was argued that the book was written in Hebrew, but by a writer whose native speech was Aramaic, and who, having determined nevertheless to write in Hebrew, was actually thinking in Aramaic when he wrote (Margoliouth, 1911). A further complication was introduced by Gordon (1947) and Dahood (*Bib.* 33, 1952), who claimed to have found strong linguistic features in Qoheleth's Hebrew which are characteristic of a northern type of speech: Phoenician, Ugaritic and Canaanite.

These questions are clearly technical ones and cannot be discussed in detail here. The translation theory has now been generally abandoned after a vigorous debate. Arguments of this kind in which an attempt is made to prove the existence of purely hypothetical phenomena—in this case, an Aramaic original—lack conviction unless the evidence put forward cannot be explained in any other way. In the case of Ecclesiastes the proponents of the translation theory adduced a number of words and phrases which in their opinion could only be explained as the infelicities of an inadequate or incompetent translator. Each of these examples was investigated by other scholars, notably by Gordis (1946, and in subsequent articles), who showed that these supposed infelicities can be adequately explained if the late date of the book, the idiosyncrasies of the author's style, and the problems posed by the quasi-philosophical nature of his material, of a kind never before treated in

Hebrew, are taken into account. The fact that the Hebrew of Ben Sira, written somewhat later, and of the Qumran scrolls is more 'classical' than that of Qoheleth merely shows that, as in his teaching, so in his language, Qoheleth was less conservative than these writers.

That Ecclesiastes contains a large number of Aramaic words—more, in fact, than any other Old Testament book except Esther—is an undoubted fact; but it is not surprising that this should be so. Aramaic, which already in the Persian period had become a kind of *lingua franca* in the western part of the empire, had become more and more the common speech of Palestine. It may therefore be assumed that Qoheleth was familiar with it, though whether it was for him a 'first language' it is impossible to say. That his Hebrew should have been strongly influenced by Aramaic is to be expected; and this feature of his language fits very well with the view that in this respect his book marks a transitional stage between the later books of the Old Testament and the Mishnah, which also abounds in words and constructions derived from Aramaic. As far as other linguistic influences are concerned, there are, as might be expected, some examples of Persian words, but none of Greek. The theory of northern or Phoenician influence on Qoheleth's language, though still supported by some scholars, is now generally regarded as problematical (see Whitley, 1979, especially pp. 111–18).

It has been suggested by some scholars that Qoheleth deliberately used traditional religious or ethical terms in new senses in order to express his own peculiar notions about the nature of the world and God. This is an exaggeration. The fact that a number of words in the book appear to have connotations which they do not have elsewhere in the Old Testament does not prove that it was Qoheleth who first introduced these new meanings. Many of these developments are attested in the Hebrew of the immediately following period and may have already taken place in the language as it was generally spoken in Qoheleth's time, and this may well be true of other words not so attested. (These questions will be considered further in the treatment of particular words in the commentary.)

The notion that Qoheleth made significant changes in the meanings of certain *theological terms* has arisen in part from the determination of some scholars to find in the book a strict theological consistency which it does not possess. Thus it has been supposed that words like *šāpaṭ*, 'to judge' (3:17), *mišpāṭ*, 'judgement' (11:9) and *ḥôṭe'*, 'sinner' (2:26; 8:12; 9:2) cannot have their normal connotations here because such meanings are inconsistent with Qoheleth's general views expressed elsewhere in the book. The prudent interpreter, however, should presume that such words are used in their usual senses unless the *immediate* context makes a different interpretation unavoidable.

The *grammatical* peculiarities of the book can mainly be explained in terms of the general development of the Hebrew language. Such features, which cannot be listed in full here, include the oscillation between the use and the omission of the definite article and between the relative particle *'ᵃšer* and the later *še–* ('who, which'). But some of the unusual and often puzzling conjunctions which appear in the book appear to have been occasioned by the complex nature of Qoheleth's sentences arising from the complexity of his thought. Earlier Hebrew speakers and writers had not found it necessary to make such subtle distinctions between different kinds of subordinate clause.

All these features—the scarcity of comparable extant literature from the latter part of the Old Testament period, the unique mode of discourse practised by Qoheleth and the undoubted idiosyncrasy of his style—combine to make the book unusually difficult to understand and to translate. With regard to the third of these features, modern commentators have been totally unable to agree about the *quality* of Qoheleth's Hebrew style: Podechard, for example, thought it poor ('*assez mauvaise*'—compare, more recently, Whitley), while Gordis characterized it as 'good Hebrew'.

Finally, there is no agreement among modern scholars about the extent to which parts of the book are to be regarded as poetry rather than prose. The fact that there is no agreed opinion about the nature of Hebrew metrics constitutes a major difficulty in this regard. Some extended passages—notably 12:1–7—at least appear to show evidence of a poetic imagination; and many of the short proverbs in the book, some of which are probably quotations of earlier wisdom sayings, have the same form as those in Prov. 10–29, which are certainly in poetical form and have that parallelism which is the one undoubted feature of Hebrew poetry. Some of these are printed as poetry in *RSV*, especially when they are arranged in short collections. On the other hand, most of Qoheleth's closely-knit arguments hardly seem to qualify as poetry, and attempts to show that the entire book is written in poetic form and metre have not been generally accepted. (On the problem of distinguishing poetry from prose in the Hebrew of the Old Testament, see Watson, 1984, pp. 44–62.)

D. LITERARY UNITY AND STRUCTURE

It is evident to any reader of Ecclesiastes that the book is not a systematic treatise. Although theological issues of great importance—such as the nature of God, the meaning and purpose of life, the moral governance of the universe, death and life after death—are earnestly discussed here, in general no progression of thought from one section to another is discernible. Rather, a certain cyclical tendency is observable: the author returns again and again to the same point and often concludes his discussions with the same recurring formulae.

Another feature of the book which strikes the reader is that it contains a number of what appear to be totally incompatible statements: for example, the categorical confession 'So I hated life' (2:17) is apparently negated by 'But he who is joined with all the living has hope, for a living dog is better than a dead lion' (9:4), and by 'Light is sweet, and it is pleasant for the eyes to behold the sun' (11:7); similarly the disillusioned remark that 'one fate comes to all, to the righteous and the wicked, to the good and the evil' (9:2), and similar comments, appear to be directly contradicted by a series of assertions such as 'God will judge the righteous and the wicked' (3:17) and 'I know that it will be well with those who fear God . . . but it will not be well with the wicked' (8:12–13).

These apparent contradictions have led commentators to pose certain fundamental questions both about the nature of the book as a literary composition and about its authorship, and in particular to wonder whether it is, after all, the work of a single author, the man known as Qoheleth, and whether it is a single, integrated work with a clear structure or simply a random assemblage of unco-ordinated material. Both of these questions are crucial for the understanding of the book as a whole.

Authorship. An earlier generation of scholars (especially Siegfried and Podechard, followed by McNeile and Barton) attempted to account for the supposed inconsistencies and contradictions in the book by means of complicated hypotheses of multiple sources, expanded editions, glosses and the like added at different times to Qoheleth's original work by persons attempting to neutralize, defend, explain or complement certain features of his thought. The early years of the twentieth century were a time when theories of this kind were particularly popular among biblical critics. It was taken for granted that a biblical writer must necessarily have been a model of consistency. Some colour was given to this kind of theory by the fact, about which virtually all commentators are agreed, that the final verses of the book—12:8–14 or 9–14—form an 'epilogue' which is the work not of Qoheleth himself but of one or more later writers, who might therefore have been the authors of some of the supposed additional material. Such extreme views about the history of the composition of the book are no longer held; however, a number of modern scholars still hold to the view that some of the more 'difficult'—that is, apparently inconsistent—statements in the book are attempts by editors or glossators to give a more 'orthodox' or traditional character to a somewhat shocking or 'heretical' book.

The issue, then, is one of consistency of thought. But it must be asked what is the standard by which such consistency is to be measured. How is it possible to formulate from the book itself, which is the only evidence which we possess, an authoritative picture of Qoheleth's thought? There is a circular argument here: the proponents of multiple authorship have first composed such a picture by omitting certain passages from consideration, and have then argued on the basis of that operation that these passages do not fit it.

Various alternative explanations have been offered by scholars who argue for unity of authorship. It has been pointed out (for example, by Galling, 1932) that the rigid concept of 'consistency' employed by the reductionist critics is not to be found in ancient Near Eastern texts but is the product of western logic first developed by the Greeks: one may add that its absence from Ecclesiastes is in fact one indication of Qoheleth's attachment to his Semitic forebears and of his independence of Greek influence. Other interpreters (Gordis; Fohrer, 1970, Coppens, 1979), on the supposition that the book was not a single composition written at one time but an accumulation of shorter pieces written over a long period of Qoheleth's life (see below), have suggested that its different parts express different moods of the author, who did not attempt to reconcile one with another. It has also been urged that the editorial process envisaged is difficult to account for: if the original book of Qoheleth's was unorthodox and unacceptable, why should anyone have taken the trouble to try—unsuccessfully!—to change its character? Finally, it has been observed that the period between the probable date of its composition and its general currency, attested by Ben Sira and by its presence at Qumran, is too short for a complex series of subsequent additions to have been made.

Each of these arguments has its merits. But the most probable explanation of the tensions within the book is that these tensions existed within Qoheleth's own mind. This question will be considered more fully below. But it may be remarked here that Qoheleth was attempting to reconcile his own experience of life and of the world with the traditional wisdom tradition which he inherited, and that he offers no universal or satisfactory answer to these problems. If he sometimes oscillates between what appear to be irreconcilable poles, he is merely expressing the tension within his own mind. Indeed, it can be shown that in some passages he is merely following precedent within wisdom circles by deliberately setting these opposite opinions side by side in order to present the problem to his readers, and also that on occasion he quotes 'orthodox' wisdom sayings in order to introduce the debate.

It would be foolish to deny that there may be passages in the book which are glosses, that is, originally comments on the text by scribes which eventually became incorporated into it. If the book were entirely free from such glosses, it would be exceptional among the books of the Old Testament. But in the body of the book (1:4–12:7) these passages are probably few in number. The wise commentator will assume that the material comes in its entirety from the hands of Qoheleth alone—though not necessarily its present arrangement—and will attempt to understand it as such before resorting to theories of interpolations.

Structure. Since Ecclesiastes is evidently not a single systematic treatise in which there is a progression from a set of premisses to a logical conclusion, it remains to be considered in what other sense it might be a unified composition. From the point of view of content, it deals with a number of distinct, though related, topics. If it could be shown that these have been arranged in some kind of logical order by Qoheleth himself, this would greatly assist the understanding of his thought; and even if—and this is extremely probable, as will be seen—the arrangement is not his own but that of an editor who undertook to put together as far as possible in an ordered arrangement a miscellaneous collection of Qoheleth's notes or *pensées*, we should at least have a very early interpretation of his thought made in all probability by someone who knew him personally.

Numerous attempts have been made to find a structure of this kind (e.g. by Ginsberg, 1955, Wright, 1968, Fox, 1977, Rousseau, 1981, Mulder, 1982). Other scholars (e.g. Galling, 1932, Eissfeldt, 1965, Kroeber) have asserted that no such structure is to be found. For Galling, the book is simply a collection of unrelated 'aphorisms' (*Sentenzen*). Between the two extremes are ranged a number of scholars (e.g. Zimmerli, 1974, Lauha, Schoors, 1982) who see some indications of purposeful arrangement, but reject the more ambitious attempts to find in the book a complete system of logical or formal connections running through the whole. The very wide divergence of scholarly opinion on this question should warn the interpreter of the need for caution.

There are two interconnected aspects of this problem: form and content. If it were possible, as is the case with some other biblical books, to determine with certainty the limits of each literary unit by form-critical methods—distinctive introductory and concluding phrases, characteristic types of utterance and the like—these units could then be studied with a view to defining their leading ideas, and it would then be clear if and how one formal unit is related thematically to its neighbours, and whether a pattern of thought can be discerned. Unfortunately, as Fohrer remarked, 'form-critical criteria are often insufficient' for the study of the structure of this book. This is not because Qoheleth does not make use of traditional literary forms: on the contrary, there is often no difficulty in identifying such forms. But this frequently fails to help the investigation of the structure of longer passages, to say nothing of the structure of the book as a whole, since Qoheleth regularly combines several such traditional forms in the course of a single argument, often in combination with his own distinctive modes of expression.

Among a number of literary forms in the book which can be traced back to traditional models are the aphorism, the admonition and the didactic narrative. The *aphorism* or short saying occurs frequently, occasionally grouped into short collections (e.g. 7:1–8; 10:1–3, 8–15), but more often introduced singly or in pairs into longer passages (e.g. 1:15, 18; 2:14*a*; 4:5, 6). These are often indistinguishable in form from the aphorisms in Prov. 10–29. Some of them are probably quotations from earlier collections picked out by Qoheleth to reinforce his own arguments, to serve as the basis of his own more nuanced discussion, or even to demonstrate the falsity of their assertions; others are probably his own composition: certainly Qoheleth had not entirely broken away from the older literary tradition which found in the parallel couplet an ideal form through which to express its meaning. This is also true of the *admonition*, in which the wisdom teacher gives advice to his pupil in the imperative or jussive mood (e.g. 5:1, 2, 4; 7:16, 17). The *didactic narrative*, either in the first or the third person (4:13–16; 5:13–17; 9:13–16), which points a moral by means of a short story, is also familiar from earlier wisdom literature (compare Prov. 4:1–5; 7:6–23; 24:30–34; Ps. 37:35–36).

But Qoheleth was by no means limited to these traditional literary forms. Admittedly some of the passages which have no real parallels in extant literature such as 1:4–11; 3:1–9; 12:1–7 may well be examples of literary types once commonplace in an extensive wisdom literature which has since disappeared (see especially on 3:1–9). There are other examples in the Old Testament wisdom books of literary forms which have no known parallels (e.g. in Prov. 1–9). What form criticism cannot illuminate and can only make allowances for is the genius of individual writers; and this is perhaps particularly true in the case of Qoheleth: his book, taken as a whole, is unique.

One formal feature of the book which is both characteristic and unique is the so-called 'broken aphorism' (*gebrochene Sentenz*: see Galling, 1934; Ellermeier; Hertzberg) in which Qoheleth expresses his peculiar critical attitude towards traditional wisdom. This attitude was not one of outright rejection: he perceived the element of truth in it, but also its failure to tell the *whole* truth, to present the world in its manysidedness. He therefore found it necessary to qualify it, sometimes drastically. This kind of argument can sometimes be easily recognized from the use of expressions like 'yet' or 'but'; but in many cases the traditional view and Qoheleth's qualifications are simply placed in juxtaposition (the *RSV* often supplies a conjunction absent from the Hebrew). Occasionally the point is made by the juxtaposition of two traditional sayings so that one qualifies the other (e.g. 4:5, 6).

Passages of this kind are often complex, made up of alternations between independent aphorisms and Qoheleth's comments on them. Occasionally we find a double qualification: what is first stated is qualified, and the qualification itself is then further qualified (4:4–6; 4:13–16; see Ellermeier), so that a balance is struck between different points of view. Such passages do not conform to a set pattern and by their very nature lack a clear-cut conclusion which can be identified as marking the end of a distinct section of the book. Here, then, problems of literary form and of continuity of thought combine to frustrate the interpreter who is looking for a clear structure for the book as a whole.

The most thoroughgoing attempt to elucidate the *inner* structure of the individual passages is that of Loader (1979). He claims to have proved that 'Excepting the epilogue, not a single palpable contradiction can be found in the book' (p. 133). He argues that Qoheleth, using familiar forms in a new way, invented a unique type of argument based on the setting in tension of 'polar opposites' (such as life and death, wisdom and folly) in order to demonstrate the futility of life. These polar structures are, he argues, to be found in virtually every section of the book. This approach has undoubtedly thrown light on many individual problems, though in some cases its application seems rather forced, and the question of the total structure of the book as a whole still remains unsolved.

On the structure and composition of the book as a whole, probably the most balanced assessment is that of Zimmerli:

1. There is no uniformity in the way in which the book has been put together. Some sections appear to be random collections of

unconnected short sayings, while in others there are clear indications of both formal and logical continuity.

2. Between these two extremes there are large tracts where some kind of continuity is a possibility, but where the divisions between one section and another are not clear-cut: here there is room for differences of opinion, and the exegete must be content to leave the matter open. (In this commentary, therefore, the division of the book into sections for practical purposes should not be taken as necessarily indicating more than a probable opinion.)

3. Although the themes of the book are for the most part closely related to one another, there is no single co-ordinating theme. (The identical verses 1:2 and 12:8, which form a framework to the thoughts of Qoheleth and ostensibly sum up his view on life in a single phrase, express the view of an editor who refers to him in the third person.)

4. Other signs of editorial arrangement include the placing of the Solomonic fiction near the beginning of the book and of the description of decrepitude and death at the end (11:9–12:7). But the rest of the material available to this editor did not lend itself on the whole to systematic arrangement.

E. THOUGHT

Qoheleth was not a philosopher. It was not his intention to construct a philosophical system. There are serious inconsistencies in his thought, and these are ultimately due to the fact, of which he was himself acutely aware, that the problems which he had set himself to solve are intrinsically impossible of solution. Although, speaking in the guise of Solomon, he states: 'I applied my mind to seek and to search out by wisdom all that is done under heaven' (1:13), he was in the end obliged to confess: 'I saw all the work of God, that man cannot find out the work that is done under the sun. However much man may toil in seeking, he will not find it out; even though a wise man claims to know, he cannot find it out' (8:17); indeed, it is God's express intention that this should be so (3:11).

Nevertheless, Qoheleth was a seeker after truth. The kind of truth with which he was concerned was truth about man and his fate in the world in which God had placed him. The standard repository of truth of this kind was the wisdom tradition, a tradition with which Qoheleth was clearly very familiar, and so it was this that he took as his starting-point. But he was not content to take its tenets for granted: he aimed to test their truth by setting them against his own personal experience of life in the Jerusalem of the third century BC. He lived in a period when the old traditions of Israelite life were breaking down. His book has been described as a running dialogue with a hypothetical 'wise man' representing the conventional wisdom which had prevailed up to that time.

Like other writers of what has come to be 'canonical' literature, Qoheleth did not see himself as a 'sacred writer'. Indeed, he seems not to have regarded his writings as carrying any kind of authoritative cachet. In this he differs notably from the authors of the Book of Proverbs, which is written in an authoritative manner and is extremely didactic in tone. In this respect he is comparable to the author of the Book of Job. Although he sometimes gives specific and practical advice to his readers, his main role is not that of a teacher in the sense of one who lays down the law to his pupils (though he *was* a teacher—see 12:9), but rather of one who presents certain fundamental problems to his readers and invites them to apply their critical faculties to them, assisting them with his own comments but not wishing to impose his own opinions dogmatically.

These facts have an important bearing on the way in which the book should be read. They relieve the reader from any obligation to see Qoheleth as either an original thinker or as one who has spoken the last word on his subject. Within the context of the surviving Old Testament books his thought is undoubtedly new and extremely daring, even shocking—though he may have had predecessors of whom we know nothing. But in terms of human thought in general, many of his ideas were not original, if by 'original' it is meant that no one had expressed them before. Some of them, for example, were already commonplaces of Greek philosophical and quasi-philosophical literature, while others are already found in much older literature such as the Epic of Gilgamesh. This does not imply that Qoheleth was consciously or unconsciously influenced by such earlier writers. It means rather that his thought is often *parallel* to that of others who had pondered on the same problems: similar human situations are likely to produce similar reflections, and indeed many later writers of many different periods were to express similar thoughts quite spontaneously and with no awareness that these thoughts were not 'original'.

In this respect, then, many of Qoheleth's thoughts are quite 'commonplace', even if they may, for him, have been 'original'. If he had been a philosopher in the Greek sense or in the modern western sense, he would no doubt have made an attempt to systematize his thought, to smooth out its contradictions, and to propound reasoned solutions to the problems which he raises. But he was not a philosopher, and he did not do so. This lack of systematization, however, does not detract from the value of his reflections or prevent them from stimulating further reflection on the part of the reader of the book.

Despite the unsystematic and sometimes contradictory character of his thoughts, it is reasonable to suppose that Qoheleth had a distinctive attitude towards life which can at least to some extent be defined. Yet it is here that the greatest divergence of scholarly opinion is found. Leaving aside the natural determination of orthodox Jewish and Christian interpreters throughout the ages to find a positive teaching in the book which conforms to the rest of Scripture and to the teaching of Church and synagogue, we find modern scholarly opinions of it ranging from an extremely negative assessment to a quite positive one. On the one hand, Qoheleth has been described in unqualified terms as a pessimist, a sceptic and even a cynic. G. von Rad, for example, wrote: 'The Preacher's book is better understood as a sceptical marginal note on the tradition of the wise men, although of course it is a very bitter one. . . . Ecclesiastes calls a halt just before the point of complete bankruptcy. . . . He sees himself suspended over the abyss of despair. . . . Nothing remained for Ecclesiastes but to submit in deep resignation to this tragic existence.' Many scholars have made similar assessments. On the other hand, a number of scholars have argued on the basis of such passages as 2:24–26; 3:12–13; 5:18–19; 8:15; 9:7–9 and of the recurring references to human life as God's gift, that Qoheleth believed that despite all its frustrations and pain life could be a joyful experience for the person who 'fears God'. For them, Qoheleth's religious faith was all the stronger for his refusal to shut his eyes to the bad things in life and for his unflinching realism.

Perhaps the chief reason for this wide divergence of opinions is that, given the fragmentary nature of the book, there is room for very different assessments of the relative importance which Qoheleth himself attached to the various statements which he makes. For example, the passages referred to in the previous paragraph commend the enjoyment of the good things which God has given mankind. Those who understand Qoheleth as a thoroughgoing pessimist for whom life presents itself as unrelieved frustration and hopelessness tend to dismiss these passages as expressing an attitude of mere '*Carpe diem*'—that is, as recommendations, born of despair, to snatch greedily at what few superficial pleasures may come one's way because life has nothing else to offer and death may come at any moment: for them it is the dark sayings of Qoheleth which express his true attitude. Yet it is equally possible to argue that it is just this series of positive statements, punctuating the book, which expresses Qoheleth's true conclusions: that it is only the person who has taken full account of the vanities of this world and faced up to them who is free to receive the divine gift of joy in simple things. This difficulty is compounded by the complexity of Qoheleth's way of arguing: in attempting to analyse the flow of thought in a single fairly lengthy passage in which opposite opinions are juxtaposed and the thought appears to flow first in one direction and then back again, it is often extremely difficult to grasp what is the major theme.

A further difficulty is created by the real or supposed ambiguity of some of Qoheleth's terminology. In several passages, for example, he speaks of 'fearing God' or of 'those who fear God'. In general in the Old Testament the fear of God or of Yahweh does not denote a state of terror but one of willing and even joyful obedience to God's will, expressed either in worship or in ethical conduct. It has, however, been argued that Qoheleth uses the expression, at least in some contexts, in a different way, laying stress on the literal meaning of 'fear': God is literally fearsome, a terrifying God who strikes his creatures without warning; the only possible attitude towards him is therefore one of terror. Clearly the interpretation of this phrase in Ecclesiastes is of the greatest importance for the assessment of Qoheleth's thought. In fact a considerable proportion of Qoheleth's vocabulary has been interpreted in a negative or reductionist sense: for example, some scholars have argued that when he speaks of God as bestowing his *gifts* on human beings, this is to be understood, not as elsewhere in the Old Testament as referring to God's beneficent care for them, but in an entirely neutral sense with no implication of a kindly concern.

All interpreters, however, agree that Qoheleth comments in a remarkably detached way on the human scene as it presents itself to him, and that wherever he looks he finds examples of a fundamental frustration: there is in almost every human endeavour a 'fly in the ointment' (10:1) which prevents the attainment of full satisfaction. Human activities, in other words, do not live up to the expectations of those who hopefully engage in them.

Work, for example, is necessary in order to make a living, and may also provide a certain satisfaction in the very doing of it; but if pursued beyond reasonable limits it becomes an intolerable burden. To *over*work in order to make not just a living but a fortune is stupid and ultimately unrewarding: it puts an unnecessary strain on the worker, and for nothing. It reduces his opportunities for the enjoyment of life while he is able to do so, and even if it does result in the making of a fortune—which is very problematical—that fortune can easily be lost. Moreover, the fruits of a life's work cannot be enjoyed after death, and even the hope that they will eventually benefit one's heirs may well be frustrated by the bad luck or the bad judgement of the beneficiaries, so that nothing at all remains to show for all the effort which has been made.

On the other hand, Qoheleth points out that the pursuit of *pleasure* for its own sake is no less satisfactory. The wealthy man who avoids the strain of work completely and opts for a life of pure self-indulgence soon finds that it palls.

These observations and others are made by Qoheleth in his role of *wise man*: that is, of one who is, in his own estimation, superior to others in his ability to observe and to draw practical and useful conclusions from what he observes: wisdom, he says, is better than folly. Yet wisdom too is ultimately profoundly unsatisfactory, not only because the wise man's advice to others is seldom taken, but above all because, like overwork and self-indulgence, it falls short of expectations. Man's mind is by its very nature finite: a wise man may be able to understand the world in which he lives far better than others, but his creator has deliberately denied to him, just as much as to others, the capability of discovering any principle which will explain why things happen as they do, or of foreseeing what will happen in the future. And this ignorance is one of the basic causes of human frustration in general. No one, in fact, is able to discern a fixed relationship between cause and effect. In particular, there is no certainty that virtue and wickedness bring their own rewards: social injustice and oppression often seem to flourish, and it appears that human life is ruled by nothing more than chance. Finally the universality and inevitability of death abolish all distinction between the wise man and the fool and between the virtuous and the wicked, and nothing is known of any life after death which might redress the balance.

The picture of the fundamentally unsatisfactory nature of human life painted by Qoheleth in these often not very original, and, it may be thought, somewhat commonplace reflections is summed up by him in the word *hebel* (*RSV*, 'vanity'), which occurs more than thirty times in this short book, comprising more than half the total number of its occurrences in the Old Testament. The precise meaning of *hebel* as used by Qoheleth has been the subject of much discussion (see on 1:2), and the word has been translated in many different ways. Ultimately, this question is a technical one of secondary importance: whatever may be the best equivalent of *hebel* in other languages, the book as a whole and the contexts in which the word occurs make it clear that by it Qoheleth is referring to the generally unsatisfactory and frustrating character of human life as he has observed it.

The main disagreements of scholars about the meaning of the book do not arise from Qoheleth's specific comments on particular aspects of human life. The crucial question is rather whether this negativism dominates the whole of his world-view, or whether it is only a foil for some other, more positive assessment of the human situation. If in fact Qoheleth's final conclusion was an encouraging one, or even if there was merely some tiny element of comfort in it, this could only be derived from outside the world, that is, from God. Qoheleth's concept of God, therefore, is the central question for the interpretation of his thought.

On this question, too, there is a degree of general agreement. Unlike many other thinkers who have lamented the unsatisfactory nature of human life—including some Greek authors with whom he has been compared—Qoheleth was no atheist, nor did he regard God as irrelevant to human affairs. He took for granted not only the existence but also the omnipotence of the one God. In this belief he did not deviate in the least from the Jewish faith of his time. This God, whom he calls (ha-)Elohim but who is in fact identical with the Yahweh of the Old Testament, is the sole creator of the world and holds the fate of every human being in his hands. Whatever happens on earth is his 'work'. Man must, therefore, recognize that all human endeavours are futile apart from him, and that all moments of happiness come from him as his gifts. He is therefore to be worshipped, and Qoheleth takes it for granted that his readers will do so.

But is this God, in Qoheleth's view, a benevolent despot or a cruel tyrant? This question is difficult to answer. Qoheleth never utters a word of reproach or hostility towards him. If an answer to this question can be obtained, it can be obtained only by looking at the evidence supplied by the picture of the state of God's world which Qoheleth has drawn, for as he himself states in 8:17, 'that which is done under the sun' is in fact God's own doing, the 'work of God'. God, then, is responsible for the state of the world, and this includes the things which Qoheleth perceives as injustice and oppression. But God's *motives* are entirely incomprehensible, and God intends to keep them so. God, then, is hidden and remote; he cannot be questioned: his will is immutable. This is why from man's point of view it seems that things happen by chance.

But, looked at from another point of view, this is not so. Everything is *given* by God in a deliberate act of giving. And here we find, in the list which could be made of those things which, according to Qoheleth, God gives to man, those apparent contradictions which make the assessment of Qoheleth's thought so difficult. God gives us our life (8:15; 12:7); but that life is short (5:18), and is even once described as an 'unhappy business' (1:13). God gives wealth to some, but even in this there may be misfortune for the recipient, for while to some he bestows the power to enjoy that wealth (5:19), to others he does not give that power (6:2). Finally, what is best for man, according to Qoheleth, is to 'eat and drink and find enjoyment in all the toil with which he toils under the sun the few days of his life which God has given him'—but he adds, '*for this is his lot*' (5:18). Similarly he says that '*to accept his lot* and find enjoyment in his toil—this is the gift of God' (5:19).

The world, then, is as God made it, and nothing can alter it. The best thing for men to do is to accept this and to enjoy to the full what *good* things God has given; and indeed this is what God *requires* of them (see on 12:1). Depending on the relative weight placed by the interpreters respectively on the negative and positive sides of statements such as these, a whole range of assessments of Qoheleth's outlook, from one of extreme pessimism and despair to one of courageous faith and radiant optimism has been made by ancient and modern scholars alike. In all these there is a tendency to confuse Qoheleth's *feelings* with his objective observations. He set down the facts as he saw them, and on the basis of these facts he put forward certain suggestions about the wisest way to conduct one's life. In contrast to what we find in other Old Testament books—especially in many prophetic oracles, in the Book of Job and in the psalms of lamentation—he virtually never reveals his own feelings. We must assume that he did not consider an account of them relevant to his purpose or of practical use to his readers. Whether he was a pessimist or an optimist, therefore, will remain a matter of opinion; what is certain is that he was a realist.

Qoheleth and Biblical Thought. Although some scholars continue to find indications in the book of substantial Greek, Egyptian or Mesopotamian influence, there is now a general agreement that Qoheleth's thought is fundamentally Hebraic. In fact it is obvious that the book could have been written only by a Jew, and by one who was not only familiar with the basic tenets of the Jewish faith but also with that religious literature which we now call the Old Testament. The list of characteristically Old Testament beliefs which he fully accepted, explicitly or implicitly, is a long one: it includes belief in a sole God who is transcendent and omnipotent, who created the world and created it a good world, and in mankind as weak and dependent on God, made from the dust and animated by him with breath, but destined after a short span of life to return to dust and to descend to the comfortless and shadowy realm of Sheol. Qoheleth was also in full agreement with biblical teaching in recognizing, within these limits, man's freedom: that it is not God but men themselves who are responsible for the present corrupt state of the world. 'God made man upright, but they have sought out many devices' (7:29).

Some of these beliefs can be paralleled from non-Israelite sources (see Loretz); but taken together they have an unmistakable Jewish flavour. It is true that the Jewish belief in God's choice of Israel and of his subsequent dealings with his chosen people is missing from the list; but Ecclesiastes shares this peculiarity with the other wisdom books of the Old Testament, Proverbs and Job. Israel's wisdom literature had always had the characteristic of being concerned with the individual member of society rather than with the nation as a whole.

But this is obviously not the whole story. Without denying the truth of the beliefs listed above or stepping outside their framework, Qoheleth has to a large extent succeeded in giving them a new perspective. Like many a theologian since his time, he adopted an eclectic approach to the biblical material at his disposal, selecting for particular emphasis certain features which especially appealed to him, while paying little or no attention to others. For example, in speaking of God in relation to his human creation he makes no mention of God's love, nor does he speak of the need to trust God, or of the possibility of close fellowship between God and man. He thus paints a somewhat bleak picture, but one which no doubt seemed to him to correspond best to his own experience and that of his own generation. All the elements of this picture, however, can be found in the Old Testament, which is by no means univocal on the subject of the nature of the deity. In fact, as has often been pointed out, Qoheleth's picture of God in his dealings with man corresponds remarkably closely to that which we find in Gen. 3: there God withdraws his presence and his intimate fellowship from man and woman and leaves them to fend for themselves in a harsh world in which the very soil has been cursed and they are faced with a life of hard toil ending only with death. The sombreness of this picture has been relieved by its subsequent incorporation into the Book of Genesis and so into the larger context in which it now stands. Qoheleth no doubt read Genesis 2–3 already in that context; but he caught its original flavour and recognized the extent to which it corresponds to the real world which we know.

Qoheleth's often repeated comments on the fact that the wicked often seem to prosper and the virtuous to go unrewarded also have a long Old Testament tradition behind them. Similar complaints had been made earlier by prophets and psalmists, to say nothing of the Book of Job, and a variety of attempts had been made to find an answer to the problem. Qoheleth made no attempt to account for this phenomenon: rather, he stressed the freedom and sovereignty of

God. He asserted with great emphasis that any attempt by puny man to discover, let alone to question, God's motives was not only ridiculous; it was to question the very nature of the omnipotent God.

Qoheleth was thus defending the Israelite doctrine of God against a corruption of it—found in such texts as Ps. 37 and parts of the Book of Job—which made the righteousness of God into a rigid principle but in doing so implicitly denied his freedom. So in this as in other respects his teaching remains within the framework of biblical thought.

F. ANALYSIS OF CONTENTS

1:1	Title
1:2–3	'Vanity of vanities'
1:4–11	The ceaseless round of nature
1:12–2:26	'Solomon's' testimony
3:1–15	Man does not know his time
3:16–22	Where is justice to be found?
4:1–3	The plight of the oppressed
4:4–6	The folly of overwork
4:7–8	The miser
4:9–12	Two are better than one
4:13–16	The hazards of power
5:1–7	Advice on worship
5:8–9	On the political system
5:10–20	The deceptiveness of money
6:1–6	Life without joy
6:7–9	A loose group of sayings
6:10–12	Man's weakness and ignorance
7:1–14	The limitations of human life
7:15	Inequities observed
7:16–18	A warning against self-righteousness
7:19	The superiority of wisdom
7:20–22	Do as you would be done by
7:23–8:1	True wisdom is inaccessible
8:2–9	Despotism and human servitude
8:10–15	Life's unfairness
8:16–17	The inscrutability of God's work
9:1–10	Enjoy your life, for death levels all
9:11–12	Time and chance
9:13–18	The limited value of wisdom
10:1–11:6	Miscellaneous sayings

11:7–8	Rejoice in the light
11:9–12:7	Make the most of youth
12:8	Editorial conclusion
12:9–14	Epilogue

COMMENTARY

on

Ecclesiastes

TITLE

1:1

Like some other Old Testament books, Ecclesiastes has been provided by an editor with a title identifying the author (compare the opening words of the books of Jeremiah and Amos, and Prov. 30:1; 31:1). On **the Preacher** (Heb. *qōhelet*), see the Introduction.

the son of David, king in Jerusalem: there can be no doubt that the reference is to Solomon, who had the reputation of having possessed unparalleled wisdom and of having been a prolific author (1 Kg. 4:29–34; MT 5:9–14). The Book of Proverbs, the Song of Solomon and the Wisdom of Solomon in the Apocrypha are also attributed to him. The phrase **king in Jerusalem** is derived from 1:12, where Qoheleth himself, following an ancient literary convention of Near Eastern wisdom literature of claiming royal authorship, presents himself to the reader in the identity of 'king over Israel in Jerusalem'. The editor who supplied the title of the book interpreted this as meaning that Qoheleth was in fact King Solomon, David's son (cf. Prov. 1:1; Ca. 1:1).

The uniqueness and peculiarity of the phrase **king in Jerusalem** has led some scholars to argue that *melek* (**king**) here has been wrongly pointed and should be read *mōlek*, 'property-owner' (Ginsberg, 1950, pp. 12–15), or, alternatively, that it is an Aramaic or Phoenician word meaning 'counsellor' (Dahood, *CBQ* 14 [1952]; Albright, p. 15, note 2). These words are unknown in Hebrew, and such suggestions are improbable. The activities described in 2:4–11 are hardly credible of any private person, and that account is clearly based on the description of Solomon's reign in 1 Kg. 3–11.

'VANITY OF VANITIES'

1:2–3

Verse 2 is clearly intended to be a summary statement of the theme of the whole book and is expressed in extremely emphatic terms. The word **vanity** (*hebel*) occurs here no less than five times in a verse which contains only eight words, four of which are accounted for by the repeated phrase **vanity of vanities**, a construction which is always used to indicate something complete, absolute or unqualified—cf. 'the heaven of heavens', Dt. 10:14; 1 Kg. 8:27 (*RSV*, 'the highest heaven') and 'The Song of Songs'. This verse, introducing the teaching of Qoheleth, recurs, in a shortened form, at the end of the book (before the editorial epilogue) in 12:8. These two verses, 1:2 and 12:8, thus form a framework for Qoheleth's sayings which is intended to leave the reader in no doubt about Qoheleth's negative attitude towards human life.

But are these two verses the work of Qoheleth himself or of an editor who added them in order to present to the reader his own interpretation of Qoheleth's teaching? With regard to verse 2, some commentators (e.g. Barton, Gordis, Kroeber) hold the former view; others (e.g. Galling, Lauha) the latter. The evidence is in favour of the latter view. First, although *hebel*, 'vanity', is one of Qoheleth's most characteristic words, the phrase **says the Preacher**, which crops up again in a similarly abrupt way at one point in the middle of one of Qoheleth's discussions in the body of the book (7:27) can hardly be other than an addition by another hand. But this then raises the further question whether the rest of v. 2 (with its repetition in 12:8) comes from Qoheleth's hand. There are good reasons for regarding it as uncharacteristic of Qoheleth's style and thought. Elsewhere Qoheleth never employs this extremely emphatic form of speech, nor does he speak in such a general way of *everything* as 'vanity': he applies the word only to specific, clearly defined situations. Consequently it cannot be affirmed with certainty that v. 2 expresses Qoheleth's own thought: the verse is undoubtedly an *interpretation* of his thought, but may well be a *mis*understanding or at least an over-simplification of it.

The question of the authorship of v. 2 is closely related to that of its relationship to the verses which follow (vv. 3–11 or 3–8), and especially to v. 3. In v. 3 the question is asked, and, by implication is answered in a negative sense, whether human enterprise (**toil**, *'āmāl*, under the sun) is ultimately rewarding or satisfying. It has been argued that v. 3 belongs closely with v. 2 in that it expresses the concept of 'vanity' (v. 2) in concrete terms (**What does man gain?**). However, if v. 2 is an editorial 'preface' to the book, and Qoheleth's words begin with v. 3, the juxtaposition of the two verses may be simply fortuitous. The thought expressed in v. 3 is not confined to the beginning of the book but occurs repeatedly, and is actually repeated in almost identical words in another passage (3:9). But there is an alternative view of the matter: if vv. 2 and 3 do in fact belong together, this may be because they are both editorial and not the work of Qoheleth. Although v. 3 is most commonly taken to be the beginning of the next section, its relationship with v. 4 is in fact not at all obvious. It may well be that the two verses

(2 and 3) together constitute a single summary statement by the editor, which he has composed by culling a number of key words and phrases from various parts of the book (so Galling; cf. Lohfink). If this is so, Qoheleth's own words begin with v. 4.

Though he may have oversimplified Qoheleth's thought in placing such great emphasis on the one word *hebel*, this editor was not entirely in error: *hebel* is indeed one of Qoheleth's favourite words. Leaving aside the editorial matter, it occurs more than thirty times in this short book—about one half of the total number of occurrences in the Old Testament. But it is not a simple matter to determine exactly what he meant by it. Its literal meaning is 'breath' or 'breeze' (so in Isa. 57:13); but it is almost always used metaphorically. In the majority of instances in the Old Testament it appears to mean what is useless or worthless; and in this sense it is often applied to false gods or idols, sometimes with the additional nuance of 'deceitful'. But in other cases it has the related but distinct meaning of what is fleeting, ephemeral or insubstantial, and in this sense is sometimes applied to human life (so, for example, in Ps. 39, *passim*). As a general rule Qoheleth appears to use it mainly in the former of these senses to emphasize the *futility* of various human activities or situations; but in some passages—e.g. 6:12; 9:9 (where it corresponds to *RSV*'s 'vain'); 11:10—it may mean no more than 'brevity'. It would be an error to make an *a priori* assumption about its meaning in any given instance: only a study of its particular context can decide.

All (*hakkōl*), used here absolutely, is most naturally taken as referring to the whole created universe (as, for example, in such late texts as Jer. 10:16; Ps. 103:19) or at least to the whole human race (as in Ps. 145:9). The whole phrase **All is vanity** is used several times by Qoheleth himself (e.g. 3:19), but in a less absolute sense: it is always some particular aspect of human life which is so characterized. Thus the use of *hakkōl* here seems to be a further example of the editor's absolutizing of Qoheleth's thought and language. Qoheleth himself took a more positive view of God's creation when he stated that God 'has made (or 'makes'—see on 3:11) everything beautiful in its time' (3:11).

Verse **3**, a rhetorical question to which the expected answer is 'None!', is made up of words and phrases characteristic of Qoheleth. Its wording is particularly close to that of 3:9.

The verb **gain** here represents a Hebrew noun, *yitrôn*. This word, which occurs ten times in Ecclesiastes but nowhere else in the Old Testament, is elsewhere rendered in *RSV* by 'advantage', though sometimes by other expressions. It is derived from the root *ytr*, meaning 'to remain over' or 'be left over', which occurs in such words as *yeter*, 'remainder'. Qoheleth himself uses other words from this root: *môtār*, 'advantage' or 'superiority' and *yôtēr*, 'advantage', 'abundance' and—in an adverbial sense—'very'. But the concept of being left over is susceptible of a number of different connotations: in post-biblical Hebrew *yitrôn* can mean 'addition', and even 'redundancy' or 'worthlessness' (the state of being surplus to requirements). Consequently it is not a simple matter to determine exactly what Qoheleth intended by it. In most instances 'advantage' may be the best translation; but it has been suggested that Qoheleth had in mind a specialized meaning of 'profit' in a purely commercial or financial sense. That such a sense existed cannot be proved; but it would be fully in accordance with Qoheleth's general remarks about the futility of the scramble to make money, expressed in such passages as 4:7–8, and would sharpen the point of the little story about a lost fortune (5:13–17; MT 12–16) where Qoheleth, using the word in a double sense, could be asking his readers to consider whether making a fortune, even if successful, can bring a *true* 'profit' in the sense of peace of mind and contentment.

toil (*'āmāl*) is yet another key-word in the book (it occurs twenty-two times), and again one which has several meanings. In general in the Old Testament it has a very negative tone: trouble, misfortune, harm. In post-biblical Hebrew, however, it simply means 'work'. There is no doubt that in Ecclesiastes it often has this later meaning, which seems to have superseded the earlier ones; but in some passages it has additional overtones (see especially the analysis in Gordis, Supplementary Note D). Especially—though not only—when associated, as here, with the corresponding verb *'āmal* (**he toils**), it has the overtone of 'hard labour' or 'toil'. In addition, as in the late Psalm 105:44 (*RSV* 'the fruit of . . . toil') it seems occasionally to have acquired the further sense of the *fruit* of labour, that is, wealth or material possessions; and occasionally it seems to mean 'skill'. However, Ginsberg's opinion (1950) that in some instances it has the specific meaning 'profit' is improbable. Clearly these different meanings are not all mutually exclusive. Only the study of the context can determine its primary meaning in each case. In this verse, 'work' or 'hard work' fits the context best.

under the sun (*taḥat haššemeš*) is another favourite phrase of Qoheleth's (it occurs twenty-nine times in the book) which is found nowhere else in the Old Testament. Its meaning, however, is quite clear: it means simply 'in the world', and is equivalent to 'under the heavens', which occurs fairly frequently in the Old Testament, and which is employed by Qoheleth himself elsewhere with precisely the same meaning (1:13; 2:3; 3:1). He uses it with regard to various aspects of human life, of good things and bad: to God's gift to men of life and enjoyment, to human work and activity in general, but also to the evil, injustice and oppression which he sees around him. Its function is to stress the universality of the human condition and of human experience. It has been thought to be a translation of the Greek expression *huph' hēliō*; but this, although the identity of the literal meaning of the two phrases is striking, is improbable. It not only occurs in third century BC inscriptions in Phoenician, but has equivalents in much earlier literature—earlier Egyptian wisdom literature and the *Epic of Gilgamesh* (*ANET*, p. 79), where, it is interesting to observe, the lines which immediately follow are strikingly reminiscent of Qoheleth's own thoughts:

As for mankind, numbered are their days;
Whatever they achieve is but the wind!

However, this thought, like the expression 'under the sun' itself, is quite commonplace and probably belonged to a common stock of ancient Near Eastern lore.

Finally, it is important to note that the subject of the rhetorical question in v. 3 is **man** (*hā'ādām*)—not in the sense of being the grammatical subject, but of being its central theme. The author has thus clearly indicated to the reader at the outset that the book which follows is primarily concerned with the human situation. The conviction expressed in v. 2 that everything is vanity is now seen to be that of one who surveys the world from the point of view of its usefulness for himself and his fellow human beings: not from God's point of view. (Cf. Zimmerli's statement (1933) that the thought expressed in v. 3 is the basic question posed by an *anthropocentric* wisdom.) But, although there is undoubtedly a sense in which much of the wisdom tradition is anthropocentric when compared with other forms of ancient Near Eastern and Old Testament literature, and Qoheleth stands firmly within that tradition, this verse, now standing so prominently at the beginning of the book, oversimplifies and distorts Qoheleth's own teaching. It does not really correspond with the thoughts of the man who began his final admonitions to his readers with 'Remember your Creator' (12:1) and ended them with 'and the spirit returns to God who gave it' (12:7).

A linguistic peculiarity of Qoheleth's should also be mentioned here. When Qoheleth uses the word *(hā)'ādām* (**man**) he does not always mean mankind in general, but often uses it as a substitute for *'îš*, the normal word for an individual (usually male) person. There are some passages where it is not clear which meaning should be attached to *'ādām*. But in this verse the generalized form of the question suggests that the wider meaning is the appropriate one.

THE CEASELESS ROUND OF NATURE

1:4–11

This passage has most commonly been understood in the light of vv. 2 and 3, as developing further the theme of human futility. But if it is in fact unconnected with what precedes, and marks the beginning of Qoheleth's own words, there is nothing in it which suggests this. It is principally the word *yᵉgēʿîm* in v. 8, translated in *RSV* as **full of weariness**, which has given colour to this interpretation; but this is a mistranslation.

The subject of which *yᵉgēʿîm* is the predicate is not 'mankind' or 'human life' but **All things**. If *yāgēaʿ*—the singular form—means 'weary', the literal meaning of the line is 'All things are weary'. There is no justification for rendering *yāgēaʿ* by 'wearisome', that is, *causing* weariness (presumably to man). But, further, the meaning 'weary' for *yāgēaʿ* is by no means well established. It is a very rare word, only occurring in two other passages in the Old Testament. The related noun *yᵉgîaʿ*, which occurs more frequently, has two other connotations beside that of weariness: hard work or toil, and the product which results from toil (e.g. in Ps. 128:2—*RSV*, 'the fruit of the labour'). In the present context it makes good sense to take the phrase 'All things are *yᵉgēʿîm*' as referring to the ceaseless 'toil' or busy activity of the natural phenomena described in the following verses (so Lohfink).

The passage is a literary unity with a clear structure. All commentators agree that v. 12 marks the beginning of an entirely new unit. The main argument is contained in vv. 4–9: v. 4 states the general theme, that within the universe there is an endless repetition of the same set of phenomena, and v. 9 concludes by adding that these cycles are entirely self-contained and unbroken by the appearance of anything new and unprecedented. The intervening verses, 5–8, illustrate the theme with examples taken from nature. Verses 10–11 reinforce the theme by refuting a possible objection: although it may sometimes appear that something entirely new has occurred, this is an illusion due to the faultiness of the human memory.

Although he may have been influenced in his choice of illustrations by current views of the universe (we may note the sequence of the four elements earth, sun, wind and sea), it was not Qoheleth's intention to give a lesson in cosmology. His sole concern was with man and his world; and here he points to the *cosmic setting* within which man has to live his life 'under the sun'. The behaviour of the elements had provided earlier wisdom teachers with analogies to human life (e.g. Prov. 25:13, 14, 23; 26:1); but the view of some commentators that Qoheleth here cites the cyclical behaviour of the elements to support the view that human life is unstable and futile is hardly correct.

Nothing in this passage suggests that there is anything *futile* about the behaviour of the elements. On the contrary, Qoheleth sees their intense activity as both predictable and positive, contributing to the stability of the earth (v. 4*b*). The reappearance of the sun each morning in its accustomed place, for example, is hardly futile or purposeless: it is rather to be welcomed, as Qoheleth clearly states elsewhere (11:7). He is here noting an aspect of the universe which embraces human life as well as the world of nature and implying that human life, despite its apparent vicissitudes, is fundamentally unchanging in character.

4. A generation goes, and a generation comes: *RSV* accepts the common view that *dôr* (**a generation**) here denotes a human life-cycle. This is frequently the case, but by no means always. In some passages (e.g. Isa. 41:4; 51:9; Ps. 72:5) it is most naturally understood as referring to periods of time without any reference to human life (it also has other meanings). The periodic or cyclical connotation appears to be primary: *dôr* is, for example, cognate with *dûr*, 'circle'. It is significant that phrases like *leḏôr dôrîm* and *leḏôr wāḏôr*, which connote an unspecified multiplicity of such periods, are frequently used as synonyms for *le'ôlām*, that is, time (past or future) in its entirety (*'ôlām* does not, however, mean 'eternity', a concept foreign to Old Testament thought and certainly to that of Qoheleth). In the present context, then, it is most natural to take *dôr* as referring to the succession of endlessly repeated natural processes described in vv. 5–7, though also embracing human events (**what has been done**, v. 9: see G. S. Ogden, 1986, pp. 91–2). The fact that **the earth remains for ever** (that is, to the end of time) provides a stable context within which these phenomena recur. The participial form of all the verbs in this verse—**goes** (*hōlēk*), **comes** (*bā'*), **remains** (*'ōmādet*)—stresses the unchanging nature of all these phenomena.

In support of the view that *dôr* means 'generation' here, it has been argued that 'come' and 'go' refer to human birth and death respectively. These euphemisms occur (though not together) fairly frequently in the Old Testament. Qoheleth himself does in fact twice employ them together in this sense (5:16 (MT 15) 6:4). Here, however, he puts the two words in the reverse order: **goes . . . comes**. If *dôr* here meant a human generation, the meaning might be that each generation as it passes away (*hōlēk*) is replaced by another (*bā'*) (in itself a hopeful rather than a pessimistic view of life?); but in the very next verse the same word *bā'* is used in a negative sense of the sun *setting*, that is, disappearing from view. It is unlikely that Qoheleth would have used the word in two such contradictory senses in two consecutive verses. It is therefore more probable that he was speaking of the positive aspect of nature's cyclical processes, pointing out that there is always a welcome reappearance of the phenomena after they might seem to have disappeared for ever. This would be particularly true of the sun, which is the first of the illustrations which Qoheleth now offers.

5. The daily course of **the sun** is now described. After it has set in the west it returns swiftly by an underground route (the earth being regarded as a flat disc) to the east where it is to rise again—a cosmological concept shared by a number of ancient peoples. The word rendered **hastens** in *RSV* (*šā'ap*) means to gasp or pant, sometimes through weakness or pain (Isa. 42:14; Jer. 14:6) but elsewhere with eagerness or desire (Ps. 119:131; Job 5:5; 7:2, and possibly some other passages). The positive sense is the more appropriate here: the sun pants eagerly towards its next appearance. We may compare Ps. 19:5 (MT 6), where, although the nightly subterranean passage is not mentioned, the sun's daily passage through the heavens is presented as a joyful progress and as a sign of strength and as one of the glories of God's creation.

The sun rises: the Hebrew as pointed has the perfect tense where the participle is to be expected in conformity with the surrounding verbs, and is somewhat unaccountably preceded by *wᵉ* ('and'). It has been suggested that the first two letters of **rises** (*wᵉzāraḥ*) have been unintentionally transposed and that the word should be emended and repointed to give the participial form *zôrēaḥ*. **hastens to the place where:** this rendering necessitates a modification of the masoretic accents; but this is preferable to the consonantal emendations which have been proposed such as that of *šô'ēp* to *šāb 'ap*. Equally improbable is the proposal (see *BHS*) to omit the last clause entirely.

6. The motions of **The wind**, in contrast to those of the sun, might seem aimless; but this is not the point which Qoheleth is making. As can be seen by comparing this verse with those which immediately precede and follow it, its point is to be found in the final clause: the wind also has its own limited **circuits** and can be relied on to remain within them, returning to the direction from which it started: it 'goes full circle', as *NEB* puts it. Its constant motion is well brought out by the constant repetition of the word *sôbēb*, **(goes) round**. The prosaic rendering of the verse in *RSV* entirely fails to reproduce the stylistic effect: the grammatical subject, the wind, is not given until the end of the second clause, but the reader has already been struck by the constant repetition of the vowel 'o', which produces a mournful or howling effect: *hôlēk 'el-dārôm w^esôbēb 'el-ṣāpôn sôbēb sōbēb hôlēk hārûaḥ*.

The plural form *s^ebîbôt* used as a noun occurs nowhere else in the Old Testament, but its meaning, **circuits**, is clear from the context. **south** and **north** simply serve as representative of all the points of the compass; east and west have already been mentioned by implication in the previous verse. It has been observed that the reference to the changeability of the wind points to a Palestinian rather than to an Egyptian setting.

7. The same cyclical movement is observable in the case of the water in the rivers (*RSV*, **streams**): the water which flows into the sea returns (*šābîm*, *RSV*, **flow**) to its original place. This interpretation, however, is not universally accepted. Part of the difficulty is that, as is often the case with poetical or semi-poetical texts, the second half of the verse is very loosely constructed. The particle (*še-*) rendered **where** in *RSV* can mean either 'to which' or 'from which': each is equally possible. Moreover, *šābîm lālāket* may mean **flow again**, but, equally, 'turn back and go'. The text, therefore, appears to offer two alternative possible interpretations: either that, as suggested above, the streams, having flowed into the sea, return to their sources in order to repeat the process, or that they simply continue endlessly to flow in the same direction towards the sea.

The first alternative is supported by the fact that the entire passage up to this point (vv. 4–6) speaks of cyclical processes in nature. The introduction of a different kind of theme at this point would be extremely unnatural and would seriously weaken the force of the argument. Moreover, the recurrence of certain key words in these four verses (*hālak*, *RSV*, **go**, **blow**, **run**, **flow**, vv. 4, 6, 7; *māqôm*, **place**, vv. 5, 7; *šûb*, **return**, **flow again**, vv. 6, 7) suggests a certain parallelism between them and a probability of an identity of meaning in each case for these words. The question how Qoheleth conceived of the cyclical movement in the case of water does not present serious difficulties. Various possible explanations have been suggested, but that of Ibn Ezra that this is a reference to evaporation is probably correct. It does not require us to believe that Qoheleth obtained the idea from Greek sources: the author of Job 36:27–28 appears also to have been familiar with it.

Against this interpretation it has been argued that on the cyclical view the phrase **but the sea is not full** has no point: Qoheleth would hardly have drawn attention to this fact as a significant phenomenon if he was about to give a rational explanation of it in the next line. In support of this objection the similarity of v. 7*b* to a line in Aristophanes's *Clouds* (line 1292–4) has been pointed out: 'The sea, although all the rivers flow to it, does not increase in volume.' This is a reference not to a cyclical motion of the water but simply to the flow of the rivers to the sea as an example of unprofitableness: it achieved nothing. The image itself is undoubtedly similar to v. 7*b*, but is capable of being applied in more than one way, and there is no reason, especially in view of the context, to suppose that Qoheleth used it for the same purpose as did Aristophanes. His observation that the sea is not full is simply part of his description of the cyclical flow of the water: *although* all the rivers flow into the sea, the sea does not overflow *because* the water returns to its source through evaporation. The phenomenon would be particularly noticeable in the case of the Dead Sea.

Further, the view that the movement of the water is represented here as in one direction only involves a dubious interpretation of *šābîm lālāket* (*RSV*, **flow again**). The normal connotations of the verb *šûb* are 'turn, return, turn back'. It is true that followed by an infinitive as here, it may simply signify the repetition of an action, as in Job's complaint *lō'-tāšûb 'ênî lir'ôt ṭôb*, 'my eye will not see good again' (7:7). But in fact this construction is only used of completed actions repeated after an interval: the agent *returns*, as it were, to perform the action a second time. *šābîm lālāket*, therefore, can hardly refer to a continuous flow of water in one direction. It could be argued that by using the word *naḥal*, which often denotes a torrent or *wadi* which flows only intermittently during part of the year, Qoheleth wished to indicate the constantly repeated annual repetition at intervals of the flow of the *wadis*; but *naḥal* does not always have that specialized meaning, and the use of the verb *hālak* (**flow**) in the participle here as in the previous verses suggests continuous rather than intermittent motion of the rivers (see Reymond, 1958, pp. 67, 111). *šābîm* then refers not to repetition but to the return of the water to its source. Verse 7*b* should therefore be rendered: 'to the place from which the streams flow they make their way back again'. It is probably implied that, like the circuit of the sun (and possibly also of the winds) the cyclical movement of water is not futile: the constant flow and redistribution of it over the earth is a wonderful and beneficial phenomenon.

meqôm še- (**the place where**): on the use of the construct form before a relative clause see GK § 130c (*še-* here corresponds to *'ašer* as elsewhere in Ecclesiastes).

8. On the meaning of *yegē'îm*, see above on vv. 4–11. The interpretation of this verse turns on this and also on the meaning of *kol-haddebārîm* (*RSV*, **All things**). The very common word *dābār* can signify either 'thing' or 'word', and each of these meanings is frequently attested in the Old Testament. The commentators are divided on the meaning of the phrase here. In favour of the translation 'all words' is the fact that the cognate verb 'to speak' (*l^e^dabbēr*; *RSV*, **utter**) occurs in the second clause, which might therefore be held to continue the theme of the first: that is, if *y^e^gē'îm* connoted weariness, and the passage began not with v. 4 but with v. 2 or 3, the first half of this verse taken as a whole might mean that speech is too frustrating to be worth while—another example of futility. Some commentators have thus seen the verse as an attack on traditional wisdom teaching—expressed, for example, frequently in Proverbs—which set a very high value on speech as a means of overcoming difficulties in life and so as a source of power. But this involves a somewhat forced interpretation of **a man cannot utter**: *RSV*'s **it** has no equivalent in the Hebrew text, so the verb has no object. Galling therefore attempted to improve the syntax by the gratuitous emendation of *lō'-yûkal* (**cannot**) to *lō'-y^e^kalleh*, which would result in the translation 'a man cannot speak effectively' (literally, 'perfect [his] speaking'). The second half of the verse would then extend the thought by adding that the faculties of sight and hearing are equally ineffective and so equally futile.

But those commentators who render *d^e^bārîm* by 'words' here have paid insufficient attention to the context: for the word *dābār* occurs again in v. 10, where, as they themselves recognize, it clearly means 'thing' and not 'word'. The 'thing' of v. 10 is clearly intended to be an example of the 'things' of v. 8: Qoheleth's point in v. 10 is that there are no exceptions to the rule for 'all things' which he has there stated.

If, then, *kol-hadd^e^bārîm* in v. 8 means **All things**, the first clause of this verse has the function of drawing together and summing up the thought introduced in v. 4 and exemplified in vv. 5–7, while the remainder of the verse stresses the overwhelming effect on the observer of the ceaseless activity of natural phenomena: they leave him speechless (there is now no need to add an object to the verb: the phrase simply means 'one cannot speak'). There is also no need to emend the text. Further, not only is the observer bereft of speech: the eye and the ear are also inadequate to take in what they perceive. **satisfied** and **filled** are here virtually identical in meaning: they signify the complete realisation of something desired or desirable (cf. Ps. 48:10 (MT 11); Ec. 6:7).

a man cannot (*lō'-yûkal 'îš*): better, 'No one can' (on this impersonal function of *'îš* see GK § 139d).

With regard to the structure of vv. 5–8, it may be observed that the triad sun, wind, water in vv. 5–7 is balanced by the triad speech, sight, hearing in v. 8. This does not affect the possibility that Qoheleth also had in mind the *four* elements in vv. 4–7.

9. It may be assumed that in the first two closely parallel lines of this verse Qoheleth intends a distinction between what *happens* (**has been, will be**) and what is *done* (**has been done, will be done**): that is, between the verb *hāyāh*, 'be, happen, occur' and the passive (Niphal) of the verb *'āśāh*, 'do'. The first line probably refers to the natural phenomena described in vv. 5–7 and the second to events or actions in human life. These actions, however, are not necessarily human actions: although Qoheleth uses *'āśāh* in the passive a number of times when speaking of human actions, in 8:17 (cf. 9:3) 'the work that is done (*'āśāh*, Niphal) under the sun' appears to be identified with 'the work of God'. But whether he has God's actions or man's in mind here, he is probably referring—for the first time—to man and his place in the world. As in nature, so in human life there is a constant movement within a prescribed circle, so that there is **nothing new under the sun**.

There is no reason to suppose that Qoheleth is here putting forward a theory that history repeats itself exactly in endless circles. He is rather drawing attention to the parallel between nature and human nature in order to point out the limitations within which man will do well to be content to live his life as an integral part of the whole 'work of God'. Like the natural phenomena, human life is what it is: to expect something radically new is foolish. Compare 6:10: man 'is not able to dispute with one stronger than he'.

10. Is there a thing . . .? (*yēš dābār*): the particle *yēš* is normally affirmative ('there is'). But the sense here is interrogative: as frequently in questions, the interrogative particle *h*ᵃ- is omitted. 'If there is' (Gordis) is less probable. In any case Qoheleth's intention is to raise and refute a possible objection to the categorical statement which he has made at the end of v. 9. In the second half of this verse he simply denies the truth of the objection: as in nature, so in human life there is no real development and no real change. In v. 11 he gives his reason for this view.

It has been supposed that in making this assertion Qoheleth is deliberately opposing the view that *God* is capable of creating something new, expressed, for example, in Num. 16:30, in Deutero-Isaiah, e.g. Isa. 43:19, and in Jer. 31:22. But it is doubtful whether he had this in mind: he does not mention God in this passage, and elsewhere he frequently emphasizes both the supreme power of God and man's inability to foresee divine intentions.

has been (*hāyāh*): an unusual but not infrequent use of the singular verb with a plural subject.

in the ages before us (*lᵉ'ōlāmîm . . . millᵉpānēnû*): with reference to the past, *'ôlam* occurs in the plural only here. The plural form may owe something to the Greek notion of the division of time into aeons. On the temporal use of *l*e- see the lexica. *mill*e*pānēnū* rather than the simpler *l*e*pānēnū* is a late usage.

11. The claim that there is novelty in life is dismissed as an illusion due to human forgetfulness: the events of the past soon pass from memory, and each generation is unaware that it is merely repeating what has been done before. As it has been in the past, so it will be again in the future. **former/later things:** these phrases could equally well be rendered 'former/later men' or 'former/later ages'; the general point is unaffected. The word *zikkārôn* (**remembrance**) sometimes means a memorial—i.e. an object or written record serving to remind later generations (or God) of something or some person; but there is no reason to suppose that here Qoheleth means anything other than the faculty of memory (cf. 2:16).

'SOLOMON'S' TESTIMONY

1:12–2:26

Although it is universally agreed that 1:12 begins a new section of the book, there is uncertainty about the point at which this section ends. Zimmerli and Lauha, together with other commentators, regard 1:12–2:26 as a section complete in itself; but Lohfink includes 3:1–15 in it, while on the other hand Galling, in accordance with his general view of the book as composed of a large number of short pieces, finds no less than six separate sections here. The question of the extent of the section is often linked with a further one: that of the extent of the 'Solomonic fiction', which also begins with 1:12. But in fact the two questions are not interdependent. It is plain that Qoheleth's self-identification with Solomon continues at least up to 2:11; but he seems deliberately to have refrained from giving a clear indication of its conclusion. The reflections attributed to Qoheleth-Solomon are not peculiar to him but are echoed throughout the book; and since the whole book is expressed in the first person singular, it is impossible to be certain at what point the 'I' of Solomon gives place to the 'I' of Qoheleth himself. Solomon is made to merge imperceptibly with the personality of the real author. So the phenomenon of the 'Solomonic fiction' provides no clues to the structure and unity of 1:12–2:26.

In fact there is good reason to regard 1:12–2:26 as a unified discourse; but it would be wrong to expect from Qoheleth the kind of logical arrangement which might be expected from a modern philosophical or theological treatise. Attempts have been made to divide the discourse into subsections on a purely formal basis:

phrases like 'I applied my mind', 'I said to myself', 'I turned to consider' etc. (there are at least twelve of these) have been taken to indicate the beginning of a new section, while the recurring comments that 'all is vanity' or its equivalent (nine times) or the apparent quotations of wisdom sayings (e.g. 1:15, 18; 2:13*b*, 14*a*) have been seen as marking the ends of sections. Such attempts are misconceived: it is clear that both here and in the rest of the book any one of these literary devices is as liable to occur in the middle of an argument as at the beginning or end of one. They certainly cannot be regarded as a consistent system of markers.

Nor is it possible to find a consistent development of thought here—in the modern sense of that phrase. The connections between one thought and another are seldom clear-cut. Yet to break the passage up into disconnected fragments would be to ignore the underlying connections of thought which bind it together and make it a comprehensive summary of all that follows in the remainder of the book.

All the principal themes of the book are treated here and are specifically related to Qoheleth's main purpose. The passage begins (1:13) with a statement that he intends to investigate 'all that is done under heaven'. In 2:3 he explains the reason for the investigation: he hopes to discover 'what is good (or 'best', -*ṭôb*) for the sons of men to do'—in other words, what course of conduct will afford them the most complete satisfaction. He has in fact already begun his consideration of the value of three options available to man in his quest for the 'good': the pursuit and enjoyment of *wealth*, the acquisition of *wisdom*, and the pursuit of *pleasure*. Each of these has its attractions, yet for various reasons each fails to satisfy. Qoheleth then announces his solution: '*Nothing* is better (*ṭôb*) for man than to eat and drink . . . (etc.)' (2:24).

The unity of the passage is to be found not only in its comprehensive treatment of themes and in its basic plan but also in a further basic motif which is related to all the others: that of *toil*, or human effort. This theme becomes more and more prominent as the passage progresses. In the seventeen verses from 2:10 to 2:26 the words 'toil' and 'toiling' (the verb *'āmal*, the noun *'āmāl* and the adjective *'āmēl*) occur in all no less than fifteen times, out of a total of thirty-four for the whole book. They are applied to all of the three activities investigated—not only to the effort to obtain wisdom and wealth, but even to the pursuit of pleasure (2:10–11). The whole section might therefore be entitled 'the futility of toil and effort'. All man's painful, strenuous efforts to achieve satisfaction for himself are self-defeating (2:22, 23).

Qoheleth's answer to the question 'what is good for the sons of men to do?' (2:3) is given in the final three verses: happiness and satisfaction (*ṭôb*) do not depend on human effort at all, and cannot be achieved by it: they can only come 'from the hand of God' (2:24, 25). It is significant that God is mentioned only at the very beginning and the end of the passage, while in the whole of the intervening verses we have a picture of *man* acting on his own for his own purposes. God may have given man an 'unhappy business' to get on with (1:13); but he has *also* (2:24) given him the possibility of enjoying life. When this is recognized, even toil loses its stressfulness and can become a source of enjoyment, but not otherwise: apart from God, it breeds only hatred (2:17, 18) and despair (2:20).

12. Qoheleth-Solomon begins with a self-introduction, following a tradition of Near Eastern—especially Egyptian—wisdom literature in which an old man, sometimes a king or one who for literary purposes claims to be a king, draws on the experiences of a lifetime to give advice to his son or successor (see, e.g., *ANET*, pp. 414–20). The use of the first person singular, however, is unusual in the introductory sentence. This is probably not, as has been supposed, an imitation of the style of the self-laudatory monuments set up by Egyptian and Mesopotamian kings, but an adaptation of the form of the wisdom introduction to fit the personal style in which the section which follows is couched. The choice of Solomon for this 'royal fiction' was made not only because he was the archetypal wise king but equally in view of his reputation for great wealth: if even Solomon, who possessed everything which a man can possess, nevertheless found all his efforts to achieve happiness and contentment profoundly unsatisfactory, how much more would lesser persons be likely to fail in that attempt! The formal style of this introductory verse has suggested to some commentators that this was originally the beginning of the book; but this cannot be proved.

On the sobriquet Qoheleth (**the Preacher**), see the Introduction; and on **king**, see on 1:1. The title **king over Israel** is less frequently found in the Old Testament than 'king of Israel', but occurs occasionally (e.g. 2 Sam. 19:23; 1 Kg. 11:37). **in Jerusalem**, together with the description which follows, identifies the speaker as Solomon without mentioning him by name. The editor who added 1:1 (see above) provided the further identification 'son of David'.

I . . . have been (*hāyîtî*): it has been supposed by many commentators that this word, which is in the perfect tense, must be translated 'I was'—that is, that it implies that the speaker was no longer king when, according to the fiction, he wrote these words. The authors of the Talmud, for whom Solomon was literally the author of the book, supposed that Solomon had been deposed by the demon

Asmodaeus. Other attempts have been made more recently to solve the supposed problem. But in fact the perfect tense may be used in biblical Hebrew to denote a state or action which began in the past but continues into the present (Driver, §§ 8, 11; GK § 106g [a]). Gen. 42:11 is another example of the verb 'to be' used in this way: there Joseph's brethren protest, 'Your servants are (*hāyû*, perfect) not spies'—that is, they have not been spies in the past, and they are not spies now. *RSV*'s rendering 'have been' is therefore correct, and the problem is an imaginary one.

13. The first half of this verse may be taken as a brief statement of Qoheleth's whole undertaking. His use of the two verbs, **to seek and to search out**, emphasizes the thoroughness of the investigation which he proposes to make. **all that is done under heaven** (cf. 1:9) does not refer exclusively, or even, perhaps, primarily, to human activity: this is made clear in 3:10–11. But the key to the meaning of the verse is to be found in the phrase **by wisdom**. Qoheleth's intention is to test the adequacy of human wisdom at its best (that is, in the case of Solomon) to discover the principles, if any, on which the world is governed. And, as 3:10–11, which are a kind of commentary on this verse, make clear, it is this attempt, rather than the human condition in general, which is **an unhappy business** (so Lauha and Lohfink, contrary to most commentators). God has **given to the sons of men** the desire to 'find out what God has done from the beginning to the end', 'yet so that he cannot find it out' (3:11). There may be a play on words in the second half of the verse: *'ānāh* (**to be busy**) has several other meanings, but *RSV* is probably right in seeing it here as cognate with *'inyān* (**business**), even though it occurs with this meaning only in this book. Following *'inyan rā'* (**an unhappy**—literally, 'bad'—**business**), however, it may be intended also to remind the reader of another *'ānāh* which denotes affliction or suffering.

14. I have seen: better, 'I observed' or 'I considered'. **all** (*hakkōl*): in some passages (e.g. 3:11; 11:5) this expression refers to the whole created universe; and it is in this absolute sense that the editor interprets Qoheleth's thought in 1:2. But here it is more probable that, as is the case frequently elsewhere, it refers to the thing just mentioned (cf. Lev. 1:9, 'the whole'; Dt. 2:36). It could thus refer either to what Qoheleth has observed or to his own investigation, which he now sees to be futile. **a striving after wind** (*r^e'ût rûaḥ*): here and on five other occasions Qoheleth uses this phrase together with **vanity** (*hebel*), and in 4:6 he uses it by itself. In 1:17 and 4:16 he uses the apparently synonymous phrase *ra'yôn rûaḥ*. Both *r^e'ût* and *ra'yôn* are peculiar to this book. It is not certain whether they are derived from the verb *rā'āh*, to tend or graze sheep or cattle, or from a verb common in Aramaic meaning 'to desire'. The former could yield the meaning 'herding (the) wind' as apparently in Hos. 12:1 (MT 2); the latter, 'striving for (the) wind'. The general meaning of the phrase is the same in either case: the pursuit of the unattainable or the waste of effort (in other passages it is closely associated with *'āmāl*, 'toil').

15. Here as elsewhere Qoheleth reinforces or sums up his preceding remarks by quoting a proverb of a type frequently found in Proverbs: a poetic couplet in synonymous parallelism. The use of rare and late words in the verse suggests that Qoheleth may have composed it himself in the style of earlier proverbial wisdom, though this is not necessarily so. The saying refers to impossible tasks (see Crenshaw, 1979), and, like others of the same kind, can be taken in more than one way, as the commentators have done. In the first line, **crooked** can be taken either in a literal or in a moral sense. The second line may mean that it is futile to try to make plans to spend what one has not got (i.e. counting one's chickens before they are hatched: for a similar meaning of the verb *mānāh*—here in the passive, **be numbered**—see 2 Kg. 12:11 ('paid it out'); Ps. 90:12). In the present context, however, the saying refers to the futility of trying, by the exercise of wisdom, to find any order in the world. This interpretation is confirmed by 7:13, where Qoheleth uses the same two verbs in connection with God's creative activity ('Who can make straight what he has made crooked?') and by 12:9, where the former of these verbs (*tqn; RSV*, 'arranging') appears to mean putting something into a meaningful order or shape. The text can thus be adequately understood without recourse to the emendations proposed by some commentators, except that **be made straight** (*litqōn*, Qal infinitive) ought perhaps to be repointed as a passive (Pual) infinitive *l^etuqqan* (Driver, 1954, p. 225), to correspond with the passive verb in the second half of the verse.

16–18 are, in a sense, parallel to vv. 12–15, but there is some progression of thought. Qoheleth is here specifically concerned to comment critically on the value of the enterprise which he has described: the devotion of all one's energies to an attempt to understand the principles by which the world is governed. His conclusion is that the enterprise is both futile and frustrating; but this is not, as some commentators have supposed, an attack on practical wisdom or natural intelligence as a guide to behaviour: he concedes a limited value to this (2:13) and counts it as a divine gift (2:26). Rather, this is a warning to those who think that the human mind is capable of finding an answer to all questions.

16. all . . . before me: this presumably refers to Solomon's predecessors; but in fact there was only one previous Israelite king who had ruled **over Jerusalem:** David. It is unlikely that Qoheleth was thinking of Canaanite kings of Jerusalem who had reigned in pre-Israelite times. Probably this is just a slip: Qoheleth was thinking of the many kings who had reigned in Jerusalem in the period of the kingdom of Judah, and had temporarily forgotten that Solomon came very early in the list.

17. and to know (*wᵉda'at*): *da'at* can be either the infinitive Qal of the verb *yāda'*, 'to know', or a noun, 'knowledge'. *RSV* follows the Masoretic punctuation, which takes it as an infinitive governing the nouns **madness** and **folly**; but the Versions take it as a noun: 'to know wisdom and knowledge, madness and folly'. But 'to know knowledge' is hardly a satisfactory phrase (the Versions conceal the tautology by using different words). Gordis's translation 'I learnt that wisdom and knowledge *are* madness and folly' is a very tortuous interpretation of the Hebrew text. *RSV* is probably correct. The reason for the introduction of **madness** and **folly** at this point is not clear; possibly it is intended to link this paragraph with the following one (2:1ff).

folly (*śiklût*): this word, which occurs only in this book, is spelled in all the other instances with a *samekh* (*siklût*). There is evidently a confusion here between two roots of almost opposite meanings: *śkl* denotes prudence or intelligence, while *skl* denotes folly. The pronunciation is virtually the same. Whatever the reason for the unusual spelling here, 'folly' is obviously correct here.

this also: a reference back to v. 14. Pride in the possession of greater wisdom than anyone else is no less futile than the attempt to use wisdom to understand how the world is governed. **striving** (*ra'yôn*): see on 1:14.

18. Here again Qoheleth concludes a topic with a proverb which he interprets in a new sense. This saying may originally have been a warning by a teacher to a pupil that education cannot be obtained without trouble and pain (*mak'ôb*, **sorrow**, should be so translated). Admonitions of this kind are found in Egyptian and Babylonian literature. The 'pain' in question may have been the result of corporal punishment, thought to be a necessary spur to the pupil's diligence (cf. Prov. 22:15, and other sayings in Proverbs). In its present context the saying is intended to give the reason for the negative judgement of the previous verse (**For** is a connecting link between the two sentences). It should be noted that such quotations of 'ready-made' proverbs in the book cannot be expected always to be perfectly congruent with the contexts into which the author has incorporated them.

2:1–11. As in his presentation of his preoccupation with wisdom (1:13), so in his account of his experiment with pleasure, Qoheleth-

Solomon first briefly describes and passes an anticipatory judgement on it (vv. 1–2) and then describes (vv. 3–10) and comments on it (v. 11) in greater detail. Verses 4–8 (9), which describe Solomon's wealth and luxury at length, are in a different style from the rest, and it has been pointed out that the passage would make adequate sense without them. But Qoheleth was quite capable of adapting his style to the matter in hand, and there is no reason for regarding these verses as an addition by another hand. They are quite appropriate as a self-description of 'Solomon in all his glory', and they help to make the point, which is clearly implied, that if even Solomon, surrounded as he was by the greatest luxury imaginable, was unable to derive any lasting satisfaction from it, such modest wealth as might be acquired by an ordinary person, however ambitious, would be even less likely to make him happy.

2:1. pleasure: this noun (*śimḥāh*) occurs eight times in Ecclesiastes, and *RSV* translates it in various different ways according to the contexts in which it occurs: pleasure, joy, mirth, enjoyment. The corresponding verb *śāmaḥ/śāmēaḥ* is similarly variously rendered enjoy oneself, find enjoyment, rejoice. There is, however, no reason to suppose that Qoheleth intended a distinction between 'joy' and 'pleasure'. For him *śimḥāh* comprises everything which makes for happiness and contentment; and as such it can only come as a gift from God (2:26; 5:18 [MT 17]; 9:7). It is because 'Solomon' has determined to seek it independently for himself that he discovers that, like his corresponding attempt to rely on his own wisdom and knowledge (1:13, 17) it proves totally unsatisfactory.

I will make a test: the Hebrew *'ᵃnassᵉkāh* would normally mean 'I will test *you*'—presumably part of 'Solomon's' address to himself. But it is really pleasure rather than himself that he proposes to test; and it may be preferable to take the verbal suffix as an indirect rather than as a direct object: 'I will make a test *for* you'. On this rare construction see GK § 117x. *RSV*, which omits 'you' altogether, apparently accepts the proposed emendation cited in *BHS*.

enjoy yourself: literally, 'look on good (things)'. *rā'āh bᵉ* frequently means to have a pleasurable experience.

2. The negative result of the experiment with pleasure is now expressed more explicitly. **laughter** (*śᵉḥôq*) is only rarely regarded with approval in the Old Testament. It often has a malicious overtone; and on the other hand, it is regarded as the sign of a fool (7:6; cf. Prov. 29:9). In 3:4 Qoheleth admits its appropriateness in certain circumstances; but here it is regarded as folly (*RSV*, **mad**) because it arises from a self-indulgence which does not contribute to genuine happiness: **What use is it?** means, literally, 'What does it achieve?' (*'ōśāh*).

3. This verse consists of a single somewhat complicated sentence; but Tur-Sinai's attempt (see Gordis) to simplify it by transferring parts of it to v. 1—involving several emendations—is unnecessary and unconvincing.

I searched: this is the same verb (*tûr*) as in 1:13 ('search out'). Together with the phrase **my mind still guiding me with wisdom** it is intended to make the point that this pursuit of pleasure is a 'controlled experiment' and not, in intention at least, mere self-indulgence.

to cheer my body: the precise meaning of the verb is not clear, although the general sense can be inferred from the context. G. R. Driver's 'sustain', based on some examples of Arabic and Aramaic usage (1954, pp. 225–6) does not make very good sense, while *NEB*'s 'to stimulate myself with wine', which is probably based on Driver's article, goes rather beyond the conclusion there drawn.

guiding me: 'me' has no equivalent in the Hebrew. An alternative rendering would be 'guiding my mind' with 'I' as the subject. A third possibility, in view of one of the meanings of the verb *nhg* in late Hebrew, is 'while my mind was behaving with wisdom'.

the few days: literally, 'the number of the days'. But *mispār*, 'number', often carries the implication of fewness (what can be easily counted). The expression 'the few days of (a person's) life' occurs again in 5:18 (MT 17) and 6:12. In this and other ways Qoheleth is constantly concerned to remind the reader of the limit set to human activities and aspirations by death.

4–9. This description of Solomon's wealth and activities does not follow 1 Kg. 3–11 in every detail, but is an imaginative description which may be partly based on the legendary picture of Solomon which had already been formed in Jewish tradition but which itself goes back in part to the account in Kings. In some respects, however, it probably reflects the luxurious style of living of Qoheleth's millionaire contemporaries.

4. I made great works: this probably refers to the various activities listed in the following verses. Gordis renders the phrase by 'I acted in grand style'. **houses:** the splendour of the architecture and furnishings of the many buildings constructed by Solomon is described in detail in 1 Kg. 6–9. **vineyards:** presumably providing the wine referred to in v. 3. Ca. 8:11 also refers to a vineyard of Solomon's. 1 Chr. 27:27 attributes the possession of extensive vineyards to David.

5. gardens: a piece of land in Jerusalem known as 'the king's garden' is mentioned in accounts of later periods (e.g. Jer. 39:4; Neh. 3:15). Qoheleth puts all these Solomonic luxuries in the plural to give an impression of unparalleled wealth and magnificence.

parks: this word (*pardēs*) is derived from the Persian *pairi-daêza*, an enclosure, and probably refers to an ornamental garden planted with exotic trees (the English word Paradise is also derived from the Persian word, via the Greek *parádeisos*). **all kinds of fruit trees:** it has been suggested that this is a reminiscence of the Garden of Eden (Gen. 2:9); but this is somewhat fanciful.

6. pools: 'the king's pool' is mentioned in Neh. 2:14. It is probably identical with the pool near the 'king's garden' of Neh. 3:15. **forest:** *NEB*'s 'grove' is a more appropriate translation.

7. born in my house: the children of slaves became the property of their parents' owner (cf. Gen. 15:3). **herds and flocks:** the absence of any reference to *horses*, with which Solomon was especially associated (see, e.g., 1 Kg. 4:26 [MT 5:6]; 10:25–29) confirms the view that Qoheleth was not simply following the text of Kings or Chronicles. **who had been before me:** see on 1:16.

8. The amassing of **the treasure of kings and provinces** suggests that Solomon made new conquests. In fact, however, he did not; and this trait may be rather a reflection of the actions of Hellenistic rulers of Qoheleth's own time. The fact that **provinces** has an article but **kings** does not has suggested to some that a word meaning 'governors of' has been accidentally omitted before 'provinces'. Dahood's suggestion that MT can be explained from Phoenician usage is improbable. The anomaly can perhaps be explained from Qoheleth's inconsistent use of the article.

singers, both men and women: a normal amenity of a royal court: compare the reference to David's singers in 2 Sam. 19:35.

many concubines: the context suggests this meaning for the completely obscure phrase *šiddāh wešiddôt*. None of the several proposed derivations of *šiddāh* is certain. The construction (a singular noun followed by the plural of the same noun) is somewhat similar to 'a girl, two girls' in Jg. 5:30 (a singular followed by a dual), and may connote a large number (so *RSV*, **many**). But *NEB* omits the two words altogether as unintelligible.

9. became great: that is, in wealth—cf. the use of this verb in Gen. 24:35; 26:13; Jer. 5:27 etc. **also my wisdom remained with me:** most commentators take this statement as a reminder to the reader, similar to that in v. 3, that all this is part of an experiment intended to test the value of pleasure (v. 1) and not simply self-indulgence. There is no doubt that the verb (*'āmad*) often has the meaning of 'remain'. On the other hand, followed as here by *le*, literally 'to' (*RSV* has **with**) it sometimes in later Hebrew means to 'stand by' or to assist someone (Gordis): hence such translations as 'and my wisdom stood me in good stead' (*NEB*)—that is, it was his wisdom which helped 'Solomon' to become rich (so, e.g., Galling, Hertzberg).

10. In vv. 1–2 Qoheleth anticipated the result of his experiment with the pursuit of pleasure, or enjoyment, for its own sake, concluding that it is ultimately worthless. He repeats this judgement in his final comment in v. 11. In the present verse, however, he is still engaged in a description of the course of the experiment itself. Having described some of the means by which, as 'Solomon', he claims to have employed his immense resources in order to obtain the maximum pleasure from life, he concludes his account by emphasizing as strongly as possible that he neglected no possible means to achieve that end. He was therefore in an unique position to draw 'scientific' conclusions from a controlled experiment. And he does not foolishly deny the reality of the pleasures which he experienced. Before he passes on to his final conclusion he frankly admits that he enjoyed the experiment while it was proceeding: his efforts (*'āmāl*) did indeed bring him pleasure, and indeed it was this which encouraged him to pursue the experiment to its conclusion. There was, after all, a reward (*ḥēleq*). This word, which literally means a share or portion (so in 11:2) is several times used by Qoheleth of the human lot, often, as here, in a positive sense (e.g. 3:22; 5:18–19 [MT 17–18]; 9:9).

11. I considered—literally, 'I turned towards', that is, 'I turned to look at'. The same expression occurs in Job 6:28. Here it indicates the dispassionate appraisal of the researcher when the experiment is concluded and the results are **all** to hand. The judgement about the pursuit of pleasure is a totally negative one, parallel to that which is made about the pursuit of wisdom in 1:17. Commentaries since Delitzsch have drawn attention to a supposed contrast of meaning between *ḥēleq* (**reward**) in v. 10 and *yitrôn* (*RSV*, 'gain' in 1:3; here, **to be gained**). It has been supposed that the former denotes only a partial, superficial or ephemeral reward, whereas the latter refers to that lasting 'profit' or advantage which gives lasting satisfaction, whose existence Qoheleth totally denies. It is doubtful whether the usage of the two words in other contexts supports this distinction. Nevertheless in these two verses there *is* a sharp contrast made; but it is a contrast between the *immediate* satisfaction produced by the pursuit of pleasure for its own sake and the lack of any *lasting* pleasure, a vital difference which is only perceived in retrospect by the observer who possesses wisdom. Qoheleth's judgement on the former is expressed in the most emphatic terms by an accumulation of expressions elsewhere employed separately in 1:9, 14, 17 (where a slightly different word is used for **striving**) and 2:1. It should be remembered, however, that this judgement is not a dismissal of joy or pleasure (*śimḥāh*) in itself, but only of pleasure consciously pursued as the main aim in life rather than accepted as a divine gift.

12. So I turned to consider: literally, 'And I turned to look at'. The meaning is the same as that of the first words of v. 11, though here the verb *pānîtî* (*RSV*, 'considered' in v. 11) is followed not by *b*ᵉ but by the infinitive *lir'ôt*, 'to see'. The phrase here marks a new development in the discussion. Having concluded in 1:17–18 and 2:11 respectively that the pursuit both of wisdom and of pleasure fails to bring lasting satisfaction, Solomon-Qoheleth proceeds to give a critical appraisal of the traditional teaching of the wisdom tradition which maintained that, on the contrary, the pursuit of wisdom is the one worthwhile goal, while folly leads to disaster. It should be noted that the objects of comparison here are not wisdom and pleasure but **wisdom** (on the one hand) and **madness and folly** (on the other). Qoheleth does not go back on his earlier conclusion (v. 3) that addiction to pleasure is a form of madness; rather, the point which he wishes to discuss in the verses which follow (12*b*–23) is whether wisdom is, after all, any better. There is thus a real continuity of thought between verses 11 and 12 (the continuity is marked stylistically by the repetition of *pānîtî*); consequently the view of some commentators (e.g. Gordis, Hertzberg) that Qoheleth is saying that 'wisdom *is* madness and folly', a rendering which is in any case difficult to justify syntactically, is to be rejected.

The second half of the verse (from **for what**) has caused difficulties for a number of commentators. A literal translation might be 'for what (is) the man who comes after the king? that which they have already done'. The difficulties are, however, exaggerated. There are two main problems: whether a satisfactory meaning can be extracted from the words as they stand, and whether, whatever their meaning may be, it fits the context. Suggested emendations include the alteration of the first clause to 'for what shall the man *do* . . .?' by the insertion of the verb *ya'ᵃśeh*, and the change of 'they have done' to the singular **'he has . . . done'** (so *RSV*). The latter emendation is supported by a large number of MSS. However, some commentators (Zimmerli, Hertzberg, Lauha) see no need for emendation: either the absence of the verb in the first clause is to be explained as a case of aposiopesis, (see GK § 167a; 117 l) or alternatively the clause may be rendered by 'What sort of man . . .?'; and the plural 'they have done' is to be taken as impersonal, equivalent to 'has been done' (GK § 144 g).

On the other hand, some commentators hold that v. 12*b* as a whole interrupts the sequence of thought between 12*a* and v. 13, and either has been misplaced from after v. 19 or is a later addition based on the thought of vv. 18–23. This view is, however, opposed by Gordis and Hertzberg, who try to make sense of it as it stands. It is true that its relevance is not very clear. It may be that 'Solomon' is claiming, in an 'aside', that his researches have been so complete that his successors can be no more than his imitators. (There may be an indirect reference here—in the mind of Qoheleth—to Rehoboam, though he does not fit the role of imitator of Solomon particularly well.) The difficulty with this view is that the word **for** (*kî*) leads the reader to expect an explanation of the preceding statement, which does not appear to be the case here. The problem remains unsolved.

Finally, the reference to the king has been taken (by Budde, Galling and Lauha) to be a later addition to the text, the word now pointed *'aḥarê*, **after**, having originally been intended to be read *'aḥaray*, 'after me'. This emendation is unnecessary. It is perhaps surprising that 'Solomon' should refer to himself as 'the king'; but there may be a nuance here which is lost to us.

13–17. 'Solomon' now sets out his findings (**Then I saw** in v. 13 picks up the 'I turned to see' of v. 12). His arguments and conclusions occupy vv. 13–23. The first part of the exposition (vv. 13–17) is the first example in the book of the so-called 'broken aphorism' which is characteristic of Qoheleth's style (see the Introduction, p. 21). The form of this type of argument is flexible; here it consists of an affirmation based on experience (v. 13) which is then supported by a quotation of an earlier wisdom saying (v. 14*a*) but then drastically modified, though not negated, by a quite new consideration (v. 14*b*). These general observations are then applied to the writer's own case (v. 15); and after a further explanation (v. 16) a conclusion is reached which is both general and personal (v. 17). (See Whybray, 1981, p. 448.)

13–14. Verse 14*a* (to **darkness**) is universally recognized as a quotation. In every respect—theme, language, poetical form, antithetical parallelism, brevity and striking imagery—it can be paralleled many times with sayings in the Book of Proverbs (Whybray, 1981, pp. 437–9). According to Gordis, v. 13—apart from the introductory words **Then I saw that**—is also a quotation of the same kind; but this is manifestly not the case. Its theme is virtually the same as that of v. 14*a*; but in every other respect v. 13 is characteristic of Qoheleth himself. It contains two words, *yitrôn* (*RSV*, **excels**) and *siklût*, **folly**, which are peculiar to him; it is in prose and lacks the neat parallelism characteristic of Proverbs; it is long-winded and clumsy (a literal translation would be 'wisdom has an advantage over folly like the advantage of light over darkness'—*RSV*'s use of the verb **excel** conceals this); and the use of the imagery of **light** and **darkness**, borrowed from the saying which follows, lacks the liveliness and directness of v. 14*a*. There can be no doubt that as elsewhere Qoheleth has here first stated the theme in his own words and then backed it up by a quotation.

13. Although **darkness** is sometimes used in the Old Testament as a symbol for death (e.g. 11:8 and Job 10:21) and **light** as a figure for life (cf. the expression 'see [the] light', Ps. 49:19 [MT 20]; Job 3:16 and elsewhere in the sense of 'to live'), Qoheleth is not for the moment concerned with the thought of death. The meaning of the verse is exactly the same as that of 14*a*.

14. darkness here is a metaphor for (spiritual) blindness. The **fool** is like a blind man who stumbles as he **walks** (cf. Prov. 3:23; 4:19); the **wise man**, on the other hand, **has eyes in his head:** he can see, and is therefore able to avoid disaster. This metaphor occurs frequently in the Old Testament. The saying is characteristic of many in the Book of Proverbs in that it is concerned simply to record the common experience of daily life in which common sense is an asset which some people lack. It does not probe further; and Qoheleth is able to assent to it as far as it goes. But there is more to be said; and now Qoheleth introduces for the first time the thought, characteristic of him, that the wise man is after all no more able to control his ultimate fate than is the fool.

and yet I perceived: perhaps better, 'but *I* know': the force of the word *gam* here is probably emphatic rather than adversative (see Labuschagne, 1966). **one fate:** i.e. the same fate, that is, death. The thought, expressed in virtually the same way, recurs in 3:19 and 9:2–3; but the motif of the certainty of death as overshadowing all human activities and pretensions is never far from Qoheleth's mind. **fate** (*miqreh*) in Qoheleth's thought, as elsewhere in the Old Testament (Ru. 2:3 ['happened']; 1 Sam. 6:9; 20:26) does not signify an impersonal or malignant force but is a 'neutral' term signifying simply what happens—in v. 15 *RSV* renders it by the verb 'befall', and in this verse the corresponding verb *qārāh*, literally 'meet', is rendered by **comes**. The idea that this is an instance of Greek influence on Qoheleth has been generally abandoned. **all:** better, 'both'; cf. 7:18.

15–16. 'Solomon' now applies his general insight to his own personal situation. It is rather strange that whereas 1 Kg. 4:29–34 (MT 5:9–14) and the Book of Proverbs make much of Solomon's lasting fame as a paragon of wisdom, he is represented here as gloomily convinced that he will be forgotten after his death and that all his wisdom will be wasted. Presumably Qoheleth held the same view about his own literary reputation. He laments his mortality because despite his superior wisdom he will be forgotten like the merest fool.

15. why then have I been so very wise?: the question which 'Solomon' here puts to himself contains an element of deep regret about his wasted life—cf. Job 3:11, and also the use of *lāmmāh*, 'Why?' in the psalms of lamentation (on this meaning of *lāmmāh* see Jepsen, 1967; Barr, 1985). **been . . . wise** (*ḥākamtî*) would be better rendered by 'become wise': that is the meaning of the verb *ḥākam* in almost all its occurrences in Proverbs (Prov. 6:6; 8:33 etc.). 'Solomon' regrets not that God has given him the gift of superior wisdom but that he has spent so much of his time *acquiring* wisdom.

16. 'Solomon' now makes explicit the reason for the negative conclusion reached at the end of v. 15. It is the common fate of **wise man** and **fool** that they will both (*hakkōl, RSV,* **all**—cf. v. 14) ultimately (*le'ôlām*; *RSV*, **enduring**) be forgotten. Here Qoheleth is once again opposing—or at least modifying—a traditional belief: that some men (specifically, the righteous) 'will be remembered for ever' (*le'ôlām*, Ps. 112:6). He does not, however, explicitly deny the possibility that the dead may be remembered for some time to come: **in the days to come** is a vague phrase which does not necessarily mean 'soon after death'. But that even the wise man, being dead, will ultimately be **forgotten** is enough to make 'Solomon' despair.

How . . .!: this sentence is more than just an exclamation: it is a lament. **seeing that . . . long:** the word *bešekbār* is a complex and unique form, of which the first part (*beše-*) corresponds to 'seeing that' and the second (*-kebār*) means 'already'. Nothing in the text corresponds to *RSV*'s **long**. *NEB* reads *bešekkerōb* and translates the phrase by 'as the passing days multiply'; but this is improbable and unnecessary.

17. So I hated life: Zimmerli's comment that this is an 'unheard-of statement' in a wisdom context is hardly correct: Job's impassioned curse on the day of his birth (Job 3) is a classic exposition of the same thought. At an earlier period Ahithophel, 'David's counsellor', a 'wise man' *par excellence*, (2 Sam. 16:23) committed suicide in despair (2 Sam. 17:23)—almost the only example of suicide in the Old Testament. Disgust with life is expressed in the literature of other peoples of the ancient Near East, as in the case of the Egyptian 'man weary of life' who welcomes death (*ANET*, p. 407)—though for him there was an expectation of a better life afterwards. For Qoheleth, suicide is not an option because it is precisely death that he fears most. Certainly Qoheleth's statement is a rejection of the traditional viewpoint expressed in the Book of Proverbs, where 'life' is richly and positively commended as the one thing worth having, and as attainable through wisdom. There is, however, no doubt that in different moods Qoheleth's attitude towards life varies. Against this verse it is necessary to set not only the several passages (beginning with 2:24–26) in which he recommends the enjoyment of life to the full, but also 9:4–6 and 11:7–8, which speak very positively of its value. (4:2–3 and 6:1–6 are not general statements about life in general, but are concerned with particular cases in which death or non-existence would be preferable to life.) In evaluating the present passage it should be borne in mind that Qoheleth is probably still speaking in the persona of Solomon, who is here engaged in describing the progress of his past thoughts. This is a personal account of his emotional reaction, as the words **to me** indicate. His final conclusion is expressed in vv. 24–26. On the interpretation of the final sentence of the verse see on 1:14.

18–23. In this passage 'Solomon' gives an additional reason for his disillusionment: not only will his wisdom eventually be forgotten, but his material possessions, which he has striven so hard to accumulate, may well be frittered away by his heirs, leaving no trace. This theme, to which Qoheleth returns again and again (4:7–8; 5:13–17 [MT 12–16]; 6:1–2) clearly betrays the interests of Qoheleth himself: his preoccupation with his personal possessions and what will become of them after his death is characteristic of the Hellenistic age, the age of the 'self-made man'.

18. The repetition of **I hated** (*weśānē'tî*) from v. 17 makes a formal link with the previous passage which corresponds to a continuity of theme. **toil:** *'āmāl* here must mean primarily the *fruit* of toil, i.e. wealth or material possessions (see on 1:3) in view of the word **leave:** one cannot bequeath one's toil as such. However, the use of the corresponding adjective *'āmēl* (*RSV*, **had toiled**) in connection with it shows that the stress is upon the labour involved in acquiring this wealth: it is *new* wealth. **under the sun** here adds nothing to the sense: it is almost a cliché with Qoheleth in association with certain phrases; in association with 'toil' it occurs also in 1:3; 2:20, 22; 5:18 (MT 17); 9:9. See on 1:3.

19. who knows . . .? (*mî yôdēa'*): equivalent to 'no one can know'. However, Crenshaw's assertion that 'Qoheleth's use of *mî yôdēa'* functioned to call in question the entire wisdom enterprise' (1986, p. 286) overstates its significance. Speculation about the reason why Qoheleth did not know who would be his heir—e.g. that he had no children or that he was a bachelor—is pointless. Moreover, taking the question as supposedly posed by 'Solomon', a reference to Rehoboam here (cf. 2:12) is also unlikely because Solomon knew who would succeed him and presumably knew whether he was a fool (so Barton). Galling explains this apparent ignorance of the identity of the heir by supposing that the whole passage is fictitious—simply an example of a certain type of wisdom saying (he is presumably referring to passages like Prov. 4:3ff; 7:6–9; Ps. 37:35–36) in which the first person form is used as a pedagogical device. This, however, is improbable unless the frequent use of the first person throughout the book is to be taken in this way.

all for which I toiled: Heb. has 'my *'āmāl* (for) which I toiled (*'āmaltî*)'. As in v. 18, this is a reference to wealth acquired by hard work.

20. So I turned about (*w^e sabbôtî*): this expression seems to be equivalent in meaning to the *ûpānîtî* of 2:11, 12. **gave my heart up to despair:** literally, 'to cause my heart to despair'. But 'despair' is probably too emotive a rendering. The verb *y'š* means to accept with resignation a situation which cannot be helped (as when, e.g., David anticipated that Saul would 'give up' looking for him, 1 Sam. 27:1). In the present verse, as in v. 19, it is his *wealth* rather than his toil whose loss through death 'Solomon' regrets: the expression *h^e'āmāl še'āmaltî* (*RSV*, **the toil of my labours**) is virtually identical with that discussed in v. 19. The point of the verse is that he now recognizes and accepts what he has complained about in v. 19 as an unalterable fact of life: he has 'given up'.

21. because: this can hardly be the correct translation of the particle *kî*, since the clause which it introduces is a general statement which does not function as an explanation of Qoheleth's personal concern about what may happen to his *own* wealth after his death. It is probably an 'emphatic' or 'asseverative' *kî* meaning 'yes, indeed' (see Schoors, 1981 and the literature cited there), apparently introducing yet another and even more depressing example of the futility of human effort and achievement: that these will benefit not the person who has worked so hard and effectively, but someone who has done nothing at all to deserve his good fortune. However, if this is the correct interpretation the **sometimes** (*yēš*) is surprising: this is surely *always* the case. Two solutions have been offered to the problem. The use of *'ādām*, 'a man', twice may suggest that Qoheleth is here not deploring the inheritance by a son (or near relative) of a father's fortune, which was generally regarded as an excellent and desirable thing (e.g. in Prov. 13:22) but cases when for some reason property may be inherited by a stranger (as perhaps also in Ps. 39:6 [MT 7]). The alternative explanation is that the verse does not refer to inheritance of a dead man's property at all, but to the loss of a man's property during his lifetime through trickery or seizure (so Lohfink). (The verb translated by **leave** in *RSV* is the neutral *nātan*, 'give, hand over'.) There are references elsewhere in the book both to the oppression of the weak by the powerful (4:1) and to commercial losses (4:13–17). Lohfink also renders *rā'āh rabbāh* (**a great evil**) as 'a *frequent* evil', commenting that arbitrary seizure of property by members of the ruling class was frequent in third century BC Judaea (on the meanings of *rab*, see Berlin, 1981).

kišrôn (**skill**), a word peculiar to Qoheleth, may also mean 'success' or 'advantage', as in 5:11 (MT 10). Cf. also 4:4.

22. 'Solomon' now adds a further and even more disillusioned consideration: it is bad enough that all that a man has worked to acquire has to be left behind when he dies to be enjoyed by someone who gets it for nothing; but, says 'Solomon', even during his life it cannot be properly enjoyed because he is forced, or driven, to lead a life not only of **toil** but of **strain**—that is, the mental strain caused by the always unsatisfied ambition to acquire even more (on the meaning of *ra'yôn*, see on 1:14). Thus when a balance is struck it turns out that such a man **has** nothing (the question is a rhetorical one implying a negative): his wealth in fact gives him no pleasure and no advantage.

23. Like the previous verses, this is not a comment on the human condition in general, as most commentators suppose, but a continuation of 'Solomon's' reflections on a particular kind of man: the man who, like 'Solomon' himself, is possessed by a restless ambition to achieve something—whatever it may be—for himself, and who puts this 'business' (*'inyān*, **work**) before everything else (compare the treatment of the same theme in 4:7–8; 8:16–17, where also the word *'inyān* is a key word). Such a man bears the burden of constant worry during the working day and of inability to relax at night (*lō' šākab libbô* means literally 'his mind does not go to bed'). It has been suggested that the first part of the verse (to **rest**) is a popular proverb characterizing the type of the merchant (Lauha). Lohfink sees it as a possible reference to the bankrupt forced into slavery for debt. The rhythmic nature of the sentence and the occurrence of the same word-pair (**pain, vexation**) as in 1:18 might suggest this; but in its present form it is hardly a complete saying as it does not identify the person to whom it refers. If it is an adapted quotation it is likely to have originally referred to just the kind of person whom Qoheleth has in mind.

24–26. The sudden reintroduction of God into the discussion at the end of a protracted passage (1:14–2:23) which was wholly concerned with man's efforts to shape his own destiny and the futility which results from these is crucial for the understanding of the whole of this section of the book. It was already recognized by the earlier wisdom teachers that 'man proposes but God disposes' (e.g. Prov. 19:21; 21:30); but this awareness had functioned as little more than a note of caution against arrogance: in general it was believed that wise and righteous behaviour would duly receive divine blessing and reward (so Proverbs, *passim*). Qoheleth here and indeed throughout the book makes the subsidiary theme central. 'Solomon' now understands the reason for the uncertainty of human life which he has repeatedly bemoaned in the preceding verses: everything, good or bad, which happens to a man comes from the same source: **the hand of God**, who is not bound to any law, but acts as he **pleases**. This enables 'Solomon' to adopt a quite new attitude towards **joy** or pleasure (in the Hebrew the same word, *śimḥāh*, is used in v. 26 as in vv. 1, 2 and 10). In contrast to the ephemeral and deceptive pleasure achieved by deliberate self-indulgence, the unsought pleasure given by God is the 'good' (*ṭôb*) which 'Solomon' was seeking (v. 3): in fact *ṭôb* occurs no less than four times in these three verses, giving an emphasis which can hardly be accidental—in *RSV* it is concealed by **better** (v. 24), **enjoyment** (v. 24), **pleases him** ('*ṭôb* before him', v. 26) and **pleases God** ('*ṭôb* before God'). This God-given pleasure is to be accepted thankfully; the same applies to **wisdom and knowledge**. It is man's determination to secure these things for himself which leads to a sense of futility.

24. than that he should: MT lacks 'than', and thus has the opposite meaning: 'man derives *no* good from . . .'. But in view of similar expressions in 3:12, 22; 8:15, and with support from some of the Versions (Pesh., Vulg. and some MSS of LXX), the commentators are almost unanimous in supposing that a *mēm* (signifying 'than') has dropped out by haplography (Loader is an exception). **eat and drink:** this is to be taken literally, though probably—as elsewhere in the Old Testament and in ancient Near Eastern literature—as standing for the enjoyment of the material things of life in general. R. Smend (1977) notes that 'Solomon' is far from advocating unbridled self-indulgence, as is clear from 7:2. **find enjoyment in his toil:** if this is the correct translation, the positive evaluation of *'āmāl* as a possible source of enjoyment here and in some other passages (especially 3:13; 5:18, 19 [MT 17, 18]) would show that Qoheleth made a distinction between work undertaken out of a frenetic desire to amass wealth, which always leads to disappointment (1:3; 2:10–11, 18–23) and simple working for one's living (or for some other reason such as creative inspiration), the enjoyment of which comes from God. Alternatively, *NEB* may be right in translating *ba'ᵃmālô* by 'in return for his labours'—though see *NEB* 5:19 (MT 18)! **also:** probably better, 'indeed' (on the emphatic use of *gam* see on v. 14).

25. apart from him: MT has 'apart from me' (so *RSV* margin). Lauha and Lohfink defend MT. Lauha regards the verse as a quotation of unknown origin added by a redactor in which God is speaking about himself; Lohfink takes it as a reference by 'Solomon' to his own exceptional opportunities for enjoyment, which are not to be taken as typical of the human situation. Neither of these interpretations carries conviction, and most modern commentaries rightly read 'from him' with LXX and some other Versions.

can have enjoyment (*yāḥûš*): elsewhere the verb *ḥûš*, which occurs several times in the Old Testament, always means 'hasten'; but this makes no sense here. A proposed emendation to *yišteh*, 'can drink', based on LXX and some other Versions, is unlikely to be correct: it is more probable that the LXX translators, faced with an unknown word or one which made no sense, made the emendation themselves as a last resort on the basis of the conjunction of 'eat' and 'drink' in v. 24. Most commentators accept MT as it stands, regarding the verb as an otherwise unknown verb unrelated to the more common verb *ḥûš*; but attempts to discover its meaning on the analogy of words in other Semitic languages have produced a variety of different conclusions. *RSV*'s rendering may be right; but Ellermeier's contention (*ZAW*, 1963; *Qoheleth I/2*) that the word is related to Accadian *ḫâšu(m)*, 'worry, be anxious' has convinced several commentators including Zimmerli, Galling and Lauha. If this is the correct interpretation, the tenor of the verse is connected with v. 26 rather than with v. 24: both enjoyment and anxiety come equally from the hand of God.

26. The interpretation of this verse depends on the meaning of the word *ḥôṭe'* (*RSV*, **sinner**), which is the Qal participle of the verb *ḥāṭā'*. Most commentators, on the basis of a few passages elsewhere in the Old Testament (Jg. 20:16 [Hiphil]; Job 5:24; Prov. 8:36; 14:21; 19:2; 20:2; Isa. 65:20) and of usages of the same root in some cognate languages, maintain that the word here means 'to fail, miss, fall short' and lacks any religious or ethical connotations. (In some of the above cases this meaning is dubious.) On the other hand, there are 231 occurrences of the verb in the Old Testament in which it means 'to sin', together with 356 occurrences of nouns cognate with it where the meaning is undoubtedly 'sin'. Of the other occurrences in Ecclesiastes (7:20, 26; 8:12; 9:2, 18), only in 9:18 is this meaning improbable. The present verse in itself offers no evidence that the meaning of *ḥôṭe'* here is other than the usual one: it is specifically contrasted with **who pleases him/God** (*ṭôb lᵉpānāw/ṭôb lipnê hā'ᵉlōhîm*) which, both here and in its other occurrence in 7:26 simply means 'of whom God approves', without any indication of God's reason for doing so.

Lauha recognises that *ḥôṭe'* means 'sinner' here, but regards the whole verse as a later addition by an 'orthodox' redactor anxious to correct the impression that God acts in an arbitrary fashion. If *ḥôṭe'* does mean 'sinner' here, as is probable, and if the verse comes from Qoheleth's own hand, he is here apparently accepting the 'orthodox' view of divine reward and punishment. But this paradox is not peculiar to this passage: it is found elsewhere in the book, most clearly in 3:16–17 and 8:10–13. In fact it is probable that this is a paradox which arises from contradictory experiences in Qoheleth's own life, which he is unable to reconcile: God does not always act in the same way. Qoheleth duly records the contradiction. He is, however, sure that God is the source of everything that happens in human life, and also that no human reason can hope to understand God's reasons (3:10–11). His conclusion to the discussion in this section of the book is thus neither wholly positive nor wholly negative: **the work of gathering and heaping** mysteriously given by God to the sinner who insists on making his fortune in his own way is both burdensome and, in the end, futile, as he remarks once more at the end of the verse; but the man to whom God has equally mysteriously given the ability to accept his total dependence on God—that is, the one who has his approval—finds that life has its joys after all. There is thus a kind of logic here, even though it is not that of the modern western mind.

give: the verb is the same as that rendered 'leave' by *RSV* in v. 21.

MAN DOES NOT KNOW HIS TIME

3:1–15

Qoheleth now finally abandons the Solomonic fiction. 3:1 is, in a sense, a new beginning. The change of style marks the section off from what precedes. There is a further change of style in v. 9; but the continuation of the same theme in vv. 9–15 shows that vv. 1–15 must be considered as a single section. Verse 16 probably marks the beginning of a new section, although—as is the case elsewhere in the book—there is no absolute thematic break.

3:1–15 consists, then, of two parts: 1. a series of fourteen pairs of opposites, set out in rhythmical form in which each member begins with the same word (*'ēt*, **a time**), preceded by an introductory heading (vv. 1–8); and 2. a question arising from the first part (v. 9), followed by a series of three comments (vv. 10–11, 12–13, 14–15) which seek to answer this question and to explore its implications. The theme of the whole section is unmistakably and emphatically proclaimed by the occurrence of the key word *'ēt* no less than twenty-nine times in the first eight verses and also by its recurrence in v. 11*a*.

'ēt is the regular word for 'time' in biblical Hebrew. It does not have an abstract sense in the Old Testament, either in this book or elsewhere, but signifies the moment of a particular occasion or happening (e.g. in the phrase *b*ᵉ*kol-'ēt* in 9:8, where it means 'on every occasion'—*RSV*, 'always'). Sometimes, however, it has the added nuance of a 'regular' or 'appropriate' happening: the 'right' time (e.g. Jer. 8:7). In 3:1–8, 11 and also in some other passages (e.g. 3:17; 7:17; 9:12) Qoheleth uses it in this sense. Some scholars have suggested that it has here an additional meaning such as the *power to assess* the 'right' time for a particular action (Wilch, 1969) or *man's need* to make such decisions (Galling, 1961). The actual contents of these verses do not wholly support these views. But it is generally agreed that it was Qoheleth's view that the ability to decide on the appropriate time for action has been denied to man by God, who deliberately conceals it from him (v. 11). The same is true of events which befall man and over which he has no power, notably death (v. 2). (Compare also 9:12.) Consequently all man can do is to accept what God gives when he gives it (vv. 12–13). This negative view of human freedom runs counter to the teaching of the conventional wisdom literature.

1–8. The rigid structure of vv. 2–8 is not an especially unusual literary device in the Old Testament or in ancient Near Eastern literature generally. The compilation of lists (onomastica) was undertaken for a number of reasons, of which some were highly theological while others may be described as rhetorical or even merely ornamental; but in general the practice attests to an understanding of the world, both 'natural' and supernatural, as an ordered structure, and to a desire to describe this, as far as possible, in its totality. 'God-lists' were a feature of Mesopotamian religious literature, and Tablets VI–VII of the Babylonian *Enuma Elish* list and comment on no less than fifty names of a single god, Marduk (*ANET*, pp. 69–72). In the Old Testament, several extensive passages (e.g. Job 38–41; Ps. 104; 136) list the attributes or qualities of Yahweh. Natural phenomena (as in the so-called 'numerical proverbs' in Prov. 30:7–31) and human character (Prov. 31:10–31) also provided an occasion for such enumerations. Some of these passages are elaborately structured, for example as alphabetic acrostics (e.g. Lam. 1–4; Ps. 119; Prov. 31:10–31) or, as here, by the repetition of key words before each item or by syntactical arrangement or refrains (e.g. Ps. 136; 150; Isa. 2:12–16; 5:8–23; Prov. 30).

It will be argued below that there is reason to suppose that vv. 2–8 (and possibly also v. 1) are not the work of Qoheleth in his role of 'wise man' versed in the literary forms of the wisdom tradition, but are an extended quotation by him of an already existing literary piece (so Wright, 1981); on this, as elsewhere in the book, Qoheleth then made his comments. If this is the case, the possibility must be borne in mind that the original meaning of these verses may have been different from Qoheleth's interpretation of them in vv. 9–15. (See Galling, 1961 and his commentary on the meaning of vv. 1–15 as a whole.) It is in any case important to consider them first by themselves as a distinct and integral statement: as the basic proposition which constitutes the starting-point of Qoheleth's argument in this section of the book.

Set apart, then, from the comments in vv. 9–15, vv. 2–8 appear at first sight to be open to a number of different interpretations; and they have in fact been variously understood by modern scholars. The clues to their meaning must be looked for in their form, content and scope, and in the introductory statement in v. 1.

1. **For everything** (*lakkōl*): this word, together with the phrases **every matter** and **under heaven** (see on 1:3) leaves no doubt that the verses which follow (1–8) are intended to represent (though they are obviously not an exhaustive list) everything which may happen in an individual's life. The verse states that for each of these there is a 'proper' or 'best' time. The use of the word *z*ᵉ*mān* (**season**), a late word in Hebrew but which is standard in Aramaic and occurs regularly in the Aramaic parts of the Old Testament and in both the Hebrew and Aramaic portions of the Mishnah, reinforces the meaning of *'ēt* (**a time**) here. It means an appropriate time; the use of the two words together, as in poetical parallelism (which in fact this may be) adds emphasis to this view.

matter: this is the meaning of *ḥēpeṣ* here, as in 3:17; 5:8 (MT 7); 8:6. This also is a late usage frequently found in the Mishnah. Elsewhere in Ecclesiastes (5:4 [MT 3]; 12:1, 10) it is used in one of its earlier senses, 'pleasure'.

This verse does not in fact greatly assist the interpretation of vv. 2–8. It does no more than to assert that human life is not haphazard: it does not state who determines what is the 'proper time' for things to happen. While it was generally recognised that both in nature (e.g. Job 5:26; 39:1, 2; Jer. 8:7; cf. Gen. 8:22; 9:8–17) and in human life (Job 22:16) it was God who ordered the 'times', the older wisdom represented by the Book of Proverbs regularly took it for granted that in most matters the human agent was free and capable of making his own plans and carrying them out successfully 'at the right time'. There is nothing in this verse taken by itself to suggest that it is God who sets the 'times', though it could be interpreted in that way.

2–8. From the formal point of view there is an almost complete symmetry here. The verses consist of twenty-eight phrases, each consisting of the word *'ēt* followed by a qualifier which defines the particular character of the *'ēt* in question. With the exception of the last two, this qualifier consists of an infinitive usually preceded by *l*ᵉ, 'to', expanded in some cases (four times) by the addition of a further word defining the infinitive more closely (thus **a time to die**, but **a time to cast away stones**, and **a time to refrain from embracing**). The series runs on without a single interruption or explanation—there is not even a verb, nor a predicate, such as 'There is'. These verbless phrases are all arranged in pairs, connected by the word 'and'. (The final pair (v. 8) differs from the others in that *'ēt* is followed not by an infinitive but by a noun (**[for] war, [for] peace**). This syntactical variation is probably simply a way of marking the completion of the series.)

That the intention in assembling these various 'times' or moments is to represent all the vicissitudes which may occur in the course of a human life is clearly indicated not only by v. 1 but by certain characteristics of the list itself: 1. the fact that the number of items (twenty-eight, or fourteen pairs) is a multiple of seven, the number which symbolizes completion or totality; 2. the fact that they are arranged as pairs of opposites or extremes, a stylistic device frequently found in the Old Testament and elsewhere in ancient Near Eastern literature which also stands for totality (the mention of extreme limits is understood as including everything which exists or is conceivable between those limits); and 3. the fact that the first pair, birth and death, marks the extreme limits of human existence itself and so by anticipation defines the scope of the whole list.

But beyond this aim to comprehend the whole of human life it is difficult to discern any deeper purpose. The author seems to have been content to fit his observations together in a simple *formal* pattern and to have eschewed any attempt to 'point a moral' or to express, even by implication, some conviction about the nature of human existence such as is expressed in vv. 9–15. Despite attempts by scholars to demonstrate a pattern of *thought* here, it must be said that, apart from the placing of the most comprehensive pair at the beginning of the list, the order in which the individual pairs are arranged is to a large extent haphazard. It is true that, as will be shown below, in five out of a total of thirteen cases (the pairs in vv. 2, 3, 4, 6 and 8) there are thematic connections between consecutive pairs; this thematic doubling possibly points to earlier stages in the composition of the passage. But there is discernible no *systematic* attempt to make such thematic connections, no progression in real or supposed order of importance, and no thematic climax or definite conclusion. Such lack of thematic arrangement is not unusual in the wisdom literature. For example, many, if not most, of the hundreds of brief sayings in Prov. 10–29 appear—at least to the modern reader—to lack any system of arrangement *either* of form *or* of theme; and this is true also of much of the wisdom literature of the ancient Near East.

A curious feature of the passage is that some of the pairs begin with what might be called the 'positive' pole (e.g. **plant**, **embrace**, **seek**), while others begin with the 'negative' pole (e.g. **kill**, **break down**, **weep**). Loader (1969, pp. 240–2) claims that the arrangement is deliberate and precise in both its formal and thematic aspects. Classifying the items as 'desirable' (D) or 'undesirable' (U), he finds the following chiastic pattern:

D – U (twice, v. 2)
U – D (twice, v. 3)
U – D (twice, v. 4)
D – U (twice, v. 5)
D – U (twice, v. 6)
U – D (twice, v. 7)
D – U (v. 8*a*)
U – D (v. 8*b*)

This theory depends, of course, on the correctness of the classification of the items as U or D, and in particular on the much disputed meaning of v. 5*a* (see below on that verse). Moreover, the 'polar' categories themselves are by no means satisfactory: in some pairs (e.g. keeping silence and speaking, v. 7) both items are 'desirable' in different situations. In fact, however the material is interpreted, it is difficult to discern a deliberate pattern. It seems an inevitable conclusion that it was only the individual contrasts themselves which interested the author, and not, in general, the order in which they are placed.

In short, these verses are an example of the practice of collecting and recording phenomena which was an important feature of ancient Near Eastern civilization (see von Rad, *Old Testament Theology*, vol. 1, pp. 423ff.; *Wisdom in Israel*, pp. 121–4). In this they resemble the so-called 'numerical sayings' of Prov. 30 (see Roth, 1965). In these passages certain otherwise quite different phenomena are listed which have one thing in common: they are, for example, all very small, yet wise, or 'stately in their tread'. One of these passages, Prov. 30:18–19, closely resembles Ec. 3:2–8 in that each item begins with the same word: *derek*, 'the way of'.

The apparent lack of any purpose in vv. 2–8 considered in themselves other than what has been suggested above supports the view that the passage is an independent piece quoted at length by Qoheleth to serve as a 'text' for his own observations. These verses contain nothing which is particularly characteristic of his thought or his language, and are perfectly compatible with earlier conventional wisdom. The introductory v. 1, on the other hand, may come from him: it contains one word, *zᵉmān*, which is late (though not peculiar to him), one word, *ḥēpeṣ*, used in a sense hardly attested before his time, and a phrase, **under heaven**, which he uses elsewhere. But the idea which this verse expresses is not peculiar to him; and if he was in fact its author he may have added it simply for 'editorial' purposes.

2. The two pairs which constitute this verse, which refer respectively to human and plant life, have a certain thematic relationship. **to be born:** the verb *yālad* in the Qal, as here, means either to bear or to beget children, not to be born. Nevertheless *RSV*'s rendering is correct: in view of the contrast with **to die**, it is clear—though some commentaries take a different view—that the centre of interest here lies in the act of birth itself—the coming into existence of a new life—and not in the role of the parents.

to pluck up: this verb (*'āqar*) occurs in only one other place in the Old Testament (Zeph. 2:4), but it is current in later Hebrew in both a literal and a metaphorical sense: to uproot, eradicate, remove. It refers to agricultural work, the two activities mentioned being not alternative but complementary. The reference is probably not to harvesting but to the life of the vine or fruit-tree: just as there is a proper time for planting a tree, so there is also a time when it is no longer profitable and has to be destroyed (cf. Isa. 5:1–6). It may be that the saying should be interpreted metaphorically: planting is frequently so used in the Old Testament with regard to human beings or peoples, and uprooting (expressed in different words) is similarly used (Ps. 52:5 [MT 7]; Ezek. 17:9; Zeph. 2:4).

3. Here again there is a thematic connection between two consecutive pairs. **kill** and **heal** are opposites in the sense that they denote respectively the taking and the preservation of life. Moral considerations are irrelevant here. There is no point in speculating whether the killing is envisaged as taking place in battle or refers to the execution of criminals. The point is that each of these actions has its place in different situations. **break down . . . build up:** this may refer to demolition of property and rebuilding; but the expressions are too general for precise definition.

4. Once more there is a thematic relationship between two consecutive pairs in this verse, though none with the preceding or subsequent pairs. The rather rare word *rāqad* (**dance**) may have been chosen instead of the more obvious *śāmaḥ/śāmēaḥ*, 'rejoice' for the sake of assonance (*s^epōd . . . r^eqōd*).

5. The literal meaning of the first pair in this verse is clear, but there is no agreement among the commentators about the purpose of the actions mentioned. The Targum interprets the saying as referring to the demolition of a building and the subsequent preparations for rebuilding; but—apart from the fact that this theme has probably occurred already in v. 3*b*—the stones in question would not be thrown away but kept together for reuse. Some commentators think that the reference is to the need to clear away stones from a field in order to make it suitable for agricultural use (cf. Isa. 5:2) and, by contrast, to the deliberate ruining of an enemy's field by throwing stones into it (2 Kg. 3:19, 25). This is perhaps the most plausible explanation. The Midrash Rabba on this verse, followed in modern times by Levy, Gordis, Loader and Lohfink, explained the two phrases as euphemisms for indulging in and refraining from sexual intercourse, and so found a connection with the pair which follows; but there is no evidence of such a linguistic usage in the Old Testament or elsewhere in later Jewish literature. Galling (1961, pp. 7–12) suggested that the reference is to a practice of keeping stones in a bag to use in counting the items of a commercial transaction; but the evidence for this speculation is very indirect. Other suggestions have been made. Lauha rejects both occurrences of the word **stones** as glosses intended to add precision to an imprecise saying, but which spoils the rhythmical symmetry.

embrace: there is no reason to suppose that this word is used here as an euphemism for sexual intercourse, although this is a possible meaning. It is used also of gestures of affection between male relatives, and even of holding on to inanimate objects. There is consequently no reason to suppose a thematic connection with the previous pair, and there is none with what follows.

6. These two pairs are thematically related. **seek** (*biqqēš*) here means to desire or attempt to acquire something; *'ibbēd* (**lose**) usually means 'to destroy' in the Old Testament, but in later Hebrew it can mean either 'to lose' or 'to consider as lost, give up for lost'. The latter meaning makes the better contrast. There is no very obvious thematic connection between this pair and that which follows in v. 7*a*.

7. rend: this probably refers to the well-attested custom of tearing one's clothes as a sign of mourning (see, e.g., Gen. 37:29; 2 Sam. 13:31) and of repairing them when the time of mourning was over (so Midrash Rabba). But there is no reason at all to suppose that **keep silence** and **speak** also refer to mourning customs. The importance for the wise man of knowing when to remain silent and when speech, if carefully worded, is useful or helpful was a commonplace of both Israelite and ancient Near Eastern wisdom teaching (on silence, see, e.g., Prov. 10:19; 13:3; 17:27; 21:23; on speech, Prov. 15:23; 16:24; 25:11). The phraseology of Prov. 15:23 ('a word in its proper time' ['*ēt*]) links this passage very closely with traditional wisdom literature. There is thus no thematic connection between these two pairs, and none with the preceding and following verses.

8. These final pairs are thematically connected, though chiastically arranged. As in v. 3*a*, no moral judgement is made; but it should be remembered that in marking out opposite poles in these verses the author's purpose was simply to point out the limits within which human life is lived. So in this verse he did not intend to imply that every person was bound to feel hatred as well as love for others.

9. In posing this lapidary question Qoheleth begins his discussion of vv. 2–8 by giving a particular interpretation of its list of activities. In doing so he generalizes the comment of 'Solomon' (2:13) on the worthlessness of his own activities, applying it to human activity as a whole. The question is equivalent to a denial (as in the editorial 1:3): whatever efforts (**toil**) a man may make (*hā'ôśeh* means any person who engages in any kind of activity, rather than **the worker**) will in the end bring him no advantage (*yitrôn*). The reference to the long list of activities in vv. 2–8 is clear, and it is also clear that the negative judgement is related to the fact that it is stated there that each has its own appointed 'time'. The explanation and justification for the negative judgement appear in vv. 10–11.

from his toil: the Hebrew has 'from that at which he toils', which is not quite the same thing.

10. *'inyān* (**business**), a common term in later Hebrew though restricted in the Old Testament to this book, is a quite 'neutral' term and so suitable to apply to the activities mentioned in vv. 2–8, or to the object of 'toil' in v. 9. However, Qoheleth's experience of the world (**I have seen**) led him to give it an unfavourable connotation. The cause of this negative judgement lies in the fact—noted now for the first time in this section—that it is **God** who **has given** mankind its various activities. This thought is explained and developed in v. 11. **to be busy** (*la'ᵃnôt*): see on 1:13.

11. has made; **has done** (*'āśāh* in both instances): in the first of these occurrences most commentators see a reference to the creation of the world and in particular to Gen. 1. However, it is more probable that the perfect tense is used here in the Hebrew to express a general truth and should be rendered by the present tense in English ('makes', 'does') (see Driver, § 12). Despite the fact that the meaning of the word rendered **eternity** in *RSV* is extremely uncertain (see below), the general sense of the verse is reasonably clear: on the one hand, everything which God causes to happen is appropriate or fitting (*yāpeh* [*RSV*, **beautiful**] has this meaning in Mishnaic Hebrew) when the 'time' is right (*bᵉʿittô*, **in its time**); but on the other hand God does not permit man to know what God is doing at any moment (**from the beginning to the end**)—that is, to know whether what *he* proposes to do will coincide with the 'time' which God has made for it. This explains Qoheleth's comment in v. 9 on vv. 2–8: since man is totally ignorant of the appropriate moment for his actions, he cannot derive from them the advantage which he strives to gain.

The relationship of the middle part of the verse (from **also** to **mind**) to the preceding and following clauses is unfortunately obscured by the ambiguity of the two conjunctions *gam* (*RSV*, **also**) and *mibbᵉlî ʾᵃšer lōʾ* (*RSV*, **yet so that** . . . [can]**not**). *gam* sometimes means 'yet, however'; and if this is the case here the clause which follows must express some kind of qualification of what God has conferred on men according to the preceding clause; if, however, it means 'also', the two clauses are parallel or complementary, and the qualification is restricted to the final clause of the verse. Again, *mibbᵉlî ʾᵃšer lōʾ* may indicate a deliberate intention or may simply introduce a fact which qualifies the preceding clause. These ambiguities affect the interpretation of the word *ʿōlām* (*RSV*, **eternity**) and of the clause in which it occurs.

God, says Qoheleth, puts *hāʿōlām* into **man's mind** (literally, 'their mind'—that is, of **the sons of men** in v. 10). *ʿōlām* in biblical Hebrew is normally used adverbially to denote either past or future duration of time virtually without limit (so 'of old' or '[for] ever'). It never occurs independently as the subject or object of a verb. In later Hebrew, however, it occurs as a noun meaning 'the age' or 'the world'. It has been interpreted here in this way by some commentators; on the other hand, others have supposed that Qoheleth has here extended the biblical sense of the word, giving it the meaning of 'eternity' (LXX has *aiōna*). But it makes little sense in Hebrew to say that God put (or, more probably, puts) either eternity or the world into man's mind, since the Hebrew language hardly allows such an expression to be understood as an ellipsis for 'the *notion* of eternity' (or of the world). Various attempts have been made, therefore, to treat the word as a word otherwise unknown to biblical Hebrew meaning 'ignorance', derived from a root *ʿlm* denoting darkness or hiddenness. (This second root *ʿlm* is attested in biblical Hebrew, but not its supposed derivative *ʿôlām*.) Alternatively, it has been suggested that it means 'knowledge', on the basis of an Arabic root. Other such suggestions have been made, and emendations of the text have been proposed. Galling, for example, proposed to read 'into it' (i.e. the world) for 'into their heart' (*RSV*, **into man's mind**). Perhaps the most likely of the proposed interpretations of the unemended text is that it means 'ignorance' or 'darkness'. Then it would be possible to translate as follows: 'yet he puts ignorance into their minds, so that . . .'. But there is no certainty about this.

12. Just as in 2:24 but in slightly different words Qoheleth here draws a positive conclusion from a negative observation about the frustrations of human life: there it was frustration about the worthlessness of human effort; here it is the frustration which arises from man's ignorance of the 'right' time for action. The two thoughts are not entirely unrelated, since the basic cause of the frustration here is not so much man's ignorance in itself, as his determination to **find out** (v. 11) something which in fact he can never know. So the conclusion here is that one should not exhaust oneself in trying to penetrate God's secrets, but should rather accept happiness when it comes. This conclusion is made more emphatic than that in 2:24 by the addition of **I know** (or perhaps better 'I have realised').

for them (*bām*): in spite of the singular 'in *his* life' (*RSV*, **as long as they live**), emendation is unnecessary (see GK § 145m).

enjoy themselves (*la'ᵃśôt ṭôb*): this expression normally means 'do good' in the moral sense, and is so used in 7:20. However, there is little doubt that here it means to realise happiness (*'āśāh* 'make, achieve, bring about'), and is equivalent to *rā'āh ṭôb*, used of enjoyment in 2:1 and 3:13, and to *her'āh 'et-napšô ṭôb* (*RSV*, 'find enjoyment') in 2:24. As is indicated by the repetition of the word *ṭôb* three times in this and the following verse (see also on 2:24–26) and its use elsewhere in the book, Qoheleth's intention here is to lay emphasis on man's possibility of happiness.

13. The syntax of this verse is very loose. A literal translation would be 'And also, every man who eats and drinks . . ., that is a gift of God'. However, *RSV* is probably right in seeing the verse as continuing the thought of v. 12. On the other hand, its rendering, which suggests that God's gift of enjoyment is universally bestowed on human beings without exception is a misinterpretation of Qoheleth's meaning. 'Every man' is qualified in the Hebrew by 'who' (this word is ignored by *RSV*). Qoheleth means that *whenever* a person finds enjoyment available to him, that enjoyment always comes from God's hands. **in all his toil:** see on 2:24.

14. Qoheleth now adds a second conclusion (once again prefaced by **I know**) to his earlier observation on v. 11. Man's ignorance of God's plans ought to lead him not only to the grateful acceptance of his gifts when they come (vv. 12–13), but also to a proper attitude of reverence towards him. He points out that man, being ignorant of God's plans, can obviously not hope to change them, and adds emphasis to this point with the formula **nothing can be added to it, nor anything taken from it**, an ancient formula familiar to his readers from its use in Dt. 4:2; 12:32 (MT 13:1) with regard to God's commandments (the Torah).

has made it so: that is, has acted, or arranged matters. **that men should fear before him:** some commentators have argued that 'fearing God' for Qoheleth means being in a state of terror or deep anxiety. If this was indeed what God has deliberately intended, then this would be an accusation against him of deliberate cruelty towards man. But this interpretation of 'the fear of God' in Qoheleth's thought is not borne out by an investigation of the handful of other passages in which he speaks of it (5:7 [MT 6]; 7:18; 8:12, 13). Nor does the fact that he speaks of 'fearing *before* God' rather than simply saying 'fear God' imply any difference in meaning from that which the phrase has elsewhere in the Old Testament. In 5:7 and 8:12 he himself uses the shorter phrase; and in 8:12, 13 he uses the two forms interchangeably. His use of 'before' (*millip*^{e}*nê*) here may possibly suggest that he wished to add a particular nuance of *awe* to the concept (cf. the use of *lip*^{e}*nê*, 'before' in similar circumstances in Exod. 9:30; Hag. 1:12). But the idea that Qoheleth's concept of the 'fear of God' is essentially different from its usual meaning in the Old Testament (devotion to God, worship of God, or willing obedience to his commandments) is an idea derived from a particular interpretation of Qoheleth's thought in general rather than from his actual use of the phrase. His meaning is that God rightly demands 'fear' from men in the sense of recognition of his essential difference from his creatures (cf. 5:2 [MT 1]).

15. In the first part of this verse Qoheleth repeats in slightly different words what he has already asserted in 1:9–10: that human existence, like the natural order, is a closed circle and offers no opportunity for anything new to be achieved. His intention was presumably to reinforce his statement in v. 14 about the immutability of God's determination of events. The first phrase (to **been**) should probably be rendered 'Whatever occurs had already been in existence'. On the unusual use of the infinitive *lihyôt* (*RSV*, **is to be**) instead of the imperfect see GK § 114i.

The meaning of the last part of the verse (from **and God**) is obscure. The usual meanings of *rādap* (here in the Niphal participle *nirdāp*—*RSV* **what has been driven away**) are 'pursue, chase' and 'persecute'. The latter meaning, however, is hardly appropriate to the context. In Isa. 17:13 the Pual of this verb is used of chaff scattered or 'chased away' by the wind; and it has been suggested that the reference here is to the occurrences or moments of time referred to in the previous part of the verse, which have passed away and are no more. God, it is supposed, catches (*y^e^baqqēš*, **seeks**) these fleeting moments and restores them to the present time. This interpretation fits the context reasonably well, but the use of **seek** is odd: 'seek' does not mean 'find' or 'catch' (cf. Isa. 41:12, 'You shall seek . . . but you shall not find'). The absence of the article before *nirdāp* is unusual, and Driver (1954, pp. 266–7) has proposed an emendation which does not, however, materially change the meaning. It must be admitted that the absence of any direct indication of what it is that is 'driven away' makes the intention of this clause quite uncertain. It may be a quotation of a popular saying which Qoheleth has appropriated for his own use but which is no longer clear to later readers.

WHERE IS JUSTICE TO BE FOUND?

3:16–22

Qoheleth now moves to a new topic: that of the manifest occurrences of miscarriage of justice in society. Once again it is not his purpose to attack the way in which God governs—or misgoverns—the world, but to ask what is the best response that man can make in this situation. His conclusion (v. 22) is the same as that which he drew in vv. 12–13 when he was dealing with the problem of man's frustrated desire to know what God has in store for him. There is also a link between the two passages in the recurrence here of the theme of the 'appropriate time' (*'ēt*, v. 17) decreed by God for everything which happens, but of which man is ignorant.

The section begins, like the previous one (vv. 10–11) with a clear statement of the problem (v. 16). But the argument proceeds somewhat differently. The verse which follows (17) gives what appears to be a sufficient answer to the problem, derived from conventional wisdom. Qoheleth does not deny the truth of this, but reinterprets it in a negative sense (compare the same technique in 2:13–16): he questions its usefulness to human beings who will all in the end share the same fate (vv. 18–21) and who, moreover, do not know the 'timetable' which has been mysteriously but irrevocably drawn up by God (**Who knows . . .?**, v. 21; **who can bring him to see . . .?**, v. 22*b*). But it is this latter fact, man's ignorance of the 'times', which, as in the previous section, leads Qoheleth to his positive conclusion about how he should live his life (v. 22*a*).

16. Moreover (*w^e^'ôd*): according to Galling this means 'always' here and the phrase should be translated 'And I invariably saw'. But the evidence for this meaning of *'ôd* is very slight. *RSV*'s rendering, which agrees with that of most commentators, is certainly correct. The word is thus a connecting particle, probably editorial, intended to create a continuity between two of Qoheleth's otherwise separate observations—a variant on the simpler 'and', which serves the same purpose in 4:4. **in the place of** (*m^e^qôm*): it has been argued on the basis of a possible, though disputed, similar meaning of this word in Hos. 1:10 (MT 2:1) that it here means no more than 'instead of'; but it almost certainly refers here to courts of law—quite literally 'places' where one would expect to find the impartial administration of **justice**. However, Qoheleth is not asserting that the courts are *always* corrupt. The problem to which he draws attention is that justice is yet another sphere of life in which there is an apparent inconsistency which man is unable to explain (cf. 7:15). The virtual repetition of the same phrase here is probably intended to add emphasis or solemnity to the observation: the emendation of **wickedness** (*reša'*) on its second occurrence to *peša'*, a word of similar meaning, in order to produce a more varied style is unnecessary.

17. There is no need to regard all or part of this verse as an interpolation by an 'orthodox' editor, as is sometimes done. The first half of the verse (to **the wicked**) expresses a belief which was universally held in ancient Israel. The verb *šāpaṭ* (**judge**) does not necessarily denote condemnation or punishment: rather, it refers to the making of impartial judicial decisions—unlike those referred to in v. 16—which mean condemnation for the guilty (e.g. Ezek. 7:3, 8; 18:30) but vindication of the innocent (e.g. Ps. 10:18; 26:1; 43:1). This kind of divine judgement is conceived of as taking place in this world: the imperfect *yišpôṭ (RSV*, **will judge**) can refer either to the future or to the present. It is extremely unlikely that Qoheleth is here referring to a judgement of the individual after death, a very rare and late concept in the Old Testament and one to which, as other passages make clear, he does not subscribe.

The order of the words in this sentence is very emphatic: it may be rendered 'both the innocent (*haṣṣaddîq*) and the guilty (*hārāšā'*) receive their judgement—from *God*'. This affirmation does not contradict v. 16: like the prophets (e.g. Isa. 10:1–4; Am. 5:10–12; 8:4–7) Qoheleth appears to be saying that those who perpetrate injustice and oppression in contemporary society, even if they escape human condemnation, will not escape God's punishment, and that their innocent victims will similarly receive justice from him. But this conventional view is now to be radically re-interpreted.

In the second part of the verse (from **for**) the concept of the 'proper' time (*'ēt*) is reintroduced. The meaning of this sentence is reasonably clear, although the phrase **he has appointed** is an extremely dubious rendering. It is based not on the Hebrew text but on an emendation (though this is not pointed out in *RSV* margin). The Hebrew text has *šām*, 'there'; but *RSV* has followed some commentators who, unable to make sense of this, have repointed it to *śām*, which can mean 'fixed, appointed'. None of the attempts to solve this problem, either with or without emendation, has been generally accepted. Some commentators consider that the word has been accidentally transposed from the middle of v. 18 (so *NEB*). However this may be, Qoheleth appears to be attempting to account for the fact that the miscarriages of justice referred to in v. 16 seem to go unpunished by using the concept of the 'proper time' of which man is kept in ignorance: God has, as it were, 'a time to judge and a time to refrain from judging' (cf. vv. 2–8 and 8:10–13).

18. This verse is extremely difficult syntactically and in other respects. **is testing them:** this word (*lᵉbārām*) has the form of the infinitive of *bārar* (with suffix 'them'), where a finite verb would be expected. It has been suggested (by Gordis) that the first letter (*lᵉ*) is here not the sign of the infinitive but an asseverative particle meaning 'surely'; if this were so, the remainder (*bārām*) could be the perfect tense—'he has tested them'. But the existence of this construction in Hebrew is not established beyond doubt. Other commentators have proposed the insertion of *śām* (transferred from v. 17 and repointed—see on that verse), giving the sense 'God has decided (or 'arranged') to test them'. A further problem is the meaning of the verb *bārar*: 'test' is a sense hardly found in the Old Testament, and also it is not clear what reason God could have for carrying out such a test. The meaning 'set apart' (i.e. from himself), attested in the Mishnah, is more probable: God decides to show men that they are totally different from him—and are in fact (in one respect) indistinguishable from the animals. **to show them:** the Hebrew has the Qal infinitive, i.e. 'to see'. But LXX, Pesh. and Vulg. have 'show', which makes better sense, since it is more natural to suppose that it is men themselves, rather than God, who are ignorant of their true status. This meaning, in view of the general laxity of Qoheleth's syntax, can probably be obtained without emendation: 'so that they may see'—though the Versions mentioned above seem to imply the causative (Hiphil). Gordis takes this verb (*wᵉlir'ôt*) as an infinitive standing for a finite verb (GK § 114p), but it is doubtful whether there are really any attestations of exactly this type of construction. **but** (i.e. 'merely'): the Hebrew has *hēmmāh lāhem* (literally, 'they to them'), which some commentators omit altogether as a meaningless error. Others, however, regard these extremely odd words as meaning 'in themselves', i.e. 'nothing but', and intended to add emphasis to this already sombre assessment of human status.

The statement that **the sons of men . . . are but beasts** is much less harsh than it appears to be on the surface. It must be taken together with the words which immediately follow in v. 19, where Qoheleth makes it clear (**For** . . .) that he is comparing man with the animals in only one respect: their mortality. Hebrew authors frequently use metaphor (*identification* of one thing with another) without intending more than is conveyed by simile (*comparison* of one thing with another). The thought, thus understood, is not peculiar to Qoheleth and is identical, for example, with that of Ps. 49:12, 20 (MT 13, 21). In this verse Qoheleth reinterprets the conventional wisdom which he has cited in v. 17*a* to mean that it is in their *death*, which all men share with the animals, that both the righteous and the wicked *equally* experience God's ultimate, but hidden, judgement (cf. 9:1–3); and God uses the knowledge which he has given them that they must die **to show them** the reality of their lowly status and their dependence on him.

19. Qoheleth's assertion in v. 18 that men are **but beasts** is now clarified. The key word of this verse—it occurs three times—is **fate** (*miqreh*). But, as in 2:14, this is not some malignant and impersonal force. 'Fate' is simply what happens to a person or to any living creature; and the final 'happening', both for men and animals, is death. **They all have the same breath** (*rûaḥ*): the view implied here, that God gives life to both men and animals by putting breath in them, and that when this breath is withdrawn they die is the common biblical understanding of the matter: cf. Gen. 2:7 (though there the word for 'breath' is not *rûaḥ* but *nᵉšāmāh*); Gen. 7:15; Ps. 104:29 and, in Ecclesiastes, 12:7. **has no advantage:** the word *môtār*, which occurs in the Old Testament only here and in Prov. 14:23; 21:5, is equivalent to *yitrôn* (see on 1:3). The placing of the negative (*'āyin*) at the end of the phrase makes it very emphatic: 'advantage for man over against the animals is there *none*'. **all is vanity:** this is not a general condemnation of everything but a comment on mortality. *hebel* here (see on 1:2) means 'ephemeral, transitory' rather than 'worthless'.

It should be noted that certain minor emendations of the Hebrew text are necessary to make sense of this verse. *miqreh* in its first two occurrences should be repointed to the construct form *miqrēh*, and in its third occurrence should be shorn of a redundant 'and' (*wᵉ*) which precedes it in the Hebrew. These emendations all have some support from Versions or MSS and are accepted by most commentators, followed by *RSV*.

20. to one place: the reference is to Sheol: cf. 9:10. The phrase *to aiōnion topon*, 'the eternal place', is used in the same sense in Tob. 3:6. The thought of the whole verse is again completely in accordance with traditional Israelite beliefs. On man as created **from the dust** and as destined to return **to dust** (cf. 12:7), see e.g. Gen. 2:7; 3:19; Ps. 104:29; Job 34:15.

21. Who knows . . .?: As in 2:19, this expression is equivalent to 'No one knows' (see Crenshaw, 1986, pp. 280–1). The question apparently refers to an opinion current in Qoheleth's time that there was in fact a distinction between the 'fate' of men and animals, because **the spirit** (or breath, see below) of the former is in some way united with God at death (**goes upward**). Qoheleth has already by implication forcefully denied the existence of such a distinction in vv. 18–20, in conventional biblical terms. Here he slightly modifies this assertion, but only to the extent of admitting that these are matters which are beyond man's ability to discover. The question is perhaps contemptuous: those who think themselves able to pronounce on these mysterious matters which God has concealed from mankind may speculate about them if they wish, but in fact their theories are worthless. The traditional view holds good.

spirit: the word (*rûaḥ*) is the same as that translated by 'breath' in v. 19, and should be so rendered here. The view that the human personality or the 'real person' existed as a distinct entity after death is first attested later than Qoheleth's time (e.g. Dan. 12:2–3, Wis. 3:1–8 and some later Jewish literature), although the germ of the idea is perhaps to be found in the concept of the rise of the 'spirit' to God which Qoheleth here rejects.

As with v. 20, *RSV*'s translation of this verse is based on generally accepted emendations. The Hebrew reads 'Who knows the breath (spirit) of man *which* goes upwards (*hā'ōlāh*) and the breath (spirit) of the animal *which* goes down (*hayyōredet*) to the earth?' The generally agreed repointing (*ha'ōlāh, hayōredet*) makes these clauses into indirect questions, i.e. **whether the spirit** (breath) . . . **goes upward/goes down**. Many commentators believe that the pointing in the unemended text is the deliberate work of later scribes who were incensed at Qoheleth's refusal to distinguish between the fates of men and animals.

22. The conclusion (**So I saw that** . . ., cf. 2:24) is the same as that reached in 2:24 and 3:12–13, though the reasons for it are slightly different. Since even man's hope of justice is outweighed by the certainty of death and the unlikelihood that he will be able to experience anything good after death, he should make the most of whatever possibilities for a good life come his way in this world. **his work** (*bema'asâw*): see on 2:24 (*ba'amālô*). **his lot:** see on 2:10.

who can . . .?: i.e. no one can (cf. v. 21). **after him:** i.e. after his death. This repeats the thought of v. 21.

THE PLIGHT OF THE OPPRESSED

4:1–3

In this passage the theme of injustice, which was introduced in 3:16 and led to reflections about the human situation and how it should be faced, is taken up again. But the two passages are otherwise unrelated. These three verses have a character of their own: a common theme is not enough to justify the attempts which have been made to attach them either to the preceding or to the following verses. (Ogden's argument [1984], on the basis of the occurrence of the word *šᵉnêhem* (**both**) in v. 3 to treat the passage as the first of a series of 'numerical sayings', is forced.) The structure is quite simple: a brief general statement about the oppression of the weak by the strong is followed (v. 1, from **And behold**) by a poignant comment on this situation in terms of human misery, and this in turn by a reflection which questions the positive value—in such circumstances—of human life.

1. **Again I saw:** literally, 'And I returned and saw'. The same phrase recurs at the beginning of v. 7. The threefold repetition of the same root in **oppressions . . . oppressed . . . oppressors**, the use of the dramatic **behold** and of emotive words like **tears** and **comfort**, the change from prose to poetical form and the repetition of **and they had/there was no one to comfort them** (a repetition which *RSV* has obscured by translating the same phrase in two different ways): all these features combine to produce an effect of emotional intensity which is rare in Qoheleth. Despite his generalization (**all the oppressions . . . under the sun**) he was clearly writing about what he himself had seen. **to comfort** (*mᵉnaḥēm*): it is not just soothing words which are meant here but active assistance (cf. Ps. 23:4; 71:21; 86:17). Qoheleth has been criticized for contenting himself with pointing out the existence of injustice without taking or proposing action to put it right, as had the prophets of earlier times; but such a judgement is anachronistic and unrealistic.

2–3. It is commonly stated that these verses constitute a calculated attack on a traditional wisdom attitude which regarded life as the most absolutely desirable of all good things (so, e.g., Zimmerli). But this is to misrepresent what was meant in the older wisdom teaching by 'life'. The Book of Proverbs, for example, does not equate 'life' with bare existence. Its authors, who frequently refer to the poor and their misery (e.g. Prov. 14:20; 18:23; 19:4, 7) and were aware of the oppression of the weak by the strong (e.g. Prov. 28:15–16), did not regard such persons as possessing 'life' in the sense of that fullness of life which was the goal and the reward of those who followed the counsels of wisdom (e.g. Prov. 3:2, 22; 4:22; 16:22). Qoheleth's comments here, therefore, are less revolutionary than has often been supposed. For those who have failed to 'find life' (Prov. 8:35–36) Qoheleth feels, in his present mood, that death or non-existence would be preferable to their suffering. This view is not far removed from that of Proverbs; and it has to be taken in conjunction with other statements of Qoheleth about the positive aspects of life (see on 2:17).

2. **thought . . . more fortunate:** these words are represented in the Hebrew by a single verb *šbḥ* (Piel), which always means 'to praise' except in this book, and always with God (or, in two Aramaic passages in Daniel, 5:4, 23, 'the gods') as its object. This is also its meaning in later Hebrew. In this book, where it occurs twice (also in 8:15) it clearly has somewhat different connotations; and here *RSV*'s rendering is the only one which makes good sense: it is clearly used in a sense similar to that of *ṭôb*, **better**—that is, '(more) fortunate'—in v. 3.

In form, *šabbēaḥ* is almost certainly the infinitive absolute used in place of the finite verb, though its use with the subject following it as here (*'ᵃnî*) is rare (GK § 113gg).

3. Qoheleth now offers a third item for comparison. Death is better than life for those for whom life has consisted mainly of suffering, since it brings that suffering to an end (v. 2). But it now appears that those not yet born are more fortunate (*ṭôb*) still, since they have no knowledge at all of what happens in the world. The argument is tortuous. First, it is not clear why Qoheleth could not have made his point more simply. Possibly he thought that this step-by-step way of proceeding was more effective rhetorically. In any case he seems to have generally been unwilling to admit that anything was either black or white (cf. 2:13–14; 4:13–16; 9:13–16). Secondly, the point of the 'yet' in **not yet been** is not clear. Its presence shows that Qoheleth is not here referring—as in 6:3–5 and in Job 3:11–19—to children who are stillborn or who die soon after birth, but to all those who will be born in the future; but since presumably these will cease to be fortunate when they enter the world and **see the evil deeds which are done under the sun**, the comparison does not appear to be a felicitous one. Possibly the insertion of the **yet** is due to Qoheleth's reluctance, mentioned above, to attribute unqualified good to anything at all.

he who: the Hebrew *'ēt 'ᵃšer* normally denotes the object of a sentence (i.e. 'him who') rather than the subject. The question whether it can on occasion denote the latter has been much debated (see Blau, 1954; Saydon, 1964; Macdonald, 1964). Here it may be simplest to take the phrase as either the object of *šabbēaḥ* in v. 2, or of a similar verb implied but not expressed: so, e.g., 'but *I called* him who has not yet been . . . more fortunate'. The latter possibility is supported by Vulg., which has such a verb, viz. *iudicavi*. LXX and Pesh., however, treat the phrase as a nominative. The general sense is not affected.

THE FOLLY OF OVERWORK

4:4–6

This passage appears to be unrelated to vv. 1–3. It does, however, share a common topic with vv. 7–12, though attempts to find a literary unity in vv. 4–12 are somewhat forced. The common subject is 'toil' (*'āmāl*, vv. 4, 6, 8, 9).

In vv. 4–6 Qoheleth reverts to the theme of the *futility* of toil and effort which was a major theme of 1:12–2:26. As in 2:22–23 he points out the folly of making work an end rather than a means and of ruining one's life by straining too hard to make money.

4. It is questionable whether *RSV*'s translation of this verse renders its sense correctly. First, **skill in work** (*kišrôn hamma'ᵃśeh*) would be better rendered by 'success' or 'achievement' (so *NEB*)—cf. 5:11 (MT 10), where *kišrôn* refers to something gained or achieved, and the meaning of the verb *kšr* in 11:6 and possibly also 10:10. Secondly, *qînāh* (*RSV*, **envy**) here probably means 'rivalry' or 'competition': this meaning is found in the Talmud (*Baba Bathra* 21*a*), and in a positive sense: 'Rivalry (*qn't*) among scribes increases wisdom'. Thirdly, Qoheleth does not say that toil and success **come from**—that is, are motivated by—the desire to compete with others, but rather that, according to his own observations (**I saw**), they are inseparable from it (literally, they are the same thing: **come from** has no equivalent in the Hebrew).

What Qoheleth is saying here, then, is that in his experience man appears to be incapable of working or achieving anything without striving frantically to do better than others. This is probably a reflection of the entrepreneurial rivalries of his time. It was for such waste of effort that he reserved the expression **vanity and a striving after wind** (cf. 1:14; 2:11, 17, 26; 4:6; 6:9). It was not his intention to put forward the absurd proposition that toil is in itself totally valueless. This is clear both from the following verse and also from other passages (e.g. 2:10; 3:13).

5–6. The negative judgement on work expressed in v. 4 needs further explanation and qualification if it is to be relevant to the circumstances of real life. Verses 5–6 provide this, in a manner characteristic of Qoheleth: the complexity of the question is brought out by judicious quotation of traditional wisdom sayings. Often—as in 2:12–17—the saying quoted is reinterpreted and its assertion relativised by its being placed in a context consisting of Qoheleth's own reflections; here, however, Qoheleth achieves the same result by juxtaposing *two* such sayings which qualify one another (for this practice in earlier wisdom literature see Prov. 26:4–5; and for a discussion of these verses see Whybray, 1981, pp. 439–40, 449–50).

5. In every respect—language, form and theme—this verse is indistinguishable from many sayings in Proverbs. Nothing in it suggests that it is Qoheleth's work, and the commentaries agree that it is a quotation. That laziness leads to want is a frequent wisdom theme (e.g. Prov. 6:9–11; 10:4; 12:24; 19:15; 20:13; 24:30–34). In two of those passages (6:10; 24:33) the same expression (*ḥbq yādayim*, **folds his hands**) is used as here to denote aversion to work.

The precise connotation of **eats his own flesh** is unknown (Driver, 1954, p. 228). Certain other passages (Ps. 27:2 [see *RSV* margin]; Isa. 49:26; Mic. 3:3; Prov. 30:14) have been cited as shedding light on the phrase, but these are not really comparable (see Whybray, 1981, p. 440, n. 9). One or two commentaries, notably Lohfink, give the phrase a positive meaning (i.e., fools still have flesh [meat] to eat despite their idleness), but this meaning is very forced. Some unpleasant fate, probably starvation, is demanded by the context. Qoheleth used the saying to put his adverse comments on work (v. 4) into proper perspective: although work is frustrating because it leads to senseless rivalry, it would be a fool who thought that he could do without it altogether. The meaning would have been clearer if he had been able to use the modern device of quotation marks, or if he had introduced v. 5 with a phrase such as 'But don't forget the saying that . . .'; but, like other biblical writers, he preferred simple juxtaposition, leaving his readers to work out the implications for themselves (cf. again Prov. 26:4–5).

6. By means of this second quotation, also of the same type as is found in Proverbs, Qoheleth draws his conclusion: it is better to be satisfied with a little and live a peaceful life than to acquire a fortune, for ambition to achieve the latter inevitably entails so much toil and effort that it brings no true enjoyment. The final words, **and a**

striving after wind, a phrase peculiar to Qoheleth (see on 1:14) are, as the poetical metre shows, an addition made by Qoheleth himself to reinforce the conclusion.

Like v. 4, this saying has parallels in earlier wisdom, of which one strand emphasized the value of **quietness**, that is, a life free from jealousy or rivalry (Prov. 14:30, where *qin'āh* [*RSV*, 'passion'] is used; cf. v. 4 above) or disputes (Prov. 17:1). In the present context these hindrances to contentment are specifically linked with **toil**. The conclusion is an adverse judgement on the assumption of Qoheleth's contemporaries that the drive to make more and more money (**two hands full**) is well worth while even at the cost of mental strain. A tranquil life is more conducive to happiness even at the expense of wealth.

A handful of quietness; two hands full: the meaning is 'a handful *with* quietness' and 'two handfuls *acquired by* toil'. On this adverbial use of the noun see GK § 131 p, r.

THE MISER

4:7–8

Most commentators treat these verses as a part of a larger section vv. 7–12, interpreted as an exposition of the need for companionship and of the futility and danger of trying to manage one's life on one's own. But while there is some similarity at least between vv. 7–8 and 9–10, vv. 7–8 are much more closely linked thematically with vv. 4–6 and may reasonably be interpreted as illustrating the truth of the impersonal and generalizing assertion of v. 6 by presenting a particular case of a man who in toiling for his own personal gain is depriving himself of pleasure. Yet the repetition of the phrase **Again, I saw** (which occurs nowhere else but here and in v. 1 and, with a slight variation, in 9:11) suggests that v. 7 begins a new section. The difficulty of determining where the original literary units in the book begin and end is nowhere better illustrated than here. But it may reasonably be asked whether this question is really important for the understanding of the book, since each individual thought of Qoheleth's needs to be interpreted in the light of other passages irrespective of their proximity to it.

8. The case cited here is that of a rich man who sacrifices all the pleasures that he might get out of life in order to labour at amassing greater and greater wealth, never satisfied with what he has already got: in other words, a miser. Presumably such cases were commonplace in Qoheleth's world. The case is similar to that of 2:18–23, but with one difference: this man has neither a partner (**no one**: literally, 'no second person') nor relations with whom he can share his wealth or to whom he can leave it at his death. Qoheleth puts his finger on the stupidity of such behaviour by putting into his mouth the question which such people never ask: what is the point of it all? The truth of the matter has already been succinctly stated in v. 6.

The words **so that he never asks** have no equivalent in the Hebrew. They have been added by the translators (following Gordis) in order to supply a link which would not have been needed by the original readers. The putting of this question in the first person singular—a device frequently used by Qoheleth in expounding his own thoughts—adds vividness to the picture. There is no reason to suppose, as some commentators have done, that it conceals an autobiographical confession on the part of Qoheleth himself. This device, of telling a moral tale in a fictional first person singular was widely practised in the wisdom literature: cf. Prov. 7:6–23; 24:30–34; Ps. 37:35–36.

his eyes: the singular verb requires the singular 'eye', which is the reading of *Qere* and many MSS. *Kethibh* has the plural.

TWO ARE BETTER THAN ONE

4:9–12

These verses have a common theme: it is dangerous and unwise for the individual to attempt to face life alone, and simple common sense to seek the co-operation of others in all that one does (v. 9). This is illustrated by three examples, all of which concern the dangers of travel, but are also meant to be taken metaphorically: falling into a pit (v. 10), perishing with cold at night (v. 11) and attack by robbers (v. 12). The section is rounded off—somewhat incongruously—with a proverb which seems to suggest that two are not sufficient after all, and that real security can only be obtained if the company consists of three! The addition of this sentence may be due to the influence of the 'numerical proverb' with its pattern of ascending numbers (see Sauer, 1963, p. 79 and note 5).

There is thus a superficial connection between these verses and vv. 7–8: a progress from the 'one, who has no second one' of v. 7 to the **Two are better than one** of v. 9, and finally to the **threefold cord** of v. 12. But—despite the views of most commentators—there is no *thematic* continuity here: vv. 7–8 are about a self-made man who makes a success—in worldly terms—entirely on his own without the need for co-operation with others; his solitariness has nothing to do with his achievement but is mentioned only in connection with a question about its ultimate purpose. The theme of vv. 9–12 is totally different: the need for co-operation if an enterprise is to meet with success. The connection between the two passages is probably editorial.

9. a good reward for their toil: better, 'a good outcome from their trouble'. The word *śākār*, frequently 'monetary payment' for work done, here has the wider meaning of a satisfactory or pleasant outcome, as in 9:5 (cf. Ps. 127:3; Isa. 40:10 and other passages where it is simply a gift from God). Similarly *'āmāl* here can hardly mean 'toil', but rather, as frequently in the Old Testament, 'trouble'. It is not *toil* which rescues these men from danger, but the fact that, being two together, they can *help* one another.

Two; one: the article before these two words serves to specify the persons referred to in the examples which follow (GK § 126g, q, r).

10. There is no doubt about the meaning of this verse, although some commentators find the Hebrew unsatisfactory and propose emendations partly based on some of the Versions. In the first half the correctness of the plural verb **they fall** has been questioned, since clearly the kind of incident envisaged is one in which only *one* of the travellers falls or slips. However, GK (§ 124o) is probably correct in seeing the verb here as a plural denoting an indefinite singular: that is, the plural is used because such incidents may occur not just once but an indefinite number of times involving one or other of the persons. If this is correct, the phrase may be rendered 'if one of them falls', and no emendation is necessary (see Gordis).

11. lie together: the reference is still to the two travellers, not to husband and wife. Huddling together to keep warm during the cold nights which occur in Palestine was a matter of common sense or even necessity (cf. Exod. 22:26–27 [MT 25–26]; Lk. 17:34).

12. And though . . . alone: the Hebrew is somewhat obscure; but the meaning is probably 'And though someone could overpower him (who is) alone'. The rest of the sentence then forms the apodosis: '(the) two would be able to resist him'. The verb *tāqap* (*RSV*, **prevail**) is late and rare in the Old Testament but occurs again in 6:10. Its subject here ('someone') is not expressed but is impersonal (GK § 144d). On the unusual suffix (-ô for -ēhû), see GK § 60d. The imperfect *ya'amᵉdû*, **might prevail**, is potential ('would be able to')—see Driver, §37.

The final sentence has the characteristics of a popular proverb rather than of a learned wisdom saying: cf. 1 Sam. 24:13; (MT 14) Ezek. 18:2; 16:44. Qoheleth uses it in its original sense: it applies the common practical experience that only a three-stranded rope can be relied on not to snap by implied analogy to the human sphere.

THE HAZARDS OF POWER

4:13–16

This passage, which is unrelated both to those which precede and those which follow it, is one of the most difficult in the book, and has been interpreted in a variety of ways. The short saying (**Better . . . king**) with which it begins is a typical encomium of wisdom in the traditional manner; but the remainder of the passage is a rather complicated series of reflections about the realities of political power, cast in the form of an anecdote (cf. 4:7–8; 9:13–16), the details of which are unfortunately difficult to follow, but which in any case greatly qualify the original statement. Various attempts have been made to find here (as also in 9:13–16 and 10:16–17) an allusion to historical events; but it is now agreed by most commentators that all these episodes, although quite plausible in terms of the political realities of Qoheleth's time, are examples of the fictional story or 'parable' which was one of the devices commonly employed by the wisdom writers (cf. also the 'Solomonic fiction' of chapters 1–2).

13. The initial saying (**Better . . . king**) has the same form as many similar sayings in Proverbs and elsewhere. It may be a quotation, though the use of the word *miskēn* (**poor**), which is a late word found elsewhere in the Old Testament only in this book (9:15–16), suggests that it cannot have been composed much before Qoheleth's time. The remainder of the verse, which is in prose, enlarges upon the initial saying, attributing the old king's folly to senility (**no longer**). **take advice:** this verb (*zhr*, Niphal) occurs in the Old Testament only in relatively late books, but is frequent in later Hebrew. It has a similar meaning in 12:12 ('beware'). The pairing of **wise** with **youth** and of **old** with **foolish** is a remarkable reversal of traditional views.

14. The serious difficulties of the interpretation of this passage begin here. In this verse the main problems are the identity of the person referred to (**he**): and the meaning of the initial word *kî* (*RSV*, **even though**).

At first sight it might seem natural to take **he** as referring to the old king, who is the subject of the previous clause. But in the initial saying in v. 13 it is clearly not he but the poor young man who is singled out for attention; and the repetition of the reference to poverty in v. 14 (even though different words for **poor** are used) confirms the view that it is the latter who is referred to in v. 14.

But the point of the account of the young man's earlier experiences in this verse is not at all clear, and many different explanations have been given. The word *kî* has many meanings and is often difficult to interpret. *RSV*'s **even though** is supported by some commentaries, but it is difficult to see why the young man's rule should be preferable *despite* the way in which he attained to the throne. It may be that the clue lies in the meaning of the word **Better** (*ṭôb*) in v. 13. In this kind of comparative saying 'better' usually has a universal sense: it means what is more advantageous to anyone at all. But earlier in this chapter Qoheleth uses *ṭôb* in the sense of '(more) fortunate' with regard to particular persons (4:3; cf. 9:4) or even of '(more) effective' (4:9). If *kî* means 'because', or possibly 'in that', here, the sense may be that the young man who has surmounted so many initial disadvantages and achieved the supreme goal of kingship should *for that reason* be considered more fortunate—or more successful—than the old king who has occupied that position for many years but whose judgement is now failing.

If this interpretation is correct, *b*ᵉ*malkûtô* (*RSV*, **in his own kingdom**) can more naturally be rendered 'under his—i.e. the old king's—rule'. The young man in the story has evidently supplanted—presumably by revolution or at least a change of dynasty—the very king under whose rule he himself had been born in poverty.

or: this expression (*kî gam*) means 'although'. *RSV* has rendered it in this way because of its translation of the earlier *kî* as **even though**. The verse may now be translated as follows: 'in that he came from prison to the kingship, and despite his having been born in poverty under his (i.e. his predecessor's) rule'.

prison: this word *hāsûrîm* is an abbreviated form of *hā'*ᵃ*sûrîm*, literally 'fetters' (see GK § 35d).

15. The major problem of this verse has been concealed by *RSV*, which has omitted the most crucial word—'the *second* (youth)' – from its translation, relegating it to the margin and replacing it by **that**. By this omission *RSV* has identified the young man (**youth**) of this verse with the young man of vv. 13 and 14. In fact there is no reason to delete the word. Commentaries are, however, divided as to the identity of this 'second' young man. There are two main possible interpretations: first, if the young man is the same as in the previous verse, 'second' may refer to his position in government: he is 'the youth who holds the second position (in the kingdom)', that is, he is the heir to the throne. This would rule out the interpretation of v. 14 given above, that he supplanted the old king in a revolutionary coup. Alternatively, the 'second young man' is an entirely new character, a third person who supplants the previous usurper. The latter explanation is the most probable: it seems unlikely that the heir to the throne should be a nobody recently released from prison, while a usurper might well be such a person.

The rendering of *RSV* is unconvincing in other ways as well. A more probable translation might be: 'I saw that all the living who live their lives under the sun were supporting (*'im*, literally '(were) with'[*RSV*, **as well as**] a second young man (for the use of the article here see GK § 126q, r) who would take his place' (i.e. that of the first usurper; see GK § 107k for this use of the imperfect).

In other words, Qoheleth, in his role of the wise man telling his moral tale (**I saw**), has reached the 'second act' of the drama: the first young usurper is about to be supplanted in his turn by a second, who is equally (or even more) a 'wise'—i.e., clever—young man (see v. 13) who has succeeded in gaining universal popular support. **all the living who move about under the sun** is simply an ironical exaggeration like the English expression 'all the world and his wife'.

16. there was no end of all the people: *'am* here means a throng of people: the new ruler enjoyed universal popularity on his succession to the throne. But the commentators are divided on the question whether this ruler is the same as in v. 15. *RSV* clearly takes this view: **he** (i.e. the young man previously mentioned) **was over all of them**. But this phrase is susceptible of more than one interpretation. The Hebrew has a relative clause here: literally, 'all those before whom he was'. Some commentators take the word 'before' (*lip^{e}nê*) as referring either to political leadership (as *RSV*) or, more literally, as marching at the head of an adoring crowd of people, for example on coronation day. Others, however (Galling, Zimmerli, Lauha, Lohfink) take the whole verse as a general comment on the fickleness of the crowd's attitude towards *any* ruler: there is boundless support from the crowd for anyone when he attains supreme power, but . . . (Gordis improbably takes 'before' in a temporal sense and translates: 'there is no end to the people who lived before both'.)

Whichever of these interpretations is correct, the verse is a concluding comment on the disenchantment of political power. Political regimes succeed one another, and each ruler may attain to the throne on a wave of popular enthusiasm; but as the reign wears on **those who come later** will become disillusioned and find little cause for rejoicing.

The conclusion, then, is that political power is yet another example of futility (on this final phrase see on 1:14). The form of the argument is characteristic of Qoheleth (compare, e.g., 2:13–17).

The truth of the initial saying that a poor man who is clever is an improvement on an old king who is foolish is not totally denied; but the anecdote which follows qualifies it almost to the point of nullity. However hopefully a new reign or regime may begin, in the end there is little to choose between one king and another, and little satisfaction either for ruler or ruled. It is also possible to regard the passage as a further example of the questionable value of wisdom: it is the young man's intelligence which supposedly gives him an advantage, but this has now been shown to be no real advantage at all.

ADVICE ON WORSHIP

5:1–7

[*N.B. The verses in this chapter are numbered 4:17–5:19 in Hebrew Bibles. The Hebrew verse numbers will be given in square brackets.]*
5:1[4:17] begins a new section. 5:1–7[4:17–5:6] are linked by the common theme of behaviour in the Temple. The theme of vv. 8[7]ff. is quite different. Some commentators, however, regard the unit as including vv. 8–9[7–8] on account of their *form*: here for the first time Qoheleth employs the form of the admonition—expressed by the imperative, positive or negative—in which an instructor gives direct advice to a pupil. There are many examples of the admonition in Proverbs.

Qoheleth here takes it for granted that his readers take part in worship in the Temple at Jerusalem and offers advice about the way in which they should behave there. Although he says nothing which could be construed as suggesting that he disapproves of temple worship or regards it as of no importance, and even seems to go out of his way to appeal to scriptural precedent, it has frequently been alleged that he was indifferent to it (so Perdue, 1977, pp. 178–88)—an attitude supposedly characteristic of the earlier wisdom tradition, and also supposedly in line with Qoheleth's view of God as a *Deus absconditus* unconcerned with human affairs. Admittedly what he says here about worship could be called 'negative' in the sense that his aim is to warn worshippers that improper behaviour in the 'holy place' (an expression which he uses of the Temple in 8:10) is dangerous and may arouse God's anger; but this suggests anything but indifference on his part. (See also on 9:2.) Moreover, these verses should not be taken as expressing the whole of his views about worship: he is concerned here only with one particular aspect of it.

The passage consists of four distinct but related admonitions: vv. 1, 2–3, 4–5, 6–7 [MT 4:17, 5:1–2, 3–4, 5–6].

1[4:17]. **the house of God:** the reference to sacrifice later in the verse shows clearly that this is the Temple and not a synagogue. Although the usual expression is 'house of Yahweh', 'house of God' is occasionally used elsewhere in the Old Testament in this sense.

your steps: literally, 'your feet', or, more probably, following Qere, 'your foot'. This advice to 'guard the foot' has been taken, on the analogy of Prov. 25:17, to mean 'do not go often (to the Temple)'; but this is not a true analogy, as in Prov. 25:17 a quite different word is used which means 'make rare'. 'Foot', although its literal meaning is also present, here has the quite common metaphorical meaning of conduct or behaviour: Qoheleth is advising his readers to be careful when they go to the Temple (cf. Prov. 1:15; 3:26; 4:27). The reasons for this advice become apparent in the remainder of the verse and the following verses.

to draw near to listen: 'draw near' (*qārab*) is a technical term for seeking the presence of God in his Temple. Here the infinitive absolute is used, a form which is sometimes equivalent to the finite verb but very rarely to the infinitive construct, which would be required here. An alternative way of accounting for it here would be to repoint it as the *plene* form of the infinitive construct (*qᵉrōb*) and to take the first word of the verse (*šᵉmōr*, **Guard**) also as an infinitive construct rather than an imperative: 'To guard your step . . . and to draw near to hear are better than . . .'. This is made the more probable by the fact that the Hebrew text has 'and' before 'draw near', omitted by *RSV*.

draw near and **listen** (hear) are found together in Dt. 5:27, which Qoheleth may have had in mind here. There 'listen' means to hear and obey the words of God. It has been suggested that here it means to listen to and obey the instructions of the temple priests, a practice about which little is known for this period. But in view of the fact that the remainder of the passage (to v. 7[6]) is concerned with the danger of *speaking* too much, it may be simply a recommendation to preserve a receptive attitude.

is better than: 'is better' is not directly expressed in the Hebrew. But it is unnecessary to emend the text by adding the expected word *ṭôb*. On the expression of comparatives in this way see GK § 133e.

sacrifice: that is, sacrifices requested and paid for by individuals, which formed the bulk of the sacrifices offered (see Schürer II, p. 296). The view that sacrifices were unacceptable to God if they were not offered with purity of intention, and that such qualities as righteousness, repentance and obedience to God's moral commandments were more important than sacrifice was a commonplace of wisdom teaching (Prov. 15:8; 21:3, 27; cf. the Egyptian *Instruction for King Merikare, ANET*, p. 417), but was not confined to the wisdom literature (cf. 1 Sam. 15:22—which is very similar in wording to this verse; Ps. 51:17 [MT 19], etc.). Only **fools**, says Qoheleth, are unaware of this. But further, to offer unworthy sacrifices is not merely useless: it is actually doing evil. Prov. 15:8 condemns it in the strongest possible terms: it is an *abomination* to Yahweh. As frequently in Proverbs, folly and wickedness are here closely associated. The ‘fools’ whom Qoheleth has in mind are presumably those who believe that their sacrifices will automatically cancel out their sins without the need for repentance, and so are offering sacrifice which is itself essentially wicked and deserving of God’s anger. It is for this reason that he warns his readers of the need for caution in approaching God in the Temple. This feeling of awe in the presence of God is fully in accordance with the Old Testament tradition (see, among many other passages, Gen. 28:17; Exod. 19:12; Num. 17:13 [MT 28]).

that they are doing evil: the phrase *’ênām yôd*^{e}*‘îm la‘*^{a}*śôt rā‘* would normally mean ‘they do not know how to do evil’; but in the context this meaning is highly improbable. *RSV*’s interpretation is probably correct: the verb *yāda‘*, **know**, is here used in the absolute sense of mental ability, as in 9:11 (‘skill’), and the infinitive *la‘*^{a}*śôt* in the sense of ‘with regard to doing’, as sometimes in Mishnaic Hebrew (Segal, § 347). So the whole phrase may be rendered: ‘for they have no awareness of doing evil’.

2–3[1–2]. Some commentators have regarded v. 3[2] as a gloss on the grounds that the first half is irrelevant to the context. Others have defended the verse’s authenticity by suggesting that the **dream** referred to has a cultic significance: Qoheleth was warning his readers against the idea that divine revelations could be obtained through the medium of dreams experienced in the Temple. But even if this interpretation were a probable one there would still be an interruption of the main thought. Gordis’s view that the verse was a familiar saying which Qoheleth quoted in full for the sake of completeness although only the second half was relevant to his theme is probably correct. In fact, the second half by itself would be unintelligible, or at least obscure, as it contains no verb.

2[1]. This verse clearly refers to *prayer* uttered in the Temple (**before God**). Qoheleth’s advice is that one should address God in a **few** well-chosen **words** rather than pour out a torrent of **rash** and **hasty** ones. Similar advice was given at a later period by Jesus (Mt. 6:7); but it was already familiar to the wisdom tradition and is at least as old as the Egyptian *Instruction of Ani* (iv 1: *ANET* p. 420) written many centuries earlier. As a general principle applicable to speech in general it is found in earlier Israelite wisdom literature (Prov. 10:19).

God is in heaven, and you upon earth: this lapidary statement has been interpreted in quite different ways: as being entirely in accordance with the main Old Testament tradition (so Hertzberg) and as completely 'heretical' (Gordis) and a deliberate denial of Dt. 4:39's 'Yahweh is God in heaven above and on the earth beneath' (e.g. Loader). The former view is nearer to the truth. Throughout the Old Testament tradition the 'wholly otherness' of God and his readiness to draw near to his worshippers to hear and to save are held in tension. This tension is discernible in Ecclesiastes, although on the whole the former pole is stressed more frequently than the latter. It is quite erroneous to interpret this saying as meaning that prayer is useless because God is unconcerned with human affairs: Qoheleth does not advise his readers not to pray, but rather to remember God's awesome sovereignty and to address him carefully as one would a human superior.

3[2]. On the relationship of this verse to v. 2[1] see above. The first word **For** (*kî*) is a connecting link indicating that what follows is a quotation of a saying which confirms the point of the preceding verse. The saying itself belongs to a type found in Proverbs (e.g. Prov. 11:16; 25:23; 26:20; 27:17) in which the truth of the second half is supported by an analogy, the two being linked not, as in many other such sayings, by a comparative particle such as 'like' or 'as' but merely by **and**. The meaning is thus '*Just as* dreams go with overwork, *so* does the voice of a fool with too much speaking'. As with some of the other examples of this kind of saying (e.g. Prov. 11:16) the analogy is not particularly apposite or, to the modern reader, particularly effective; Qoheleth no doubt quoted it only because of the relevance to his theme of the second half, though the reference to dreams, which presumably implies restless nights, is in accordance with Qoheleth's own view of the folly of overwork expressed in 2:23.

4–5[3–4]. This third admonition is concerned with *vows*. As with sacrifice and prayer offered in the Temple, Qoheleth clearly takes it for granted that his readers will, or may, **vow a vow to God**. This practice was a very common one and continued up to the final destruction of the Temple (even St Paul made such a vow, Ac. 18:18). It consisted of making a promise to consecrate something, normally either a sacrifice or a money payment (as in Lev. 27:1–25) to God in return for the granting of a favour (for the regulations concerning vows see Lev. 7:16–17; 22:18–23; 27:1–25; Num. 6; and de Vaux, 1961, pp. 465–6). The passage is taken almost word for word from Dt. 23:21–23 (MT 22–24), which both warns that slackness in paying one's vows is a sin which God 'will surely require of you', and also points out that 'if you refrain from vowing, it would be no sin'. Prov. 20:25 also warns against the making of rash vows, and Ben Sira also echoes the thought (Sir. 18:22–23). The view of some commentators that Qoheleth's substitution of 'God' for 'Yahweh your God' in the quotation from Deuteronomy, and his speaking of God's disapproval of the fool rather than of his punishment of sinners indicate a sceptical attitude towards the efficacy of the practice of making vows is unjustified: this is simply the typical style of the wisdom writer.

6–7[5–6]. Although some commentators regard v. 6[5] as the continuation of the previous admonition about the making of vows, it is unlikely that Qoheleth would have rather pointlessly repeated what he had already said. It is more likely that this is a separate, fourth admonition about another kind of case of unwise speech in some way connected with the Temple. Unfortunately both these verses are extremely difficult to interpret. The chief difficulties are the identity of the mysterious **messenger** in v. 6[5] and the strange syntax of v. 7[6], a verse which has been dismissed by some commentators as unintelligible. As will be argued below, the latter may be a general conclusion to the whole section 5:1–7[4:17–5:6].

6[5]. Two distinct but interconnected examples of rash and dangerous speech are involved in this admonition: first uttering words which are sinful, and secondly compounding the offence by pretending that they were spoken unintentionally. **Let not your mouth lead you into sin** (literally, 'Do not permit your mouth to bring guilt upon your flesh') probably refers to such offences as are listed in Lev. 5:1, 4—failing to come forward as a witness and swearing a rash oath—and also to cursing and blaspheming. Such acts incurred guilt; but a vital distinction was made between deliberate and unintentional sin. According to Num. 15:27–31, deliberate sins (those committed 'with a high hand') could not be atoned for; but those which were committed unwittingly (the technical term *šᵉgāgāh*, *RSV*, **a mistake**, is taken by Qoheleth from this law and Lev. 4–5) could be atoned for by confession to a priest (Lev. 5:5) accompanied by a guilt- or sin-offering. How far and in what way the prescription of Num. 15:30–31 that the deliberate sinner is to be 'cut off from among his people' was carried out in Qoheleth's time is not certain; but what he envisages is the even worse offence of lying in confession to the priest, claiming that the sin was an unintentional one. Qoheleth is in no doubt about the punishment: to arouse God's anger was to invite direct divine intervention, here probably in the form of financial ruin (**destroy the work of your hands**) and perhaps also illness or death.

before the messenger: if the above interpretation is correct, **messenger** refers to the priest to whom the (in this case false) confession is made: he is God's representative or spokesman (Lev. 5:6). Admittedly the priest is elsewhere so called only in one other passage: Mal. 2:7; but the alternative explanations of the word *mal'āk* here, that he is an angel, or that he is a temple official whose business was to collect payment for undischarged vows or to report sins are less probable (see Salters, 1978). LXX and Pesh. have 'God' instead of 'the messenger', but this (despite *BHS*) is more likely to be a—mistaken—interpretation than a translation of a different Hebrew text.

you: literally, 'your flesh'. *bāśār* may mean the whole person (see Lys, 1967, pp. 124–6; *TDOT* II, p. 319).

On the unusual form *laḥ^{a}ṭî'* (**lead . . . into sin**), see GK § 53q.

7[6]. **For when . . . grow many:** neither *RSV*'s translation nor the alternative rendering in *RSV* margin can be convincingly derived from these words as they stand. In fact, they can hardly be said to form a complete sentence. There is no verb in the Hebrew text, and three nouns—**dreams**, 'futilities' (*hebel* in the plural) and **words**—stand together simply linked by *w^e* (usually 'and'), suggesting that they constitute a list. *NEB*, which regards the whole phrase as a meaningless intrusion into the text, illustrates the problem by omitting it altogether but giving a literal translation in the margin: 'for in a multitude of dreams and empty things and many words'. If the text is corrupt, the corruption must have occurred early, as the Versions offer no significant alternative reading. None of the various attempts by commentators to restore the original text on the assumption of omissions, mistaken letters, transposed words and the like, is more than purely speculative. On the other hand, several ways have been suggested of making sense of the text as it stands: one is to assign to *w^e* ('and') some other function such as 'indeed' (so Whitley, p. 50: 'for in a multitude of dreams and vanities there are *indeed* many words'), or 'then' (so Perdue, 1977, p. 186 and p. 248, note 207: 'when dreams increase, *then* so do vanities and words'—cf. GK § 143d); another is to take the whole verse as a single sentence: 'with all the dreams, follies and idle chatter this remains—fear God!' (Gordis; cf. Sir. 34:5, 'Divinations and omens and dreams are folly.')

Whatever may be the syntax of the verse, it clearly picks up the vocabulary of v. 3[2] and concludes the whole section: the emphatic **do you fear God** (on the meaning of which see on 3:14) sums up the kind of conduct which is the opposite of the stupid behaviour in the presence of God described in the previous verses.

ON THE POLITICAL SYSTEM

5:8–9

Both these verses [7–8 in the Hebrew] present serious difficulties of interpretation, especially v. 9[8]; moreover, it is unclear how they are related to one another. But they are both evidently concerned with the political—or, more precisely, the administrative—system and unrelated thematically both to the preceding and following verses.

8[7]. The theme of social injustice is here taken up again (cf. 3:16; 4:1) with particular reference to administrative corruption. As in previous passages on this subject this is regarded as something inevitable to be endured. Rather than speculating why God permits it (as in 3:17) or questioning whether for some of its victims life is worth living (as in 4:2–3) Qoheleth here explains why it is inevitable under the contemporary system of local administration, so in effect warning his readers that it is pointless to be outraged by it.

in a province: this is a possible translation; but as the word is preceded by the article here '*the* province'—i.e. the district of Judaea where Qoheleth and his readers lived—is a more probable rendering. **the matter:** on this meaning of *ḥēpeṣ*, see on 3:1.

the high official . . . a higher . . . yet higher ones: the Hebrew has in each case simply the adjective *gābōah*, 'high': the word **official** has been added by *RSV*. Clearly 'high' here means 'a person of high rank' (cf. Ezek. 21:26 [Heb. 31]), and there can be no doubt that this is a reference to an entire hierarchical system of administrative corruption which bore most severely on those at the bottom, who were exploited but had no means of exploiting others. **is watched by:** in the Hebrew the verb is active: literally, 'one person in authority watches above another person in authority'; but this 'watching' probably has a favourable sense ('protects') rather than that of 'controls' or 'oversees' (*šāmar* can have either meaning). Thus there is no reason to **be amazed** that injustice is not corrected, since appeal to a higher authority has no chance of success. An alternative view, that **yet higher ones** refers to God (a case of the so-called 'plural of majesty') does not make good sense here.

9[8]. This verse has been described, not without reason, as 'An insuperable crux' (Gordis). The Hebrew word order is different from that of *RSV*. The first half of the verse may perhaps be translated 'But the advantage for a country, in all, is this:'. The second half, which is presumably intended to state the nature of that advantage (*melek leśādeh ne'ebād*) has been interpreted in various ways, of which the two most straightforward are 'a king, for a cultivated field' and 'a king devoted to the land'; but in both cases the Hebrew is difficult. Moreover, it is quite unclear how this verse, however it is rendered, is related to verse 8[7]: that is, how the supposed advantage to be provided by the king—who in Qoheleth's time could only be the remote Ptolemaic emperor—is related to the previous verse in which no hope for change in the corrupt local administration was envisaged. It seems unlikely that Qoheleth entertained some mitigating scrap of hope that the king might intervene to put it right. Some commentators have seen in the reference to **cultivated fields** some reference to the fact that much of the agricultural land of Palestine was directly owned by the king; but there is no evidence that this was more equitably administered than privately owned land. Gordis's opinion about the impenetrable obscurity of this verse has much to be said for it.

THE DECEPTIVENESS OF MONEY

5:10–20

Most commentators treat 5:10–6:9[5:9–6:9] under a single heading. As elsewhere in the book this question is debatable and not of the first importance. However, there are good reasons for taking 5:10–20 [9–19] separately. 5:18–20 [17–19] can hardly be regarded as other than a concluding comment (cf. 2:24–26; 3:12–15; 3:22); and 6:1ff. have a somewhat different point to make.

5:10–17[9–16] set out a number of distinct reasons why wealth ultimately brings no gain to its possessors, so that it is foolish to make the acquisition of a fortune the main aim in life:

1. Wealth, far from bringing satisfaction to its possessors, only creates a restless desire to acquire more (v. 10[9]).

2. It brings no real benefit with it, but only a crowd of greedy friends and hangers-on who swallow it up (v. 11[10]).

3. It brings no peace of mind but only worries, which deprive its possessors of sleep (v. 12[11]).

4. There is no guarantee that it will not be lost again and its former possessors once more reduced to poverty (vv. 13–14[12–13]); and, finally,

5. In any case, all the effort and toil put into its acquisition

will ultimately be useless, as it cannot be taken beyond the grave (vv. 15–17[14–16]).

The *conclusion* (vv. 18–20[17–19]) is that one should simply accept and enjoy whatever God gives.

10[9]. The series begins with that which lies at the root of the whole problem: the *love* of money, that is, putting it before everything else. Qoheleth's solution, given at the end of the section (vv. 18–20[17–19]) is a direct answer to this initial point. The theme constantly occurs in the book: cf. 2:8–11; 4:7, and especially the ironical 'money makes everything possible' (10:19), which is a comment on the obsession of the age.

The first half of the verse with its neatness and compactness (*'ōhēb kesep lō'-yiśba' kesep*) sounds like a popular proverb; but it fits very well with Qoheleth's own views and is probably his own work. The idea that wealth is a cause of unhappiness rather than a sign of divine favour runs counter to traditional wisdom teaching.

nor he who loves wealth, with gain: this may be the meaning of the Hebrew, though the syntax is peculiar. An alternative rendering, based on a different pointing perhaps suggested by the Syriac (*lō' tᵉbô'ēhū* for *lō' tᵉbû'āh*) would be 'and as for him who loves wealth, it will not come to him' (Gordis).

11[10]. In the Hebrew the first half of this verse (to **who eat them**) has the same brevity and neatness as the first half of v. 10[9]: *birᵉbôt haṭṭôbāh rabbû 'ôkᵉle(y)hā*; but again the sentiment expressed is hardly likely to have emanated from the common people. It is Qoheleth himself who first puts forward a neat epigram and then makes a wry comment on it. **who eat them:** this is an unnecessarily literal translation: Heb. **eat** (*'ākal*) frequently means 'consume' in a metaphorical sense. *NEB* has 'who live off them'. Qoheleth probably mainly had parasitical friends and relations in mind, though he may also have been thinking of taxes and other expenses pertaining to a large fortune. The whole verse is of course a deliberate exaggeration.

to see them with his eyes: literally, 'the seeing of his eyes'. It is probably best to accept the reading *rᵉ'ôt* (infinitive) here with some MSS, against both *Qere* and *Kethibh*. The rich man has only the dubious pleasure of seeing his profits accumulate before they melt away again. **gain:** on this meaning of *kišrôn*, see on 4:4.

12[11]. Ostensibly the purpose of this verse is to compare the unhealthy state of the **rich** man unfavourably with that of the poor hardworking **labourer:** the latter sleeps soundly whether he has had a square meal or not, while the former, through over-indulgence at dinner, is kept awake by indigestion. But there is probably a play on words here: although the rich man has a surfeit (*śābā'*) of good things—that is, he has more than enough to satisfy him—yet, as has been pointed out two verses earlier, money does not buy satisfaction (again the root *śb'*; cf. also 4:8 and 6:3 [*RSV*, 'enjoy']). The only 'satisfaction' which the rich man gets from his **surfeit** is something which keeps him awake at night, whether a stomach-ache or, as in 2:23, worry. Qoheleth may have taken a brief popular saying about the rewards of physical labour and enlarged upon it to strengthen his general point about the deceptiveness of wealth. In any case the first half of the verse is merely ancillary to the second in its present form and should not be taken as advocating a life of industrious poverty, an idea which was very far from Qoheleth's thoughts.

13–17[12–16]. *RSV* and other modern translations are probably right in understanding these five verses as referring to the same person (**he**), that is, the rich man who loses all his money. But Qoheleth draws two distinct morals from the story.

13[12]. **grievous:** literally, 'sick' (*ḥôlāh*). Cf. *ḥᵒlî rā'* (*RSV*, 'a sore affliction', literally 'a severe illness') in 6:2. **kept** (*šāmûr*)—i.e. 'stored up', like Joseph's corn in Egypt (Gen. 41:35). **to his hurt** (*rā'āh*): that is, with the very opposite result to that which might have been expected. The idea that the possession of a fortune could lead to *mis*fortune was a shocking one, and its discovery justified Qoheleth in calling this a sick state of affairs. There is probably an ironical reference to v. 11[10], where Qoheleth has used the opposite word *ṭôbāh* in one of its customary senses as a synonym for wealth (*RSV*, 'goods').

14[13]. The first example of the 'grievous evil' of v. 13[12] is now presented: the unpredictability of apparent financial security. The case described is probably hypothetical, but based on what Qoheleth 'has seen'. As in the case of Job, the crash is presented as a total one which completely crushes the victim. **a bad venture** (*'inyān rā'*—for the emended pointing, see *BHS*): elsewhere (in the Old Testament it occurs only in this book) *'inyān* means 'work' or 'business'; here it probably refers to some kind of speculative business affair. The fact that the victim had a son who would normally have inherited his father's fortune and social position increases the 'grievous evil'. **nothing in his hand:** this could refer either to the father or the son; the context suggests the former, though both would be equally ruined.

15–17[14–16]. These verses are somewhat repetitive; but in spite of their clumsiness of expression it is perhaps possible to see in them some logical progression of thought (see Zimmerli). The person envisaged—the self-made man—is the same as in the previous verses; but a somewhat different theme is introduced: the inevitability of death. It is now a question not of a *particular* case—the *unpredictable* loss of a fortune during life—but of an *universal* fact, which in the case of the person concerned means the *predictable* loss of a fortune at death. For such a person each is **a grievous evil** which makes nonsense of all the effort and discomfort which he has endured simply to acquire what is now lost.

15[14]. **nothing . . . in his hand:** this phrase is exactly the same as in v. 14[13], but has been split into two and the intervening words added. This deliberate repetition and expansion was no doubt intended to ease the transition to a new theme. The similarity of the verse to Job 1:21 ('Naked I came from my mother's womb, and naked shall I return') is striking. **for his toil:** this may mean 'in return for his toil' (see GK § 119p) or 'from his wealth' (see Whitley, pp. 52–3, but also above on 1:3). **which he may carry away:** the Hebrew *šeyyōlēk* is probably the Hiphil (i.e. causative) jussive of *hālak* 'to go', written defectively. LXX and Pesh. apparently read the consonants as the Qal *šeyyēlēk*, 'that it may go'; but this reading is less probable.

16[15]. **This also is a grievous evil:** that is, it is a *second* evil (cf. v. 13[12]). On **grievous** (*ḥôlāh*), see on that verse. Some commentators have taken this phrase as an introductory formula as in v. 13; but this is not necessarily so. Qoheleth frequently (e.g. 1:17; 2:26) uses this type of formula at the conclusion of a reflection, and this is so here. What follows is part repetition, part expansion of a completed reflection.

just as (*kol-'ummat še-*): the form is unusual (see Gordis and Whitley, p. 53), and various emendations or repointings have been proposed; but the meaning is clear. The whole phrase is a variation of v. 15[14]*a* and serves to introduce a further reflection. **for the wind:** that is, uselessly (cf. *re'ût rûaḥ, ra'yôn rûaḥ* in 1:17, 2:26 and other passages).

17[16]. This verse has been very differently assessed by the commentators: thus Barton comments 'The MT of this verse is obviously corrupt; a translation of the present text is impossible', while Gordis and Lauha assert that it makes sense as it stands without any emendation! The first half may be translated literally as 'And also all his days he eats in darkness'. If 'eats' may be taken in a metaphorical sense, *RSV*'s **spent all his days** may be correct; others, however, take it literally: 'all his days he has eaten (his food) in darkness'—perhaps an exaggerated way of referring to the man's miserly economies. This is rather improbable. But in any case there seems to be no need to follow LXX and read *we'ēbel*, 'in mourning', for *yō'kēl*, 'he eats' (so: 'all his days (were) in darkness and mourning and . . .'). **darkness** may be a metaphor for unhappiness or misery (cf. Am. 5:18).

In the second half *RSV* has followed LXX: **grief** in the Hebrew text is a verb, not a noun, and **sickness** in the Hebrew has a suffix—literally '*his* sickness'—though it might mean 'sickness is his lot', according to Brockelmann, who understands the word as a 'single-term nominal sentence' (§ 13a). If this is allowed, this part of the verse (from **and grief**) may be translated as it stands: 'and is in great trouble; and sickness and resentment are his lot'.

Whatever may be the correct interpretation of the verse in detail, it is clear that Qoheleth's intention was to emphasize the futility of an obsessive devotion to money-making by piling up a series of exaggerated expressions of misery, thus providing an effective contrast to his recipe for happiness in the verse which follows.

18–20[17–19]. The alternative which Qoheleth proposes to the futile pursuit of wealth is the same as that which he sets against other attempts to secure the future (cf. 2:24–26; 3:11–12; 3:21–22): to accept the fact that man can achieve nothing at all by his own efforts and can only obtain whatever God chooses to give him. Only in this way can he have **joy in his heart**.

18[17]. This verse is virtually a paraphrase of 2:24; 3:12–13 and 3:22. The chief differences are the more solemn beginning, **Behold, what I have seen**, the addition of **and to be fitting** after **good** (*ṭôb*, 'better' in the other passages) and the expression **the few days of his life**.

to be good and fitting: if this is the correct interpretation of *ṭôb 'ᵃšer-yāpeh*, the syntax is strange: *'ᵃšer* does not elsewhere have this meaning. It has been suggested that this is a Graecism; but this view is now generally regarded as improbable. It is probably better to render the phrase '. . . I have seen to be good: that (*'ᵃšer*) it is fitting to eat and drink'. This is a late but not infrequent use of *'ᵃšer* (GK § 157c). On this meaning of *yāpeh* (**fitting**), see on 3:11. *rā'āh ṭôbāh* (**find enjoyment**) is a variant of *rā'āh ṭôb*, the form found in 2:24 (see also on 2:1). **his lot:** on this word (*ḥēleq*), see on 2:10.

the few days of his life: Qoheleth does not disguise this limitation of man's possibility of enjoyment. It is precisely this limitation which adds point to the advice to enjoy life as much as possible.

19[18]. Qoheleth now applies the general statement of the previous verse to the particular case of the rich man. **also** here has the sense of 'moreover'. His intention is to correct any impression which the reader might have received from the previous section that he regards wealth as an evil *in itself*: on the contrary, he says, God when he bestows riches on a person also bestows the **power to enjoy them**. It is implied, however, that this enjoyment depends on the recipient's willingness to see them in their true character as **the gift of God** rather than as obtainable only through his own desperate efforts which have been dismissed in vv. 16–17[15–16] as 'toiling for the wind': in other words, he must be able to **accept** them as **his lot**.

Every man . . . toil: this is grammatically an incomplete sentence. The meaning is 'Whenever God gives . . .'. Qoheleth does not of course pretend that wealth is given to every one: he is dealing here only with the particular matter of wealth and its problems.

enjoy: literally, 'eat' (*'ākal*). For this meaning see, e.g., Prov. 18:21. It is interesting to note that this verb occurs five times (vv. 11, 12, 17, 18, 19 [MT 10, 11, 16, 17, 18]) in this section, though with different meanings.

20[19]. This concluding verse picks up and draws together the main thoughts of the whole section. The answer to the evils usually associated with wealth—greediness, dissatisfaction, worries about losing it all, the strain of overwork, the thought of death as putting an end to the 'good life'—is to live in the present and to take full advantage of happiness when it presents itself. In this way one will not spend much time dwelling on (*RSV*, **remember**) life's frustrations (or its brevity, v. 18[17]), because joy will fill one's whole being. The thought is similar to that of 3:10–13: it is not denied that the 'evils' described in the previous verses are sent by God (cf. also 1:13); but joy is also a divine gift and one which can put them into the background provided that the right disposition is there.

keeps him occupied (*ma'ᵃneh*): various other meanings of this word have been proposed (see Gordis). *'ānāh* has several different meanings (see on 1:13). It is probably best to follow *RSV* in giving it the same meaning here as in 1:13 and 3:10, but as a Hiphil rather than a Qal participle. MT as pointed lacks the suffix **him**; but the consonants should perhaps be repointed as *ma'ᵃnēhū*, a defective spelling of *ma'ᵃnēhû*. **with joy in his heart:** literally, 'with his heart's joy'.

LIFE WITHOUT JOY

6:1–6

With all his emphasis on the importance of enjoying whatever God makes possible, Qoheleth does not forget that there are evils in the world which cannot be explained away (cf. 4:1–3). Having addressed those to whom God has given not only wealth and possessions but also *power to enjoy them* (5:19[18]), he now speaks in very negative terms of the situation of those to whom **God does not . . . give . . . power to enjoy them** (6:2). The theme is similar to that of 5:10–17[9–16], but the sombre picture is this time unrelieved by any suggestion of a way out. The motif occurs three times, and the impact is increased by the use of three different expressions for the enjoyment which is beyond the grasp of the unfortunate persons involved: *'ākal*, v. 2; *śāba‘ min-haṭṭôbāh*, v. 3; *rā'āh ṭôbāh*, v. 6. The verses which follow (7–12) are equally sombre in tone, but are not closely related to vv. 1–6.

Qoheleth is here not so much presenting concrete examples to illustrate his theme as reflecting on various hypothetical circumstances, no doubt based on real cases, in which the possession of those supposed advantages in life most prized by traditional wisdom teaching—wealth, social position, a large family, long life (the gifts of wisdom according to Prov. 3:16 and 8:18)—proves ultimately valueless.

1. **There is an evil:** compare 5:13, 'There is a grievous evil'. Some MSS have 'grievous' (*ḥôlāh*, literally 'sick') here too; but this is probably a scribal accommodation made to link the two passages. **upon men:** on the meanings of *hā'ādām* in this book see on 1:3. Here the context shows that it refers to mankind in general: Qoheleth is about to describe an evil which may afflict anyone. **lies heavy upon:** this Hebrew expression (*rab ‘al*), which occurs again in 8:6, is unusual, and its meaning is not certain. Another possible translation would be 'is prevalent' (Gordis; cf. Vulg. *frequens*). The reference to 'an evil' probably refers to everything described in vv. 2–6.

2. The first case cited is that of a wealthy man who for some reason is unable to derive enjoyment from his fortune himself, and also has to leave it to a stranger. No indication of the reason why he is unable to enjoy his fortune is given: sickness, temperamental incapacity, worry—as in 5:12[11]—and other reasons have been suggested. The precise meaning of **a stranger** (*nokrî*) has also been variously assessed. The word usually means a foreigner, that is, a non-Jew; but this is not always the case, and here it may refer simply to someone outside the immediate family (see Humbert, 1939).

honor (*kābôd*): this word can also mean riches. It has been suggested that it cannot mean 'honour'—that is, social standing or esteem—here, because honour cannot be inherited. Exactly the same list occurs in 2 Chr. 1:12 with respect to God's gifts to Solomon; but there also *kābôd* is ambiguous. Honour is, however, the more usual meaning.

a sore affliction (*ḥ^{o}lî rā‘*): literally, 'a severe illness' (so LXX); but especially in view of the metaphorical use of the adjective *ḥôlāh* in 5:13[12] a literal meaning is extremely unlikely. **enjoy(s):** for a similar meaning of *'ākal* ('eat') see on 5:11[10].

3–5. The opening words (**If a man**) indicate that this is a second case distinct from the previous one. This man, like the first, is wealthy (he possesses *ṭôbāh*, **life's good things**); but he also has two additional advantages: a large family, so that there will be no possibility of the alienation of his property into the hands of strangers, and an unusually long life. He thus ought to be the happiest of men according to traditional notions. Yet his case is judged by Qoheleth to be the most wretched of all: his life, long as it has been, is reckoned to be such a tragedy that it would have been better if he had been still-born (**an untimely birth**) and so missed it altogether.

Two reasons are given for this totally negative judgement. The first is that, like the man in 5:10[9], his appetite is not satisfied by his wealth (*napšô lō'-tiśba' min-haṭṭôbāh*; *RSV*, **he does not enjoy life's good things**). The second—if the text is correct; see below on v. 3—is that he **has no burial**. These two circumstances appear to be unrelated and so to weaken the argument. But it would seem that Qoheleth has omitted some information about the case without which the modern reader cannot fully understand his point. It is possible that he had in mind an actual case well known to his original readers of a wealthy man who for some reason fell foul of the authorities in his old age and so ended his life in ignominy.

3. so that the days of his years are many: this clause appears to be a virtual repetition of the previous one. Its function is not clear: repetition for emphasis is hardly a convincing explanation. The syntax is strange (*w^erab šeyyiyhû y^emê-šānâw*). Gordis takes it as a concessive clause: 'however many the days of his years may be. . . .'.

and also has no burial: the apparent incongruity of this clause in its context has led to various suggestions for textual emendation. Gordis and Galling proposed to repoint the negative *lō'* as *lū'* (for *lû*) and so to give the phrase a positive sense: '*even if* he *have* an elaborate funeral', while Zimmerli believes the clause to have been accidentally transferred here from v. 5, where it would refer to the still-born child. Crenshaw takes it as anticipating the following verse: 'even if it does not have a burial, . . . the still-born is better off'. However, *RSV* is probably right. To be denied a burial, though considered a dreadful fate, was not entirely unknown: cf. 2 Kg. 9:33–37; Jer. 22:18–19. It may have been the fate of convicted criminals.

4. In 4:2–3 Qoheleth asserted that both those who are already dead and those who have not yet been born are more fortunate than the victims of oppression. Here, echoing Job 3:16–18, he uses an even stronger image to emphasize the futility of a life lived without enjoyment and ended in ignominy. To be like 'the still-born child that never sees the sun' was to be especially cursed (Ps. 58:8[9]). Its birth, says Qoheleth, is totally meaningless (*hebel*), and unlike the living who after death may expect to be remembered, it is totally forgotten—this is the meaning of **in darkness its name is covered:** 'name' here, as often, means 'memory' or 'remembrance' (cf., e.g., Exod. 3:15; Dt. 9:14), and 'covered in darkness' means 'hidden (from men's minds)' (cf. Isa. 60:2).

5. has not seen the sun: that is, has not lived (cf. 7:11 and Job 3:16, 'see the light'). Elsewhere (11:7) Qoheleth expresses his particular delight in the ability to see the sun. **or known anything:** in the Hebrew 'known' has no object. Without an object the verb *yāda'* can mean simply 'have knowledge' (cf., e.g., Isa. 44:9; 45:20). Some commentators take it here as a second verb governing 'the sun', and so translate 'or known it'. But this is not the most obvious interpretation. **yet it finds rest rather than he:** the Hebrew is very succinct, and has no verb (literally, 'rest to this one rather than that one'), but is not impossible. Gordis, on the basis of the Hebrew of the Talmud, renders 'satisfaction' rather than 'rest'. That a foetus which has never lived should be thought of as enjoying either rest or satisfaction seems strange, but precisely the same idea occurs in Job 3:16–18.

6. Even though he should live: if this is the meaning, 'he' refers to the subject of v. 3; and in that case *hakkōl* (**all**) should probably be rendered 'both'—that is, both the man in question and the foetus are destined for the same ultimate end. But it is more likely that the verb is impersonal: 'Even if someone should live . . .'. **a thousand years twice told:** that is, more than double the length of the life of the longest lived person recorded in Scripture, the patriarch Methuselah (969 years, Gen. 5:27). The reader is perhaps invited to contrast the lives of patriarchs such as Abraham, who 'died in a good old age' (Gen. 25:8) with the case in question.

enjoy no good: this expression (*rā'āh ṭôbāh*) is the same as in 5:18[17], where *RSV* renders it by 'find enjoyment'. **the one place:** see on 3:20. This reference, in the concluding words of the section, to death as the common fate of all has been interpreted as an unrelievedly bitter comment on the worthlessness of life; but this is a misunderstanding of Qoheleth's purpose here, as a comparison with the thought of 3:16–22 and 5:10–20 shows. In each of those two passages also the portrayal of the unhappy lot of some unfortunates is followed by a reminder that death puts an end to the hopes of all alike; but these thoughts lead to a recommendation to make the most of any opportunities that may be offered during life. The same pattern is followed here, but the concluding advice remains implicit: the tragic cases in which the enjoyment of life has for various reasons been impossible ought to encourage the reader more than ever to seize whatever such opportunities may be offered.

A LOOSE GROUP OF SAYINGS

6:7–9

Although these verses have been regarded by most modern commentators as in some way constituting the conclusion to 5:9–6:9—generally supposed to have the uselessness of wealth as its principal theme—it is in fact difficult to find any thematic connection between them and the preceding verses. In addition, they do not appear themselves to have a single unified theme. There is perhaps some logical connection between vv. 7 and 8*a*; but the Hebrew of v. 8*b* and of v. 9*a* is difficult, and there is no agreement at all about their meaning. Verses 10–12, on the other hand, have somewhat more thematic cohesion and are probably best considered separately.

7. This verse is identical metrically and syntactically with many sayings in Proverbs; and there is also a partial thematic parallel, using the same words **appetite** and **mouth**, in Prov. 16:26. If it is a quotation of an older saying its original purpose may have been to make the rather trite observation that a man's labour is never done because hunger is perpetually present and needs to be satisfied. In the context of Qoheleth's world, however, it would mean something rather different and less literal: that the drive for ever greater profit never by itself brings satisfaction (cf. 4:8; 5:10[9]).

There is an alternative explanation of the verse which, if correct, would connect it with v. 6 and the previous verses. This is to understand **his** (twice) as referring to **the one place** of v. 6—in other words, to Sheol. In the Old Testament (e.g. Prov. 27:20; 30:16; Isa. 5:14; Hab. 2:5), and elsewhere in the literature of the ancient Near East, death or the underworld was personified as an insatiable devourer swallowing up men and women into his mouth. However, the verse makes perfectly good sense without this interpretation; and *māqôm*, **place**, can hardly be said to have a **mouth** or an **appetite**. It would have been more natural for Qoheleth to use the word Sheol (which he uses in 9:10), if this had been his meaning.

8. The meaning of the first part of this verse (to **the fool**) is clear, but its connection with v. 7 is less so. As in 2:14–17 Qoheleth here questions whether the wise man has any advantage over the fool; but it is not clear why, if he wished to stress the universal application of the preceding aphorism by citing pairs of contrasting types who despite the difference between them are no exception to the general rule, he should have chosen to cite this particular pair rather than, for example, the more obvious one of rich and poor. (It has been argued that the second part of this verse *does* present a contrast between rich and poor, but see below.) It is probably best to regard this sentence (from **For what** to **fool**) as unrelated either to what precedes or to what follows.

Ellermeier (1963) quotes Ehrlich (VII, p. 80) as commenting, with particular reference to the second part of this verse, that 'only the gods know' what it means! *RSV*'s translation is fairly literal if a somewhat loose syntax is allowed, and if the otherwise unknown phrase *lahᵃlōk neged haḥayyîm* (literally, 'walk in the presence of the living [or, of life]') can in fact be held to mean **to conduct himself before the living**. If the question is intended to be parallel with the preceding one, **And what . . .?** may mean 'And what advantage . . .?' But there are two difficulties with this interpretation: first, there is no contrast here, as the text stands, between two human types as would be expected from the preceding question: only the poor man is mentioned. Secondly, no one would expect the poor man to be in an advantageous position, so the question appears pointless.

Numerous attempts have been made to solve these difficulties. Particular words have been interpreted in different ways. Lauha's rendering of *'ānî* (**poor man**) as 'humble' or 'pious' yields a sense which might well be expected of Qoheleth, that even the religious man fares no better than the wise man, in that he also is not exempt from human frailties. Gordis's 'who has got on in the world' for **who knows how to conduct himself before the living** makes the poor man into a newly rich one! Other commentators suggest emendations of the text. Among these, the addition of 'than (he)' (*min-*) either before **the poor man** (Hertzberg) or before **who knows how . . .** (Kroeber) produces the expected contrast between *two* different men. Even more radical is the emendation of *'ānî* (**poor**) to *'ᵃnî*, 'I' (Galling, Ellermeier), which gives an entirely different sense: 'To what purpose do I understand . . .?' But none of these emendations is supported by any of the ancient Versions. No entirely satisfactory interpretation has been produced, and this is probably a text which became corrupt very early and whose original form can no longer be recovered.

9. The first half of this verse (to **desire**) has the brevity and form of a traditional saying; but whether it is a quotation or not, its meaning is quite uncertain. There is general agreement that the sight of the eyes (*mar'ēh 'ênayim*) denotes what is immediately and concretely obtainable, and, by implication, pleasurable (cf. 11:9). It is the other term of the comparison whose meaning is disputed. *RSV*'s translation of *h^alok-nāpeš* by **the wandering of desire**, which corresponds to the view of most commentators, makes the saying an implicit recommendation to be satisfied with what one has: a bird in the hand is worth two in the bush! This accords well with Qoheleth's general views: cf. 5:18–20[17–19] and perhaps 6:7. But although *nepeš* frequently means 'desire' or 'appetite' both in this book and elsewhere in the Old Testament, it is doubtful whether this interpretation of the phrase is correct. There is no justification for translating the other word, *hālak* (normally 'go') in the particular sense of 'wander'. In fact *hālak* in this book—and also elsewhere in the Old Testament—several times means 'to depart' in the sense of 'to die' (3:20; 5:15[14], 16[15]; 6:4, 6; 9:10; 12:5); and since in biblical Hebrew *nepeš* very frequently means 'breath' or 'life', *h^alok-nepeš* here may well be a circumlocution for dying (cf. the use of *nepeš* with *yāṣā'*, 'go out' in that sense in Gen. 35:18). If this is so, the saying would mean that life should be enjoyed to the full because it is at the very least preferable to the inevitable onset of death, another sentiment characteristic of Qoheleth.

The **this** of the second part of the verse appropriately refers to the immediately preceding phrase whatever interpretation of the latter is adopted. Although on either interpretation there are echoes here of sentiments expressed by Qoheleth in several of the preceding verses, there is no obvious connection between this verse and v. 7.

MAN'S WEAKNESS AND IGNORANCE

6:10–12

These verses to some extent share a common theme in that they assert the helplessness of man in a world which he does not understand. It has been argued that a kind of progression of thought can be found in the passage: for example, the argument might be that since man's nature was determined from the first and he is powerless to change it (v. 10*a*), it is fruitless to argue with God about it (10*b*–11). Consequently man is bound to remain ignorant of the future: both his future as an individual in this life and also future history beyond his lifetime (12). But such an interpretation assumes the existence of more logical and consistent connections between the individual parts than are actually apparent in the text. Moreover, the verses exhibit no stylistic coherence. Loretz (p. 231, note 63) is probably right in his view that the passage is simply a group of independent short sayings on somewhat similar themes 'which should not be forced into a logical connection'. It should be added that as a group they also have no obvious connection with the surrounding material.

10. has already been named: that is, by God. In Hebrew thought the giving of a name was believed to determine the character of its recipient, and also to give power to the namer over the named. These thoughts lie behind Adam's naming of the animals in Gen. 2:19–20 and the account of God's creative acts in Gen. 1:6, 8, 10; cf. also Isa. 40:26. What Qoheleth is saying here, then, is that everything has its immutably determined character, and that this includes man.

and it is known: again, known to God. **what man is:** other renderings are 'what each man will be' (Galling); 'that he will only be a man' (Lohfink). Gordis and *NEB* take **man** with the following clause (ignoring the Masoretic accents): 'a man cannot contend . . .'. Despite these differences the general sense is clear. In view of the previous reference to the significance of names, it is probable that Qoheleth was inviting the reader to remember the meaning of the word *'ādām* ('dust from the *'ᵃdāmāh*, ground', Gen. 2:7; cf. Ec. 12:7). **one stronger than he:** once again, presumably God (rather than, e.g., death). *taqqîp*, 'strong', occurs nowhere else in the Old Testament, but is found in rabbinic Hebrew, and the verb *tāqēp*, 'to be strong' is attested in biblical Hebrew. On the form of the word here, see *BHS*. **dispute:** this meaning of the verb *dîn* is also unique in the Old Testament, but occurs in later Hebrew. In biblical Hebrew it occasionally means to plead (a cause), a meaning which is not far removed from its meaning here.

The whole verse, and especially the second half with its admission of the futility of puny man's attempting to dispute with an all-powerful God, inevitably calls to mind the situation dramatically portrayed in the Book of Job, where Job, after a titanic struggle to present his case to God, eventually submits (42:1).

11. In the Hebrew this verse begins with *kî* ('For'); but this, unless it has an asseverative function here ('Truly . . .'), is probably an editorial attempt to link vv. 10 and 11 together. In fact there is no obvious connection between the two verses: v. 11 does not illustrate or elaborate the truth of v. 10, but is an unrelated general comment, wholly consonant with the teaching of earlier traditional wisdom, on the folly of talking too much and without due caution (cf. Prov. 10:8, 14, 19). The elegant brevity of *RSV*'s **The more words, the more vanity** is not, however, matched by the cumbersome Hebrew, which is entirely in Qoheleth's own prose style. **What is man the better?:** the expression *mah-yōtēr lᵉ-* is the same as in v. 8 where it is used with reference to the wise man, and has the same meaning: 'what advantage has . . .?'

12. These two questions emphasize man's ignorance of the future: both the future of the individual in this life and the course of future history. **after him:** the addition of **under the sun** makes it clear that this is not a reference to life after death for the individual but to future events in this world. **who knows . . .?:** the implication, as in other passages beginning with this phrase (e.g. 3:21), is that *God* **knows what is good for man** but has withheld that knowledge from him (cf. 3:11). It is Qoheleth's view (v. 10) that each person's destiny is known—to God. So in saying that we cannot know what is good for man he is not contradicting earlier statements such as 5:18[17], but rather confirming them: since man cannot by his own knowledge know what is good for him he must—it is implied—accept submissively what God sends him. On the reference to **the few days of his vain life**, see on 5:18. On the possibility that *hebel* (**vain**) may denote brevity rather than futility, see on 1:2–3.

which he passes like a shadow: the Hebrew word *ṣēl*, 'shade' or 'shadow', when used metaphorically has both negative and positive senses: it can stand for insubstantiality on the one hand, or for either a pleasant existence ('in the shade') or protection (cf., e.g., 'in the shadow of Shaddai', Ps. 91:1; also Ps. 36:7 [MT 8] and elsewhere) on the other. In Ecclesiastes *ṣēl* has a positive meaning in 7:12, but not in 8:13. LXX here—and also in 8:13—has '*in* shade/shadow', and it is possible that this points to the original reading. If so, 'that he should spend them in the shade'—i.e. pleasantly—might be a better translation.

For who can tell . . .?: the translation of *'ᵃšer* by **For** is usually defended by reference to a supposedly similar usage in Dt. 3:24, but this explanation is somewhat dubious. In any case it makes no sense to link the two questions in a causal relationship. They are really parallel. There seems to be no particular reason for this second question except to produce additional evidence of human ignorance. Only God could **tell man what will be after him under the sun**, but he does not do so.

THE LIMITATIONS OF HUMAN LIFE

7:1–14

It is agreed by most commentators that these verses form a distinct section of the book. They end with a general conclusion that it is God's intention that **man may not find out anything that will be after him** (v. 14), a conclusion remarkably similar to that of the previous section (6:12*b*). But if it is their aim to provide a reasoned argument to support this conclusion, it must be confessed that they go about this in a very roundabout way. At first glance they appear to consist mainly of a number of unrelated wisdom sayings indistinguishable from parts of the Book of Proverbs, to some of which further comments have been added. Nevertheless, although some of these sayings are probably quotations from earlier wisdom collections, the section as a whole bears the unmistakable stamp of Qoheleth's own views about the limitations of human life. As elsewhere in the book he has made use of traditional wisdom for his own purposes, mingling his own comments with older material in a way which sometimes makes it difficult to distinguish the one from the other.

Attempts to see a logical progression of thought throughout the section are probably wasted. The section is held together partly by the repetition of certain forms—especially the 'Better-saying'—and partly by the repetition of a number of key words: **good/better** (*ṭôb*), eleven times, **wise/wisdom**, six times, **heart**, five times, **fool**, four times, **sorrow/anger** (*kʿs*), three times, and **laughter** and **house of mourning**, twice each. But neither the repetition of forms nor that of key words forms a strict pattern. Rather, the occurrence of a word in one context seems to have suggested, by association, other contexts in which it could be used. Thus the occurrence of **wise** and **fools** in v. 4 apparently suggested a further series of sayings containing those words (vv. 5–12) which are not, however on precisely the same theme. Verses 13–14 form the general conclusion to the section.

1–4. These verses are closely related thematically and formally. In each a negative state—**death, mourning** or **sorrow**—is said to be preferable to a positive one—**birth, feasting, laughter, mirth**. In the first three the same formal pattern occurs ('X is better than Y'), while in the fourth the preferred state is indicated by its being associated with **the wise** as against **fools**. By means of these paradoxical—if not absurd—inversions of common assumptions Qoheleth seems to have intended to administer a shock to his readers with the hope of opening their eyes, through a sober recognition of human mortality, to the limitations of an existence bounded by death. We may assume from the pointed references to **feasting, laughter, mirth** and **song** that he was addressing a particular group of persons who, perhaps through a misunderstanding of Qoheleth's own advice (as given in 2:24 and parallel passages) had given themselves over to thoughtless and irresponsible buffoonery or dissipation.

1. The first half of this verse—only four words in the Hebrew—bears the marks of a popular saying: terseness, a memorable form, play on words (*šēm*, **name** and *šemen*, 'oil' [*RSV*, **ointment**]; two meanings of *ṭôb*, **better** and **precious**). *RSV*, like other translations, is unable to do justice to the neatness and simplicity of *ṭôb šēm miššemen ṭôb*. Taken by themselves these words have a meaning similar to that of Prov. 22:1: to be esteemed by others is more rewarding than are the luxuries provided by wealth. But in the second half of the verse this admirable sentiment is given a clever but bizarre reinterpretation by Qoheleth, who, taking the phrase **A good name** to refer to a person's reputation *after death* (as, e.g., in Job 18:17; Prov. 10:7), reaches the conclusion that **the day of** one's **death**, when one's reputation is complete and cannot be spoiled by last-minute follies and sins, must be preferable to **the day of** one's **birth**, when the future is entirely unknown (cf. Sir. 11:21–28). Elsewhere (2:18–23; 6:2–3) Qoheleth *denies* that what a person achieves in life will endure or be highly regarded after his death. Irony, however, is not always consistent. In twisting the meaning of such popular sayings, Qoheleth undoubtedly had his tongue in his cheek.

2. The thought of death is now taken up in a different way. The saying in the first half of this verse may be an older saying simply expressing disapproval of over-indulgence at parties such as wedding feasts which Qoheleth has then reinterpreted by laying stress on the other side of the comparison. (Jer. 16:5–9 suggests that the contrasting of these two occasions may have been commonplace.) **this** clearly refers to death, although the word itself does not occur in the verse. Qoheleth's meaning is that it is salutary for all men to be brought face to face with the reality of death, which is the only fact about them about which there can be no doubt (cf. 9:5). It is this which **the living** should (*RSV*, **will**) **lay to heart** (**it** in this phrase is not expressed in the Hebrew, but this is the most probable meaning). Qoheleth clearly believed that, although 'the wise man dies just like the fool' (2:16) and so in the end has no advantage over him, continued awareness of mortality affects the *quality* of one's life, giving it a seriousness which enables one to avoid the pitfalls into which the fool's conduct leads him. Again it is important for the reader to recognize that he is not here contradicting what he says elsewhere about the enjoyment of life: the empty, raucous laughter of fools (cf. v. 6) is of a quite different order from the quiet enjoyment of God's gifts which Qoheleth recommends in 2:24–26 and elsewhere, in which 'the *heart* is made glad' (cf. v. 3).

3. This verse seems to consist of two originally independent sayings which Qoheleth has juxtaposed, joining them with the causal particle **for** (*kî*). The first, which consists in the Hebrew of only three words, is paradoxical in form, but originally expressed a sententious attitude similar to that of v. 2*a*, that it is better to face up to the vexations of life than to assume an attitude of carefree levity. The second saying has been interpreted by some commentators (and *RSV*) as conveying the moral—or psychological—message that suffering has a salutary effect on the character of the sufferer. But this somewhat modern interpretation pays too little attention to the actual wording of the saying. Like v. 1*a* this consists of only four words, and these comprise two pairs of opposites: bad/good, outside/inside (*RSV*, **sadness/glad, countenance/heart**). Taken by itself it has nothing to do with human emotions, but means simply that appearances may be deceptive: 'when the outside (*pānîm*) is bad (*berōaʿ*) (e.g. of a fruit), the inside (*lēb*) may be good'. Consequently one should not judge anything simply by its outward appearance. But each of the four words is ambiguous, and Qoheleth has reinterpreted them all in terms of human behaviour. *NEB* gives a correct rendering: 'A sad face may go with a cheerful heart.' Seen in this way the second saying serves to reinterpret the first saying by suggesting a distinction between the outward appearance and the hidden inner reality.

4. There is a close resemblance between the wording of this verse and that of v. 2*a*, but the use of antithetical parallelism rather than of the 'Better-' form and the association of **the wise** and **fools** respectively with the two activities sharpens the tone. One saying may originally have been a variant version of the other. The reason for quoting both versions may have been nothing more than emphasis.

5–6. Two more originally independent sayings (notice that one speaks of the '*song* of fools' and the other of their *laughter*) have been juxtaposed here by Qoheleth and connected by the causal particle **For** (*kî*). The concluding clause of v. 6, **this also is vanity**, is Qoheleth's own comment on the situation. One reason for the juxtaposition of the two older sayings is probably the fact that together they present a whole range of assonance and alliteration: *šîr* (**song**), *kesîlîm* (**fools**), *sîrîm* (**thorns**), *sîr* (**pot**), *kesîl*. The thoughts expressed in both cases are those of traditional wisdom literature (cf., e.g., Prov. 13:1; 15:31; 17:10; 25:12; 26:9; 29:9). Verse 5 appropriately serves to cap the thought of v. 4, but goes further in introducing the notion of a **rebuke** from the **wise** man who has learned a lesson about life from his association with the 'house of mourning' and is therefore able to warn others. His solemn words contrast sharply with the meaningless **song of fools** (there is no justification for translating *šîr*, song, there by 'praise' or 'flattery').

Verse 6 with its image of **the crackling of thorns under a pot**, made more striking by the onomatopoeic language, brings home clearly the futility of the fool's meaningless **laughter**. The final comment that **this also is vanity** is unfortunately ambiguous. Qoheleth would certainly have characterized the laughter of fools as vanity, but his comment may have a wider scope. He may have intended by this phrase to qualify the whole of the preceding argument, in which wisdom is commended over against folly. Such a qualification, implying that in the end the difference between wisdom and folly will count for nothing, is found elsewhere in the book, especially in 2:13–16. This interpretation may perhaps receive some support from v. 7, if that is interpreted as also throwing doubt on the superiority of wisdom.

7. Apart from the possible link with the final words of v. 6, it is difficult to see any connection between this verse and what precedes it. Moreover, if *RSV*'s translation is correct, the two halves of the verse itself do not seem to constitute a convincing parallelism. It has been suggested by Delitzsch and some later commentators that the verse is only the second part of a saying whose first part—which was perhaps something like Prov. 16:8—has somehow dropped out. But there is no trace of such an omission in the ancient Versions, although it has been argued that a fragment discovered at Qumran (4QQoh[a]) implies something of the kind (Muilenburg, 1954). Another suggestion is that the verse has been misplaced, having originally stood after v. 12. Still other commentators have argued that there is in fact a satisfactory connection with vv. 5–6: that the verse is intended to qualify the impression which might be given by v. 5 that the wise man is always impervious to mundane temptations—a proceeding which would be characteristic of Qoheleth. But in spite of the use of the particle *kî*, 'for' (*RSV*, less probably, **Surely**) at the beginning of the verse, it is probably best not to assume too much in the way of a logical progression of thought.

The internal problem of the connection between the two halves of the verse is more serious, as parallelism would be expected here. However, there is some evidence that *'ōšeq* may mean 'extortion' rather than oppression (cf. Lev. 6:4 [MT 5:23]; Ps. 62:10[11]), or, alternatively, 'slander, false witness' (see Driver, 1954, pp. 229–30), either of which meanings would provide a fair parallel with the second half of the verse. 'Drives mad' would be a better translation of *y*ᵉ*hôlēl* than **makes . . . foolish**. But the second half of the verse is itself problematical: both the grammar and the order of words are unusual. Several of the ancient Versions, including LXX, took the last word *mattānāh* (*RSV*, **a bribe**) as the object rather than the subject of the verb, and some of these (Theodot., Vet. Lat., Vulg.) translated it by 'his strength', probably reading it as *motnōh* (see Driver, 1954, p. 229; cf. Whitley, pp. 62–3). The meaning would then be 'and destroys his strong heart'. However, the phrase as translated by *RSV* has verbal affinities with the warnings against taking bribes in Exod. 23:8 and Dt. 16:19 with which Qoheleth will have been familiar, and may therefore be correct.

8. There is no obvious connection between this verse and v. 7. Its two halves, each of which is an independent saying complete in itself, are not necessarily related to one another (there is no **and** to connect them in the Hebrew). Of the two, the second presents the least problems. In view of v. 9, which counsels self-control under provocation, it is most naturally interpreted as advocating caution (*'ārēk*, **patient**, means literally 'long', that is, slow—cf. 'slow to anger' in Prov. 14:29) as opposed to the quickness to take offence which characterizes the **proud** man.

In v. 8*a* the word *dābār* can equally well mean **thing** or 'word, speech'. It has been argued that if the two halves of the verse are intended to be similar in meaning, the latter sense is the more probable: caution is advocated here too in that since speech may be dangerous, it is better to have brought it to an end safely than to be just beginning to speak—cf. the many recommendations to speak little or not at all in the Book of Proverbs, e.g. 10:19*b*; 13:3*a*; 17:27–28; 21:23. But if this is what is intended here it is expressed in a very tortuous manner. It is more natural to take *dābār* as meaning 'thing': the meaning would then be that there is a satisfaction in completing a task or an action which exceeds the hopes with which one begins it (*'aḥ*ᵃ*rît*, **end**, frequently signifies the final result or accomplishment of an action or series of actions, e.g. Prov. 14:12; Isa. 46:10; Dan. 12:8). There may then be a kind of connection with the first half of the verse in that self-control is needed to carry through any project. Whether Qoheleth is their author or not, the two sayings are entirely characteristic of conventional wisdom and show no sign of reinterpretation.

9. This verse, which is in the form of an admonition rather than of a statement (the two most frequent forms in the Book of Proverbs), is similar in theme to v. 8*b*. It also is entirely in accordance with conventional wisdom: cf., e.g., Prov. 12:16. (*ka'as*, **anger** or, perhaps better, irritation or vexation, is used here in a different sense from that which it has in v. 3 [*RSV*, 'sorrow']). Lauha, however, considers that in placing the saying here Qoheleth intended to give it a new interpretation: the anger referred to is now anger *against God*. Since what God has ordained cannot be changed (v. 13), it is folly to kick against one's lot.

10. This verse, which is clearly a personal comment by Qoheleth himself though expressed in the same admonitory form as the previous verse, continues and particularizes the thought of vv. 8–9: to complain—whether to God or to fellow human beings—about the degeneracy of the times is to show a lack of patience and self-control which is the mark of a fool rather than of a wise man. Lohfink, however, regards the verse as a deliberate criticism of the conventional wisdom quoted in verses 8–9: Qoheleth is opposing the conservatism of his fellow 'wise men', whose thinking is tied to the past, by pointing out that to say, in effect, that 'earlier' is synonymous with 'better' and 'later' with 'worse' contradicts their own wisdom as expressed in v. 8*a*, that the end of a thing is better than its beginning. This interpretation, to which there is no specific pointer in the text, is oversubtle. But the thought is in line with Qoheleth's belief that 'there is nothing new under the sun' (1:9) and that man 'is not able to dispute with one stronger than he' (6:10).

11. Four quite different views have been put forward about the meaning of this verse: 1. As in *RSV*'s rendering, *'im* (**with**) has here its most usual meaning of 'together with, accompanied by': that is, it is stated that the possession of wisdom, if unaccompanied by wealth, confers no **advantage** (cf. 9:15–16) (Barton, Gordis). 2. The text is corrupt: 'than' (*min-*) should be restored before *'im* (as supposedly in Pesh.), giving the sense: 'Wisdom is better than the possession of an inheritance' (Hertzberg, Galling). 3. *'im* here means 'just like', as in 2:16 (*RSV*, 'as') and in some other passages in the Old Testament: so the advantage of wisdom is *equated* with that of money (Kroeber, Zimmerli). 4. Interpretation no. 3 is correct, but the second half of the verse should be understood as meaning 'and *even more of* an advantage (than money) to the living', thus radically modifying the statement in the first half and making wisdom preferable to money after all (Lauha, Lohfink).

Of these four interpretations the second has the disadvantage of dependence on a conjectural emendation—in other words, should be regarded as a last resort. The fourth reads more into the text than is actually stated. The first and the third are perhaps equally probable from the linguistic point of view. But whether Qoheleth is here saying that wisdom by itself is useless or that it has some advantages over wealth must depend on the interpretation of v. 12, which purports to pursue the point in more detail. In 9:15–16, as stated above, Qoheleth opposes the conventional view that 'wisdom is better than jewels' (Prov. 8:11) and that her 'fruit is better than gold' (8:19; cf. also 16:16).

those who see the sun means the living (cf. 6:5). By using this expression here Qoheleth may be reminding the reader once more of the point which he makes elsewhere about the uselessness of both wisdom and riches when one is faced with death.

There appears to be no connection between this verse and v. 10 except the catchword **wisdom**.

12. The meaning of the first half of this verse is disputed. A literal translation would be 'For in the shadow (*b^{e}ṣēl*) of wisdom—in the shadow (*b^{e}ṣēl*) of money'. This might mean that wisdom and money both (equally?) provide some kind of protection against adversity, and it was so interpreted by several of the Versions, which may or may not have had before them a different Hebrew text in which *k^{e}ṣēl*, '*like* the shadow', stood for *b^{e}ṣēl* in the second, or perhaps in both, of its occurrences. Hertzberg's view that Qoheleth is here saying that wisdom is so superior to wealth that it makes wealth superfluous is difficult to understand: the phraseology indicates equivalence rather than differentiation. This may be a quotation of a saying which rebukes the arrogance of the rich who think that 'money makes everything possible' (10:19). But Qoheleth caps this with another saying which points out that wisdom does after all have one advantage which wealth does not have: **wisdom preserves the life of him who has it** (cf. Prov. 3:13–18).

This understanding of the verse tends to confirm one particular interpretation of v. 11*a* (see above): that it equates the value of wisdom with that of money. Verse 12*a* explains the meaning of v. 11 by presenting wisdom as a *protection* against adversity no less efficacious than wealth. The thought that wisdom is in fact *more* valuable than wealth is reserved until the end (v. 12*b*). Thus Qoheleth has once more built up a case for the great value of wisdom, only to throw doubt on it in the next verse (13).

13. The preceding verses (1–12) have been mainly devoted to the making of comparisons between different modes of life in order to determine which of a series of alternative courses is 'better' than the others. The rather random assortment of sayings has often been reminiscent of conventional wisdom. At the same time it recalls the behaviour of 'Solomon' in 1:12–2:26 when he tries one thing after another. The conclusion reached in vv. 13–14 is similar to that reached by 'Solomon'. Verse 13 brings the discussion to an end with a jolt with the repetition of the saying quoted in 1:15*a* that 'What is crooked cannot be made straight', put this time in an even more pointed form: certain things are indeed **crooked** in human life and cannot be made **straight** by human beings because it is **God** himself who **made** them so. The value of all attempts to discover the better course of action—of which, as in 1:12–2:26, wisdom is rated as the best—is thus radically relativized by the wise man himself as he turns to **Consider the work of God.**

14. The conclusion which Qoheleth draws from his consideration of the world which God has created is one which is found elsewhere in the book: that man must accept things as they come and make the most of good fortune when God sends it, while reconciling himself without rancour to the bad when it comes in its turn. **be joyful:** better, 'be glad'—no contradiction is intended between this advice and the earlier rejection of shallow merriment in vv. 3–5. **consider:** literally, 'look'. This verb is one which Qoheleth frequently uses to refer to his own reflections on life. **as well as** (*lᵉʿummat*): literally, 'corresponding to'. *NEB* renders the word by 'alongside'. **so that**: in Hebrew this expression (*ʿal-dibrat*) would most naturally mean 'because'; but this is probably an Aramaism (cf. Dan. 2:30; 4:17 [MT 14]). **so that man may not find out . . .:** this clause is almost identical with 3:11*b*, and also very similar to 6:12*b*. **after him:** this word occurs also in 3:22 and 6:12, but not necessarily with the same meaning in each case. Here it is tempting, with *NEB*, to render it by 'next': 'what will happen next'; but it is difficult to see how it can have this meaning.

INEQUITIES OBSERVED

7:15

This verse is taken by almost all the commentators to be the beginning of a new section: 7:15–22. According to this view, the practical advice of vv. 16–17 is based on the general observation made in v. 15: 'Since there is no correspondence between virtue and happiness and between vice and misery, men should avoid either extreme' (Gordis). But there are objections to this interpretation of vv. 16–17 (see below). Alternatively, v. 15 has been held to be the concluding verse of the previous section. But here also there are difficulties. The opening words of v. 15 give the impression of beginning rather than closing a section (cf. 3:16; 4:1; 6:1); and its theme—the inequities that are observable in daily life—is different from that of v. 14, which is concerned with man's ignorance of God's plans rather than with injustice. Verse 15 may therefore be an isolated short *pensée*.

The observation which Qoheleth makes in this verse is similar to that of 3:16, but in this case no discussion follows the bare statement. By his phraseology (**there is,** *yeš*) he seems to have wished to avoid a total denial of the conventional view that virtue and vice receive their due rewards: he merely says that he knows of cases where this does not happen (see on 9:11).

In my vain life: literally, 'in the days of my *hebel*'. Here *hebel* probably means what is insubstantial or brief (see on 1:2). **everything:** as in 2:14 and 7:18, *hakkōl* here probably simply means 'both (i.e. all) of two': so 'I have seen both of these things'.

A WARNING AGAINST SELF-RIGHTEOUSNESS

7:16–18

It is stated in many of the commentaries that in vv. 17–18 Qoheleth advocates the 'golden mean' in human behaviour: that is, that he teaches what is in fact an immoral doctrine that, while excessive wickedness is not advisable, it equally does not do to be too virtuous. But, as will be shown below, this is a serious misunderstanding of his meaning. (For a more detailed treatment of these verses, see Whybray, 1978). His warning is not against righteousness and wisdom, but against *self*-righteousness and *pretensions* to wisdom. Verse 18 adds force to his advice by identifying those who follow it with those who 'fear God'. This is clearly the end of the section: v. 19 enunciates a new theme.

16. This verse and the next are closely parallel both in form and content and have a quasi-poetical character. **Be not righteous:** the elliptical form (*'al-tᵉhî ṣaddîq*) rather than the simple verbal form *'al-tiṣdaq* (compare the parallel *'al-tirša'* in v. 17) suggests that the meaning is 'Do not *claim* to be a *ṣaddîq*', that is, a righteous person; similarly, the use of the Hithpael of the verb in **do not make yourself overwise** suggests that it is pretension to wisdom rather than actual possession of wisdom that is meant: compare a similar use of the Hithpael ('pretend to be ill') in 2 Sam. 13:5.

overmuch, overwise: the implication of '*too* much' in *RSV* is a misunderstanding of the adverbs *harbēh* and *yôtēr*. 'Very righteous' and 'very wise' would be better translations. **why should you . . .?:** this construction connotes a strong warning: 'if you do, you will certainly . . .'. **destroy yourself:** this is a vague expression, but Qoheleth was no doubt thinking of some major catastrophe which would befall the self-satisfied: compare Prov. 16:18, 'Pride goes before disaster, and arrogance before a fall'. As in 5:6[5] Qoheleth counsels prudence, despite his awareness (v. 15) that retribution does not necessarily follow upon wrong conduct.

17. Here Qoheleth is concerned to guard against the possibility of being misunderstood. To claim perfection of virtue or wisdom may be to invite disaster, but to go to the other extreme and abandon oneself to extreme wickedness or folly (on **overmuch**, see on v. 16) is at least equally disastrous. Thus in these two verses Qoheleth recommends a moderate course, but not, as is usually thought, one of moral neutrality or indifference. Rather, he means that recognition of the impossibility of achieving perfection ought not to lead to the abandonment of standards altogether. Such erratic and antisocial behaviour will not be tolerated by society but will have fatal consequences.

18. this, that: i.e. the two pieces of advice given in vv. 16 and 17. **shall come forth from them all:** 'all' means 'both' here, as in v. 15. If 'come forth' means 'escape'—a normal meaning of the verb *yāṣā'*—the sense would be that it is possible to escape the disastrous consequences threatened in vv. 16 and 17 by avoiding extremes of conduct. But Gordis suggested that *yāṣā'* may have a special, idiomatic sense here sometimes found in Mishnaic Hebrew, of satisfying or being quit of an obligation. If this is correct, Qoheleth's meaning would be that it is a characteristic of the person **who fears God** (see on 3:14 for the meaning of this expression in Qoheleth) that he carries out equally the two recommendations in question.

THE SUPERIORITY OF WISDOM

7:19

The taking up in this verse and v. 20, in reverse order, of the themes of v. 16 (righteousness and wisdom) may perhaps be a deliberate editorial device; but there is no continuity of thought here at all. The thought of wisdom's superiority over political sagacity or military strength is a commonplace of the wisdom literature (cf. Prov. 21:22; 24:5), and occurs, though in a qualified form, elsewhere in this book (9:16–18). The verse may be a quotation, although the use of the rare term *šallîṭ*, 'ruler', which occurs in the Old Testament only once outside Ecclesiastes, makes this unlikely.

gives strength to: this verb (*'zz*) is normally intransitive. LXX and the Qumran fragment have 'helps' (reading *ta'ᵃzōr* for *tā'ōz*), but the idea of strength is more plausible. It is probably best to retain

MT and take it as transitive. In that case 'to' (*l*[e]) must be taken as the sign of the accusative under Aramaic influence. **ten rulers:** some commentators have suggested that this refers to a specific form of contemporary government by a group of ten officials; but it is probably simply hyperbole: cf. 'Am I not more to you than ten sons?' (1 Sam. 1:8).

DO AS YOU WOULD BE DONE BY

7:20–22

At first sight v. 20 appears to be an isolated saying: the theme of the admonition which follows in v. 21 seems to be quite unconnected with it. But v. 22 reverts to the earlier theme, that no one is without faults. If these three verses form a single literary unit, it is not clear what is its main point: the need to recognize human frailty in oneself, or the consequences of listening to gossip. This is a problem which occurs frequently in the interpretation of Ecclesiastes, and is due to the author's peculiar method of argument. Probably, as elsewhere in the book, reflection on the commonplace dictum of conventional wisdom which he cites in v. 20 suggested to Qoheleth a connection with the thought about listening to gossip, a connection which he then set out in v. 22. It is possible that the thought of v. 20 may itself have been put into his mind by v. 16, although the interposition of the unrelated v. 19 makes this rather doubtful.

20. This verse begins with the particle *kî*, which often means 'because'. But *RSV* is probably right in translating it by **Surely**. The thought itself is commonplace: cf. 1 Kg. 8:46; Ps. 143:2; Job 15:14–16; Prov. 20:9.

21. Do not give heed: as elsewhere (e.g. 5:4[3]; 7:16) Qoheleth here acts in the role of wisdom teacher, warning his readers against imprudent conduct rather than teaching a moral lesson. **cursing:** this verb (*qillēl*) may mean no more than that the slave grumbles about his master or disparages him; this would be disagreeable to overhear. **your servant:** properly, 'your slave'. Qoheleth takes it for granted that his readers would own domestic slaves, though Crüsemann's assertion (1979, pp. 98–9) that the verse reflects a contemptuous lack of interest in slaves as human beings is quite unjustified.

men say: literally, '*they* say'. The verb is impersonal: see GK § 144f. **lest:** on this meaning of *'ᵃšer . . . lō'*, see GK § 165b.

22. The order of the words is unusual in the Hebrew, and the word 'also' occurs twice: literally, the verse reads: 'For also many times your heart knows that you also have disparaged others'. **many times** clearly goes with 'you have disparaged', and is probably placed near the beginning of the verse for emphasis. The function of the first 'also' is to introduce a further thought. This is an implied recommendation to overlook the slave's misconduct on the basis of the original remark in v. 20 about the universality of human frailty. This is a rare insight into Qoheleth's views on personal relationships, which comes close to that of the Gospels (cf. Mt. 18:35).

TRUE WISDOM IS INACCESSIBLE

7:23–8:1

The sequence of thought in these verses is hard to follow, and some commentators have split them into several sections. But despite digressions and obscurities they are held together by the theme of Qoheleth's unavailing effort to understand how the world is governed. The reiteration and also the variety of the verbs denoting intellectual effort, especially in vv. 23 and 25, the eightfold repetition of the verb *māṣā'*, 'find out', and the two occurrences of *ḥešbôn*, 'sum' (vv. 25, 27), show this to be the main theme. This 'wisdom' which Qoheleth seeks is clearly of a different order from the practical and conventional wisdom which Qoheleth claims elsewhere to possess (e.g. in 1:16–18; 2:13–16), but which he frequently dismisses as having only a relative and very limited value. As in 1:13, the wisdom discussed here is that intimate knowledge of the divine activity itself, which Qoheleth admits in 3:11 that God has deliberately reserved to himself.

23. All this: this could refer either to what precedes or to what follows, depending on the view which is taken about the demarcation of the sections. **I have tested by wisdom:** as in 1:13, where the same phrase *baḥokmāh* is used, the test really amounts to a test *of* (conventional) wisdom—that is, of its adequacy to solve fundamental questions. (This is so whatever may be the correct interpretation of the particle *b*ᵉ, **by**, here: as instrumental, as introducing the object of the verb [cf. GK § 119 l] or as relational: 'concerning, with regard to'.) **far from me:** that is, 'beyond my grasp' (*NEB*). Qoheleth is here using the concept of wisdom or 'being wise' in two different senses: in a superficial sense he is wise, while in a deeper sense he is not.

24. Qoheleth now makes explicit what he means by 'it' in v. 23: it is **That which is**. This phrase occurs in 1:9; 3:15 and 6:10, where it means 'what happens', i.e. phenomena in general. But, as Barton observes, 'the context makes it necessary to understand it here as that which underlies phenomena'. Man's inability to penetrate to this mystery is expressed very forcibly. To the 'horizontal' metaphor 'far' Qoheleth now adds the 'vertical' one 'deep', which he emphasises further by repeating it: **'deep, deep'** (*'āmōq 'āmōq*). This word has the connotation of 'impenetrable, unsearchable' also in Ps. 64:6 (MT 7). **who can find it out?**: this is a forceful way of saying 'No one can . . .'. The recognition that God's ways are totally mysterious is of course not new. It was a fundamental aspect of the Israelite's concept of God, and also occurs in the wisdom literature (e.g. Prov. 30:1–4). Its classical expression in terms of wisdom is in Job 28; but it is presupposed throughout that book. But there was another, more optimistic trend in wisdom thought which understood wisdom as the agent which revealed God's secrets to mankind. Thus Qoheleth's view is quite opposed to the confident attitude of Prov. 8, where personified wisdom, who was intimately associated with the creation of the world and knows its secrets (vv. 22–30) makes herself available for men to 'find' her (vv. 17, 35).

25. This verse closely resembles 1:17, but the addition of **and the sum of things** (*weḥešbôn*) suggests a deeper or more rigorous investigation. *ḥešbôn*, which in the Old Testament occurs only in this book (here and 7:27; 9:10 [*RSV*, **thought**]; on the similar *ḥiššābôn* see on 7:29) has the meaning 'account, sum'—in the literal sense—in later Hebrew. Here the phrase '**wisdom and the sum (of things)**' is probably a hendiadys: the kind of wisdom which Qoheleth has sought is not the superficial, conventional, 'practical' wisdom but something which makes sense of the whole of 'That which is' (v. 24). Qoheleth is describing here the process of thought, of which he has anticipated the conclusion in v. 24: that the attempt is beyond human possibility of achievement.

The second half of the verse is probably corrupt. At least one of the three words **folly, foolishness** and **madness** may have been added to the original text (there is a similar duplication in the **know, search out** and **seek** of the first part). *reša' kesel* . . . (*RSV*, **the wickedness of folly** . . .; cf. LXX and Pesh.) could equally well be rendered by '(that) wickedness *is* folly . . .' (literally, 'to know wickedness (as) folly') or '(that) folly is wickedness'. Qoheleth may mean that to seek wisdom is to recognize that ultimately folly and wickedness come from the same source; but this is uncertain. It is clear, however, that Qoheleth sees an enquiry into the nature of human wisdom and folly to be an important part of his enquiry into the 'sum of things'.

I turned my mind: literally, 'I turned, I and my heart'. Some commentators accept this; others suppose a word to have dropped out and emend the text to 'I turned and *set* my heart . . .'. Many MSS, Targ. and Vulg. have simply '*in* my heart' (*bᵉlibbî* for *wᵉlibbî*).

26. The unexpected introduction of this reference to **woman** into the discussion has perplexed commentators from very early times. If this verse is in fact part of the section which begins in v. 23 and not the beginning of an entirely new section, it can only be understood as intended to be in some sense a particular illustration of some point which has been made in vv. 23–25; but the connection is not easy to discover. The problem is complicated by uncertainties about the meaning of the verse taken by itself. In particular, it is not clear (1) whether Qoheleth is talking about women in general or about a particular type of woman; and (2) whether or not at least part of the verse is a quotation from conventional wisdom.

RSV implies that the reference is to a particular kind of woman: the immoral woman against whose temptations men are constantly warned in ancient Near Eastern wisdom literature and specifically, in the Old Testament, in Prov. 2:16–19; 5:3–6; 6:24–26; 7:5–27. But if, as elsewhere in this book, the particle *'ᵃšer* (**whose**) here means 'because, for', we may render 'I found more bitter than death—woman: for her heart . . .'; in other words this would simply be a male indictment of women in general (so, e.g., Gordis). Such an interpretation might find support in the further statement about women in v. 28; though on the other hand 9:9 suggests a different attitude towards women. But the phrase **woman** (is) **more bitter than death** (or possibly, 'stronger than death'—on this possible meaning of *mar*, see Whitley, p. 68; Lohfink, 1979, p. 281) may be a quotation from a conventional saying (cf. 'Love is as strong as death', Ca. 8:6) which Qoheleth has elaborated, perhaps ironically, quoting it without necessarily agreeing with it.

Most commentators, including Hertzberg, Kroeber, Galling, Loader, find the explanation of the reference to the woman in the second half of the verse: it is only God who can protect men from her temptations, and—as is stated again in 2:26, where the same terms **he who pleases God** and **sinner** are used—his reasons for doing so or refraining from doing so are hidden. Thus the example of the temptress confirms Qoheleth's view expressed in vv. 23–24 about the inadequacy of ordinary human wisdom, and also illustrates the barrenness of Qoheleth's stated attempt (v. 25) to penetrate further and to 'seek the sum of things': all he has found is that he has *not* found it! (cf. v. 28). (For an alternative and very elaborate explanation of the verse in its context see Lohfink in the article cited above.)

27. Behold, this is what I found: Qoheleth now begins to sum up the result of his investigation. This is indicated by the use of the past tense (*māṣā'tî*) in contrast to the 'I found' of v. 26, which is a participle (*môṣe'*, literally 'I am/was finding'), which refers to a process which is still continuing. **adding one thing to another:** there is no verb in the Hebrew, which has simply 'one (thing) to one (thing)'. But *RSV* gives the meaning correctly. **to find the sum:** the same word (*ḥešbôn*) is used here as in v. 25 ('the sum of things'). Lohfink describes this process as 'inductive thinking'—in other words, Qoheleth is saying that in order to arrive at the principles governing the universe he is not content with simply repeating conventional aphorisms learned by heart, but tries to form his own conclusions on the basis of phenomena which he has himself observed.

says the Preacher (*'āmᵉrāh qōhelet*): the verb is feminine; but all commentators agree that this is an error due to wrong word-division: the final letter of the first word (*h*) properly belongs to the second, and is the definite article, so that the phrase should be, as in 12:8, *'āmar haqqōhelet* (the verb now being masculine). Elsewhere in the book *qōhelet* has no article and so gives the impression of being a personal name. The occurrence of the article in these two cases confirms the view that the word is in fact a title or a *nom de plume*.

Apart from the initial 'I, Qoheleth' of 1:12 this is the only passage in the body of the book where the name occurs; and, like the references in the prologue and epilogue (1:1, 2; 12:8, 9, 10) it refers to him in the third person. The reference here in 7:27 may be the work of an editor, or a later gloss; its purpose is not clear. It has been suggested on the one hand that it is intended to indicate that the view just expressed about women is a 'private' opinion of Qoheleth's which carries no authority (Galling, Lauha), and, on the other, that it is intended to stress the central importance of the theme of this section in the teaching of Qoheleth as a whole (Lohfink). Neither theory is particularly persuasive.

28. In v. 25 Qoheleth stated his intention, as part of his search for the 'sum of things', to discover why, if God 'made everything fitting in its time' (3:11), human folly and wickedness should exist. In v. 26 he finds that only by the grace of God can one avoid temptation. In v. 29, however, he absolves God from responsibility for human corruption: men have corrupted themselves. In the context of this train of thought the second half of v. 28 (from **One man**) appears, at least at first, to be an intrusion; and this may be the case: it may be a gloss based on a mistaken interpretation of v. 26, making a further comment on the depravity of woman.

More probably, however, this is a conventional saying quoted by Qoheleth himself (so Kroeber, Galling), possibly to emphasize the seriousness of the problem which he is discussing, and which he has sought repeatedly to solve: the apparent universality of human depravity and folly. Whether this is the point of the saying is, however, uncertain. The commentators, in interpreting it, have failed to notice that it *does not state what it is* that the speaker has sought, and which he has, or has not, found in his extensive research (**One man among a thousand** is of course hyperbole)! Nor does the context make this clear. Most commentators have assumed that the saying means that Qoheleth has not found—with one exception!—any 'true' or 'trustworthy' person (cf. Prov. 20:6; 31:10); but this is merely a guess. Whatever the saying means, it may in fact not be specifically directed against women: there is little difference between the judgements on the two sexes, and the slight variation in wording may simply be for stylistic reasons. The meaning is that the speaker has 'found' virtually no person, whether man or woman, who corresponds to whatever he has been looking for.

One man: whether *'ādām* here means a person of either sex or specifically a man has long been disputed: Qoheleth uses the word in both senses. The parallelism *'ādām* || *'iššāh* suggests the latter. But in fact it makes no difference to the general sense.

29. this alone: Qoheleth has not found the 'sum of things' (v. 28). Now he admits that he has found out only one small thing. But what this is depends on the meaning of the two words *yāšār* (**upright**) and *ḥiššᵉbōnôt* (**devices**). *yāšār*, when used of material things, means 'straight, smooth, level'; but Hertzberg's opinion that here, where it is used of human beings, it has no ethical content but means 'simple, uncomplicated' can hardly be accepted. In all such cases it appears to have an ethical or religious connotation: 'righteous, pious'. To be '*yāšār* in God's sight' is to be approved by him. In contrast with this state of men as God made them, they have deliberately invented (**sought out**) numerous *ḥiššᵉbōnôt*. This word occurs in the Old Testament only here and in 2 Chr. 26:15, where it refers to weapons for use in siege warfare. The connection between these two meanings and with that of *ḥešbôn* in vv. 25, 27, which is a closely related but probably distinct word, is that they all refer to the results of human ingenuity (the verb *ḥāšab* means 'think, calculate, plan' etc.). The fact that Qoheleth chose to use this word immediately after the two occurrences of *ḥešbôn* suggests that he intended it to bear a double meaning (Zimmerli, Lohfink). On the one hand it stands for the mental corruptions by which man has distorted the originally upright nature given him by God: Qoheleth may have had in mind Gen. 2–6, with its account of the progressive corruption of mankind through temptation and acquisition of the knowledge of good and evil (3:22) and the subsequent development of technology (4:17–22), culminating with the statement, introductory to the story of the Flood, that the universal evil of men's thoughts (*maḥšᵉbôt*—again the root *ḥšb*) of man caused God to regret that he had made man (6:5–6). On the other hand the word points to the futility of the attempt—of which Qoheleth's own experiment recorded in these verses is an example—to discover by wisdom the 'sum of things'.

8:1. This verse presents almost insuperable difficulties to the interpreter with regard both to its intrinsic meaning and its connection with its context. Some commentators (e.g. Barton, Kroeber, Gordis, Zimmerli) regard it as the beginning of the next section (8:2ff.) about behaviour in the presence of the king: a wise man will not show his true feelings, but will try to preserve an amiable expression on his face. Others (e.g. Hertzberg, Galling) attempt to interpret it as the conclusion to the previous section (see below). Lohfink divides the verse, taking the first half (up to **of a thing**) with 7:23–29 and the remainder with 8:1ff., while Lauha regards the whole verse as a gloss, but is uncertain whether it is attached to what precedes or to what follows.

The references to 'wise' and 'wisdom', together with the absence of any reference to the king compared with the specificity of 8:2 suggest that the verse is in some way connected with the preceding and not the following verses. In that case—if it is not simply a gloss—it ought to constitute the conclusion of vv. 23–29; and in fact its first part can be so interpreted without too much difficulty. The two questions beginning with **Who?** are equivalent to emphatic negatives: 'No one is . . .; no one knows . . .' (see Whybray, 1971, pp. 19–26). **Who is like the wise man?**: this may mean 'Who is a *really* wise man?'—see GK §118x on this use of *kᵉ*. (The form *kᵉheḥākām*, in which the article is not assimilated, is not unusual in the later books of the Old Testament: see GK § 35n. An emendation, on the basis of Vulg. and some other Versions, giving the reading 'Who is a wise man in this [i.e. the above] sense' (*mî kōh ḥākām*), is unnecessary.) Qoheleth thus concludes his attempt to discover the 'sum of things' by a categorical denial that he or anyone else possesses the kind of wisdom required for the task.

the interpretation of a thing (*pēšer dābār*): the word *pēšer* occurs nowhere else in the Hebrew part of the Old Testament, but it is found in the Qumran literature, where it refers to the interpretation of the hidden meanings of biblical texts, and its Aramaic equivalent occurs in Daniel in connection with the interpretation of dreams. In Gen. 40–41 the cognate form *pitrôn* and the corresponding verb *pātar* are used in the account of the interpretation of dreams by Joseph. Here it may be either a problem (*RSV*, **thing**) or a word or saying which Qoheleth declares to be impossible of interpretation: *dābār* has both meanings. The former meaning makes good sense: no one is able to grasp the ultimate meaning of things which God has hidden from man. Some commentators, however, favour the meaning 'word, saying'. Hertzberg follows Ewald in rendering the statement by 'Who knows the interpretation of the [following] sentence:'. This has the advantage of making an otherwise problematic connection between the two halves of the verse (see below).

The second half of the verse clearly expresses a positive view of wisdom which contradicts the negative view of the first half and appears to weaken the force of the whole section. It is best to regard it either as a gloss or as a quotation by Qoheleth of a conventional wisdom saying for a special purpose. 'Making the face shine' is an expression used elsewhere only with God as the subject: it denotes his gracious approval (e.g. in Num. 6:25). But here it probably has a somewhat different sense: the face is an index of the feelings; and a bright face is a sign of happiness or contentment (Prov. 15:13; and cf. Ec. 7.3). The meaning of the parallel statement **and the hardness of his countenance is changed** is uncertain. A different vocalization (cf. from some of the Versions) would give a quite different meaning: 'but he who is hard-faced (*'az* for *'ōz*) is hated (*yiśśānē'* for *yᵉšunne'*)'.

This saying (from **A man's wisdom**) can hardly express Qoheleth's own thought, and its poetical form suggests that it originated elsewhere. If it is not simply a gloss, Hertzberg's suggestion (see above) may be right: that it is quoted by Qoheleth as an example of a type of wisdom saying which is so far from the truth that no one, however wise, can make sense of it.

DESPOTISM AND HUMAN SERVITUDE

8:2–9

Whether or not there is a link with v. 1, this section has affinities with the previous section. Qoheleth first takes up the conventional wisdom teaching concerning the problems of dealing with unpredictable *human* monarchs (vv. 2–5) as an analogy and starting-point for a wider discussion of man's helplessness in the face of *divine* unpredictability (vv. 6–9). The phrase (**the**) **time and way**, repeated in vv. 5 and 6, links the two parts together. The fulcrum on which the whole section turns is v. 5: this confident assertion of traditional wisdom that the wise man can circumvent the threat posed by the whim of the despot by knowing how to 'manage' him is cited by

Qoheleth only to be rejected: not only in his dealings with human kings but also in the management of every aspect of his life, man, however 'wise' he may be, is helpless because he does *not* know 'the time and way'.

2. In the Hebrew text this verse begins with the word 'I' (*'anî*), which *RSV* leaves untranslated (see *RSV* footnote). It makes no sense in the context, and is not represented in the Versions. It is probably a textual error. Various suggestions have been made to account for it: that it is a corruption of the accusative particle *'ēt*; that it is a corruption of *benî*, 'my son', or of *'āmartî*, 'I said'; or that it is a partial dittography of the last word of v. 1.

Keep the king's command: this admonition could also be rendered 'Observe the king's face'—that is, try to assess the king's mood from his expression (cf. Prov. 16:15). On the other hand, the king's absolute power and the need to fear and obey him are frequently stressed in Proverbs (14:35; 16:14; 19:12; 20:2; 24:21). But it is not clear to what king Qoheleth can be referring: Israel no longer had a native king, and Qoheleth's readers were hardly likely to have personal contact with the remote Ptolemaic emperor in Alexandria. Two possibilities remain: that 'king' is used here loosely to refer to local governors; or—more probably—that Qoheleth is simply repeating commonplaces of earlier Israelite—or international—wisdom as a basis for his more general reflections about the dangers and unpredictability of life.

be not dismayed: in the Hebrew text these words are part of the next verse, where they begin a new sentence. *RSV* here follows LXX in agreement with some commentators (Budde, Galling, Zimmerli). Whichever reading is adopted, *RSV*'s rendering of the verb is hardly correct: 'Do not be hasty' would be a better translation.

because of your sacred oath (literally, 'on account of God's oath'): the meaning of this phrase is disputed. The oath in question may be one of loyalty sworn to the king *before* God (Lauha, Gordis, Galling), an oath sworn to the king *by* God, confirming his authority (Hertzberg), or an oath which had to be taken before the king as judge in a lawsuit—a risky procedure as the king could not be relied on to be impartial (Zimmerli).

Probably the simplest solution is to retain the verse-division of the Hebrew: the king is to be obeyed because disobedience would entail the breaking of a solemn oath of loyalty, which would bring disastrous consequences on the rebellious subject: so, 'Obey the king, especially on account of your sacred oath' (on 'especially' as a translation of *we* [*RSV*, **and**] see GK § 154a, note 1b).

3. The meaning of the first half of this verse (to **unpleasant**) is very uncertain, partly owing to the doubt about the point at which it begins (see on v. 2) and partly because of the ambiguity of several of its constituent words. On the first point, if the Hebrew verse-division is followed, the first admonition is negative: '*Do not* go *hastily* from his presence' (on the construction with two verbs see GK § 120c). On the second, the verb translated by **delay** in *RSV* ('*āmad b*ᵉ, literally 'stand in') may also mean 'persist in' or 'take part in', and the rather general phrase **when the matter is unpleasant** (*b*ᵉ*dābār rā'*, literally 'in a bad matter') may refer to what is dangerous or disastrous (for whom?), or may be a euphemism for a plot or rebellion against the king (Waldman, 1979). Finally, **go from his presence** (literally, 'go from his face') could also be interpreted as meaning 'be disloyal' (so Hertzberg and Lauha; cf. Hos. 11:2).

Whatever conduct is recommended in the first part of the verse must clearly be consonant with the motive for it stated at the end: that the king **does whatever he pleases**—that is, that he is both all-powerful and accountable to no one for his actions. *RSV* interprets the verse as simple advice to the courtier to waste no time in carrying out the king's commands even when the errand is an unpleasant one. This, however, involves a somewhat strained interpretation of **go from his presence**. Of the alternative interpretations, that which takes the verse to be a warning against conspiracy is perhaps the most probable: 'Do not be in a hurry to desert him and involve yourself in a plot which is bound to fail, since he will always get his own way' (cf. Prov. 20:2; 24:21–22; 25:2).

4. This verse confirms the last clause of v. 3. It may be a popular saying (so Zimmerli and Lauha), though the use of the rare and late word *šilṭōn* (**supreme**) suggests that it was coined not long before Qoheleth's time. The root *šlṭ*, signifying power or authority, occurs fairly frequently in the later books of the Old Testament, but *šilṭōn* itself occurs only here and in v. 8. In Sir. 4:7 it occurs as a noun meaning 'ruler'. Here it is probably to be taken as a noun meaning 'power' or 'authority': to say that the king's word 'is power' is comparable to the English expression 'his word is law'.

The second half of the verse (from **who may say**) is virtually identical with Job 9:12*b*, where it refers to God.

5. This verse has clear verbal links with the preceding verses: **obeys** (*šômēr*) is the same verb in the Hebrew as 'Keep' in v. 2, and **harm** (*dābār rā'*) is repeated from v. 3 (*RSV*'s 'unpleasant matter'). As it expresses a view directly opposed to that of the verses which follow, it has been taken by some commentators to be a gloss. But it is in fact a further commonplace of traditional wisdom, cited by Qoheleth as a dictum to be attacked. It is concerned with ways in which the wise courtier can successfully accommodate himself to the arbitrary will of the ruler: either by unquestioning obedience (cf. Prov. 13:13; 19:16; 24:21–22) or, more subtly, by knowing how and when to put in a persuasive word (**the time and way**—cf. Prov. 14:8; 15:23).

Some commentators take *dābār rā'* to refer, as in v. 3, to a conspiracy, or, more generally, to an evil deed, and also take *mišpāṭ* (**way**) in its more common sense of 'judgement'. This would open the way to several alternative interpretations of the verse: that the obedient man will steer clear of involvement in intrigue because, as a wise man, he will be aware of the probable penalty, that he will be afraid of divine retribution if he does wrong, or that he may take comfort in the knowledge that even tyrants have only a time to rule and must face God's judgement. The interpretation suggested above, however, best accords with the conventional wisdom which Qoheleth is attacking.

6. The first half of this verse repeats the statement in v. 5 about the **time and way** and appears to confirm and even extend its validity: there is a time and way for **every matter** (on this meaning of *ḥēpeṣ* see on 3:1). Of equal significance, however, is the fact that the statement (up to **way**) is also a virtually word-for-word repetition of 3:1. These verses (6–9) radically re-interpret the phrase 'time and way' in terms of Qoheleth's general view which he expresses elsewhere, but especially in 3:1–15, that although there is a 'right time' for everything, it is known only to God, who has concealed it from his creatures, so rendering them helpless and unable to plan or exercise control over events. Thus the statement of v. 5 that 'the mind of a wise man will know the time and way' is radically rejected.

The second half of the verse must be interpreted in the light of the first and of v. 7. The word translated as **trouble** (*rā'āh*) can also mean 'wrongdoing, evil', and is so taken by some commentators, who interpret the statement as referring to the universality of human sin; but the verbal similarity of the phrase to other passages, especially to 2:21 and 6:1, where, as here, *rā'āh* is qualified by *rabbāh* (**heavy**) defines its meaning here as disadvantage or misfortune. This interpretation is confirmed by v. 7, which makes it clear that it is man's ignorance rather than his sinfulness with which Qoheleth is concerned here.

One of the difficulties in the interpretation of this verse and of v. 7 is that each of the four clauses which they comprise is introduced by the same ambiguous particle *kî* (*RSV*, **For, although, For, for** respectively). Each must be interpreted according to its context. In this verse the word is best rendered on its first occurrence by 'For' and on its second by 'but'.

7. what is to be: that is, the future course of events. **for who**

can tell . . .?: that is, no one (except God) can predict the future. **how:** this word (*kaʾašer*) normally means 'as' or 'when'. Its precise force here is uncertain, but the general sense is clear. Emendation to 'what (will be)' is unnecessary.

8. Here Qoheleth makes use of the device of the so-called 'numerical saying' (cf. Prov. 30:4, 11–14, 18–19, 21–31) to demonstrate by means of four examples that man's inability to predict the future is all of a piece with his general helplessness in every aspect of his life. The first three of these begin with the same word *ʾên*, literally '(there) is not'; the substitution of another word for 'not' (*lōʾ*) in the final clause is a stylistic variation to end the series, which is also held together by an incomplete but recognizable rhythmic pattern. Although there is some uncertainty about the precise meaning of some of the items in the list (see below), their general purpose is not in doubt.

No man . . . the spirit: the Hebrew text is fuller, with a double occurrence of the word *rûaḥ* (**spirit**): 'No man has power over the spirit, to restrain the spirit'. Some commentators (Zimmerli, Galling, Lauha) regard the second half of the clause, 'to restrain the *rûaḥ*', as a gloss added to make clear the meaning of an original text which read simply: 'No man has power over the *rûaḥ*.' This emendation would give the verse a perfect symmetry, but is purely speculative. In any case it does not materially affect the sense.

There is, however, an ambiguity here: *rûaḥ* (**spirit**) can also mean 'wind'. Elsewhere Qoheleth uses it in both senses (e.g. wind, 1:6; 11:4; spirit or breath of life, 3:19, 21; 11:5; 12:7). Here either meaning makes good sense: on the one hand, the theme of the wind as beyond man's control is echoed in 1:6, where the wind is taken as an example of the unalterable movements of the natural world; on the other, the thought that man is powerless to prevent the departure of the breath from the body (cf. 12:7) would neatly parallel the next clause, which states that he has no **authority over the day of death:** in other words, he can neither prolong his life nor determine when he will die.

discharge: in the Old Testament this word (*mišlaḥat*) occurs only here and in Ps. 78:49 (*RSV*, 'company'), where it probably means a deputation or delegation. In later Hebrew it means mission, substitution or divine visitation. The root *šlḥ* has the connotations 'send' and 'release'. In connection with **war** the most natural meaning of the word would be either exemption or release from military service, although other meanings have been proposed, including immunity (for civilians as well as combatants) from the effects of war, and negotiations (not possible once the fighting has begun). Release or discharge rather than exemption is the more probable meaning here.

In earlier times when Israel had its own army certain classes of men were exempt from military service (Dt. 20:1–8), and later Judas Maccabaeus is said to have observed this law (1 Mac. 3:56). But in Qoheleth's time Jewish soldiers would have been mercenaries serving in foreign armies to whom such exemptions presumably did not apply. Alternatively, Qoheleth may have meant that—whatever exemptions may have been allowed beforehand—there was no possibility of discharge once a campaign had begun (the Hebrew reads not **from war** but '*in* war').

The point of the last example (**nor will . . . given to it**) is not entirely clear. It has, however, a certain similarity to the previous example in that, unlike the first two, which are concerned with human helplessness in general, it cites a particular example: just as those involved in warfare cannot escape from it, so also with those involved in doing evil: they cannot ultimately escape the consequences of their wickedness. Some commentators regard this as the climax of the series: the person who recognizes no law but does exactly as he pleases might be expected to be an exception to the general rule that man is always the victim of circumstances; but even he will eventually be overtaken by them. This would then be one of a series of passages (2:26; 3:17; 8:12–13; 11:9 in particular) in which, in apparent contrast with what he maintains elsewhere, Qoheleth expresses his belief in divine judgement.

Other commentators (e.g. Budde, Galling, Zimmerli), finding this thought unsatisfactory, suppose that there is a textual error here: that *reša'* (**wickedness**) is a mistake for *'ōšer*, 'wealth', which contains the same letters but in a different order. But it is difficult to see how this emendation, which is speculative, improves the sense.

9. All this: Zimmerli and Galling take this to refer to the following rather than the previous verses, and so to mark the beginning of a new section. But a comparison with similar cases (especially 7:27), together with the use here of the verb *šālaṭ* (**lords it**), which picks up *šilṭōn* (**supreme, authority**) in vv. 4 and 8 and *šallīṭ* (**has power**) in v. 8, makes it probable that the verse belongs with vv. 2–8. It is in fact a summarizing verse which draws together both the remarks about tyranny in vv. 2–5 (**lords it over man to his hurt**) and the general observations of vv. 6–8 about human helplessness (**all that is done under the sun**).

while man . . .: better, 'at a time when man . . .'. Qoheleth points out that the context for his general observations is the age in which he and his readers live, which he regards as notorious for its cruel tyranny (cf. 4:1–3). Thus in this final comment Qoheleth makes clear his attitude towards political authority as it manifested itself in his time: on the one hand he counsels obedience and submission to it on the grounds of prudence, while on the other he does not hide the fact that he regards it as brutal and tyrannical—as a particular, concrete example of human servitude in general.

to his hurt (*l^e ra' lô*): compare 'for our/your good' (Dt. 6:24; 10:13). Emendation to a verbal form ('to do him harm') is not necessary.

LIFE'S UNFAIRNESS

8:10–15

This is the first of a series of sections comprising 8:10–9:12, all of which are concerned to question the conventional belief that righteousness and wickedness unfailingly receive their due rewards.

In 8:10–15 two totally opposed views on this question seem to stand side by side: while in v. 12*a* it is conceded that a habitual 'sinner' may attain to the long life conventionally reserved for the wise or righteous, v. 13 declares unequivocally that the life of the 'wicked' person who does not fear God will be short and miserable. Three main solutions to this difficulty have been proposed. Some commentators, including Galling and Lauha, regard vv. 12*b*–13 as a gloss added to the book by a later editor to protest against Qoheleth's 'heretical' view. According to others (e.g. Loretz, p. 123; Loader), Qoheleth quotes or cites the traditional view only to refute it in v. 14. But Gordis and Hertzberg among others hold a third view: that although vv. 12*b*–13 express a point of view which Qoheleth cannot accept without serious qualification, he does not reject it entirely. It is the frequent exceptions to the rule which lead him to characterize this aspect of human life as 'vanity' (vv. 10, 14), and to recommend once more the joyful acceptance of whatever things God sees fit to bestow (v. 15). The argument is similar to that of 3:16–22.

10. The Hebrew text of this verse has clearly suffered some corruption and hardly makes sense without some emendation. The emphasis on the wicked's being **buried** is particularly strange, since burial of the dead was the normal practice, and there is no suggestion in the text that these funerals of the wicked were in any way extraordinary. The majority of modern commentators (Gordis and Lohfink are exceptions) emend *q^e bûrîm*, 'buried' to *q^e rēbîm*, 'draw near', in the sense of worshipping at the temple (cf. 5:1[4:17]). This fits well with the context: **the holy place** certainly refers to the Jerusalem temple (cf. a similar meaning in Lev. 7:6; the suggestion of Gordis and others that it means 'cemetery' here is improbable).

Clearly Qoheleth's intention is to depict the wicked as respected citizens who piously frequent the temple precincts. The second half of the verse as rendered by *RSV* makes an appropriate continuation of the thought of the first. But the correctness of *RSV*'s translation is by no means assured. **were praised** is a translation not of MT but of a variant (*wyštbḥw*) found in a few Hebrew MSS and presupposed by LXX and other Versions. MT has *wyštkḥw*, 'are forgotten'. This can hardly refer to the wicked: if it is a correct reading, it suggests that this part of the verse does not refer to them, but to their opposites, the righteous. Qoheleth would then be contrasting the undeserved reputation of the wicked with the equally undeserved contempt suffered by the righteous. This interpretation is supported by the phrase which *RSV* translates by **where they had done such things. such things** is a very vague expression since no specific actions of the wicked have been mentioned; and the word so rendered (*kēn*, taken by *RSV* in the sense of 'thus, so') can also mean 'right(ly)'. The sentence may then be rendered 'while those who do right are forgotten in the city'. If this interpretation is correct, the verse makes a contrast between the treatment of the wicked and of the righteous: the former are honoured, while the latter are forgotten. It is this situation which Qoheleth regards as *hebel*, **vanity**.

11. Qoheleth here pursues the theme of the apparent immunity from censure or punishment of the wicked, pointing out its bad effects on human conduct generally: it encourages others to behave like them. However, he does not go so far as to assert that wickedness is never punished: he qualifies his criticism by the use of the word **speedily**, which implies that punishment will, or at least may, eventually overtake its perpetrators, even though it is often delayed. But it is precisely this delay which encourages other evil-minded persons to think that they will not suffer for their deeds. Qoheleth thus agrees up to a point with the teaching of earlier wisdom writers (e.g. in Proverbs, Job and some of the Psalms), who acknowledge the fact of the present prosperity of the wicked but take comfort from the thought that they will eventually come to a bad end; but his conclusion is quite different from theirs: the postponement of retribution is in itself a positive cause of evil.

The word *pitgām* (**sentence**) is a late borrowing into Hebrew, a Persian loanword which in the Hebrew parts of the Old Testament occurs only here and in Est. 1:20, but is found several times in the Aramaic parts of Daniel and Ezra, where it always refers to a human command or decree, and also in later Aramaic. Here it is not clear whether the sentencing authority referred to is human or divine; if the latter, it has been argued that this is an implicit criticism of

God for allowing evil to proliferate. But such criticism would be uncharacteristic of Qoheleth.

12–13. On these verses, see above on vv. 10–15 as a whole. The first part of v. 12 (to **his life**) probably belongs to the previous sentence: it is doubtful whether **Though** is a possible translation of *'ᵃšer*, which should be rendered by 'for'. It is *because* sinners appear to get away with numerous misdeeds that others are encouraged to imitate them. It is also doubtful whether **and prolongs his life** is a correct translation. **his life** is missing from the Hebrew; and although this omission seems to have been a permissible idiom—it occurs also in 7:15—the phrase as a whole (*ma'ᵃrîk lô*) is not without difficulties. Further, it is strange that Qoheleth should use the idiomatic form here while employing the full, normal form (*ya'ᵃrîk yāmîm*) in the very next verse. LXX may be correct in taking the verb here in its alternative sense of 'postpone': the sinner is able to persist in his wicked deeds only because God in his patience postpones the punishment.

As has been stated above, it is uncertain whether vv. 12*b*–13 (from **yet I know**) cite a view with which Qoheleth totally disagrees, or whether he regards this traditional view as a generally valid view to which, however, there are lamentable exceptions. Some commentators have taken the use of the participle rather than the perfect tense (**I know**) as indicating scepticism: Gordis renders the phrase by 'though I know the answer that . . .'. But it cannot be denied that these verses are composed in Qoheleth's own personal style.

a hundred times: Hebrew has simply 'a hundred' in what appears to be, irregularly, the construct form. Whatever the reason for this, the meaning is clear and emendation—e.g. the substitution of *mᵉ'ōd*, 'very much' for *mᵉ'at*—is probably unnecessary.

like a shadow: on the possible meanings of this expression, see on 6:12. Here it has a negative meaning. It refers not to the prolongation of life, as *RSV*'s translation suggests, but to the whole phrase. The meaning is 'neither will he prolong his days but will be like a shadow'. LXX seems to have read 'in shadow' (*bᵉṣēl* for *kᵉṣēl*); but MT is correct.

14. Qoheleth now returns to the theme which he had introduced in v. 10: although he has not entirely abandoned the traditional belief that justice will ultimately prevail, he points out that human existence is rendered fundamentally unsatisfactory (note the threefold recurrence of *hebel*, **vanity**, in v. 10 and twice in this verse) because, judging at least by appearances, there are exceptions to the rule. The use of the word *yēš*, **there are**, here shows that he regards them as inexplicable exceptions and no more; but they are enough to leave men in a state of uncertainty about their future.

deeds of (*ma'ᵃśēh*, twice): this word is in the singular, and refers not to human actions themselves but to the *consequence* of the behaviour of righteous or wicked (cf. Isa. 32:17; Hab. 3:17, where it means 'fruit' or 'effect'). A better translation would be 'what is due to'.

15. Compare the similar verses 2:24–26; 3:12–13, 22; 5:18–19 [MT 17–18] and also 9:7–10 and 11:9–10. It is perhaps noteworthy that each time the commendation of enjoyment occurs in the book it is expressed with increasing emphasis (see Whybray, 1982), here by the use of the verb *šbḥ* (Piel, **commend**), which elsewhere in the Old Testament means 'praise' (cf. its meaning in 4:2). The meaning of *yilwennû* (**will go with him**) is somewhat uncertain; but the thought is unlikely to be very different from that of 2:24 and 3:13.

THE INSCRUTABILITY OF GOD'S WORK

8:16–17

In this short passage Qoheleth reiterates a theme which appears frequently in the book, often expressed in similar words (cf. especially 3:11; 7:14, 24, 27–28). In its present position it may be seen as a comment on the previous section: the reason for the apparent unfairness frequently experienced in life is beyond human understanding. It also has some relevance to the passage which follows. But the three passages are all self-contained and lack any structural link. Verses 16–17 may have been placed here by an editor who wished thereby to give a more systematic presentation of Qoheleth's thought.

16. how . . . see sleep: *RSV* implies that it is the business that is done on earth that prevents sleep. But although elsewhere (2:23; 4:7–8; 5:12, 17 [MT 11, 16]) Qoheleth speaks of the strain and inability to rest from which the overbusy man suffers, he is here concerned with a much wider issue. Most commentators have rightly seen that the sleeplessness referred to here is connected with man's unceasing but fruitless attempt by the exercise of wisdom to understand the ways of God (cf. 3:10–15). Thus this phrase is either a parenthesis which interrupts the sentence (**When . . . then . . .**) or has been misplaced from v. 17, which would then read: 'then I saw . . . that man, *even if* (*gam; RSV*, **how**) *his eyes find sleep neither by day or night*, cannot find out . . .'. The latter proposal also accounts for the lack of a subject governing the verb **see** (*RSV*'s indefinite **one** is hardly satisfactory).

17. I saw: better, 'I considered', as in 1:14 and other passages. It is important to note that Qoheleth here equates **the work of God** with **the work that is done under the sun**. God controls the events of human history. **cannot find out:** that is, cannot understand the logic which governs God's actions.

However much: the probable meaning of this particle (*bešel 'ašer*) is 'because'. *bešel* is a late expression perhaps modelled on an Aramaic usage, found also in Jon. 1:7, 12 in the sense of 'on account of'. The phrase is thus a continuation of the previous sentence, giving it extra emphasis: man cannot understand '*because* a man may toil in seeking, *but* . . .'. **toil in seeking:** that is, try hard to find.

ENJOY YOUR LIFE, FOR DEATH LEVELS ALL

9:1–10

Some commentators consider that v. 1 is the final verse of the previous section, summarizing its conclusions. Some support is thought to be given to this view from the initial words *kî 'et-kol-zeh* (**But all this**), which recall similar introductory phrases in 7:27, 29; 8:9. But if so the 'summary' which follows is of inordinate length, and 9:1–10 are best taken as a separate section. *kî* does not necessarily mean 'but': it is used elsewhere in the book as an asseverative particle emphasizing what follows; and *zeh*, **this**, has a future rather than a past reference also in 7:27, 29. That the passage ends with v. 10 is certain, since v. 11 clearly begins a new section: compare **Again I saw** (literally 'I turned and saw') with 4:1, 7.

The first part of the section (vv. 1–3) pursues the same theme as 8:10–15; but from v. 4 onwards Qoheleth turns from a general discussion of the inequities inherent in human life to one of his favourite themes: the levelling effect of death, to which all are destined (cf., among other passages, 2:16; 3:19–21). But—in contrast with his mood in 4:2–3, where his brooding on the sufferings of the oppressed led him to exclaim that death or non-existence is preferable to life—he here puts forward the view that, despite everything, life is preferable to death, and goes on in vv. 7–10 to recommend, in even stronger terms than in the comparable passages in 2:24–26; 3:12–13, 22; 5:18–19 [MT 17–18], the full enjoyment of the pleasures which God bestows. But it is significant that at the very end of the passage he reminds the reader once more of the inevitable cessation of all further activity in the total annihilation which death brings. Here Qoheleth expresses most clearly the positive side of his thought: that the awareness of mortality ought to give men a new zest for life rather than drive them to despair.

1. **examining:** the Hebrew has an infinitive construct preceded by *wᵉ*, 'and'. Possibly this stands in the place of a second finite verb which continues and strengthens the force of the first: 'I laid to heart and examined' (see GK § 114p). But the form of the infinitive, *bûr*, is difficult. The word occurs nowhere else, though it has been thought to be cognate with the more common verb *bārar*. However, *bārar* hardly means 'examine, test' in the Old Testament (see on 3:18), though in late Hebrew it can mean 'sort out, sift'. LXX and other Versions presuppose a quite different text: *wᵉlibbî rā'āh*, 'and my heart saw', for MT's *wᵉlābûr*. The commentators are divided on the question.

their deeds (*'ᵃbādêhem*): a late word of Aramaic origin which occurs only here in the Old Testament.

whether it is love or hate: literally, 'neither love nor hate'. It is not clear whose love or hate is meant here: that is, whether man does not know whether *God* loves or hates him, or whether even his *own behaviour* (**their deeds**) is outside his control so that he is unable to determine whether *he* should love or hate. Another possible explanation of the phrase is that 'love' and 'hate' constitute an example of merismus, in which a pair of opposite terms are used to signify the whole range of items lying in between: that is, man does not know *anything* (on merismus, see Watson, 1984, pp. 321–4).

Everything before them is vanity: the words **is vanity** do not correspond to anything in the Hebrew text, which has simply 'Everything (is) before them'. *RSV* has followed Pesh. (cf. also LXX), which took the first word of v. 2 as belonging to this verse, but must have read *hebel*, 'vanity', instead of MT's *hakkōl*, **Everything**. This reading has been accepted by a number of commentators. Others regard MT as correct and as making good sense. But there is no agreement on the meaning of **before them**. Hertzberg correctly pointed out that this cannot refer to the future—as in Gordis's translation, 'anything may happen to them'—because Hebrew *lipᵉnê*, 'before', when it refers to time, always refers to the past and never to the future. He renders the phrase by 'everything lies before their time', meaning that men's fate is predetermined. But this would not be a very clear way of expressing this thought. Lauha, however, citing Gen. 13:9—'Is not the whole land before you?' – and similar passages, maintained that 'before' here means 'at one's disposal'—though he is among those who link the phrase with an emended v. 2: 'everything which is at their disposal is vanity'.

Each of the above proposals has its strengths and weaknesses. The solution of the problem is partly linked with that of the text and meaning of the opening words of v. 2 (see below). Fortunately the general sense of the verse is reasonably clear: God controls men's lives absolutely, and men are left in ignorance of what is going on.

2. *RSV* accepts the emendation of the first word of this verse to *hebel*, taking it with v. 1 (as noted above). If this emendation is not accepted, the verse reads, literally, 'All is as to all. There is one fate for the righteous . . .'. 'All is as to all' has been taken by some commentators to be meaningless, and some emendations have been proposed. But Gordis's view of the phrase as an idiom meaning 'one fate awaits all men' (comparing similar repetitive phrases in Exod. 3:14; 4:13—the latter reading literally 'send by whom you will send') avoids emendation and makes reasonable sense.

to the good and the evil: the Hebrew lacks the reference to evil. This has been supplied by *RSV*, following a number of commentators, from LXX and other Versions, on the grounds that the other items in the series all consist of contrasting pairs. Other commentators solve the problem in the opposite way, by omitting **to the good** as a gloss. The Hebrew text as it stands is not impossible, though it is stylistically unsatisfactory.

righteous/wicked; good/evil; clean/unclean; sacrifices/does not sacrifice: the choice of opposite pairs here, which appears to line up the offerer of sacrifice with the righteous and the good, may suggest that Qoheleth's attitude towards temple worship was more positive than has often been supposed. To interpret this reference to sacrifice as meaning that it was a matter of indifference to him because it had no effect on one's ultimate fate (Perdue, 1977, p. 188) would imply that he was also indifferent to righteousness and goodness, which is manifestly not the case. See also on 5:1–7. **swears/shuns an oath:** there were evidently differences of opinion in Qoheleth's time about the propriety of taking oaths, as there were on the question of offering sacrifice (on the attitude of the later Essenes to this practice, see Schürer II, p. 568; see also Mt. 5:34–37).

The **one fate** to which Qoheleth refers here is death: the wording is almost the same as in 2:14 (see the commentary on that verse with regard to the meaning of *miqreh*, fate). Here Qoheleth is *not* referring to injustices in this life, but to death as the great leveller.

3. The meaning of the **one fate**, repeated here from v. 2, is now made explicit: all men must **go to the dead** (the Hebrew is more dramatic here than *RSV*: literally, 'and afterwards—to the dead!'). 'Going to the dead' simply means joining the company of the dead in Sheol, where no positive thought or activity is possible (cf. v. 10).

after that: the Hebrew *'aḥ^a^râw* usually means 'after him'. Possibly the suffix is intended in a neutral sense: 'after it', referring to the life just described; though this would be unusual in view of the absence of a precise antecedent. In fact neither the grammatical explanations which have been offered nor the emendations which have been proposed are entirely satisfactory, though see Gordis *ad loc.* and GK § 135 q, r.

also . . . while they live: Galling and Lauha regard this sentence as a gloss, added in order to relieve God of any implied responsibility for human mortality by blaming it on human sinfulness: cf. Gen. 3:17–19; 6:5–8. But there is no need to deny these words to Qoheleth. As the juxtaposition of **while they live** and **after that** shows, his intention was to depict the sorry state (**This is an evil**) of human beings *both* (*RSV*, **also**) during life *and* after death.

4. This verse has been seen by some commentators as ironical. But there is a logical progression from v. 3, which implicitly raises the question: if the state of both living and dead is so wretched, what is there to choose between them? Qoheleth here replies that, despite everything, life is greatly preferable to death, precisely because of the uncertainty of the former: in life there may still be things to enjoy in the future (vv. 7–9), whereas in death all possibility of further change of fortune is impossible (vv. 5–6).

he who: better, 'whoever'. On this meaning of *mî–'ᵃšer*, see GK § 137c. **is joined:** *Kethib* has *yᵉbuḥar*, 'is chosen'; but this makes no sense. *RSV* with the Versions and virtually all modern commentaries follow the *Qere*, *yᵉḥubbar*. **hope:** this word, *biṭṭāḥôn*, occurs elsewhere in the Old Testament only in 2 Kg. 18:19 (= Isa. 36:4), where it means 'trust'. The meaning 'hope', however, is found in the Talmud.

a living dog . . . a dead lion: this is probably a popular saying quoted by Qoheleth with approval as a support for his view—although the inconsistency of its use of the article suggests that, if it is an exact quotation, the saying was of recent vintage. The **dog** was the most despised and wretched of animals according to ancient Near Eastern ideas, whereas the **lion** was then as now the 'king of beasts'. Qoheleth is saying, then, that life, however wretched, is preferable to (**better than**) death. The *lamedh* preceding *keleb*, dog, may either be the 'emphatic lamedh' (Brockelmann, §31a; Nötscher, 1953) or may mark a casus pendens: 'with regard to a living dog, it . . .' GK § 143e).

5. In vv. 5–6 Qoheleth develops and defends his assertion (v. 4) that life is preferable to death. To him the knowledge of the inevitability of death is a valuable asset which will be lost at death, because **the dead know nothing** at all. Some commentators have seen this

'defence' as bitterly ironical, on the grounds that this knowledge is more likely to cast a blight on the lives of the living than to enhance the positive quality of life; and indeed elsewhere (2:14–17; 3:19–21; 5:15–17 [MT 14–16]) Qoheleth seems to put forward very much that point of view. Yet in each of these cases (2:24–26; 3:22; 5:18–20 [MT 17–19]) he reaches quite a different conclusion: it is because of this knowledge that life should and can be enjoyed to the full. So also here (vv. 7–10). Qoheleth's argument here, then, is a serious one and not ironical.

A second disadvantage of death, according to Qoheleth, is that the dead **have no more reward**, an assertion whose meaning is made clear in the next phrase: **the memory of them is lost** (literally, 'is forgotten'). The point is emphasized with a play on words between **reward** (*śākār*) and **memory** (*zēker*). Qoheleth, who accepted the traditional valuation of the importance of the reputation left behind by a person after his death (cf. 7:1), nevertheless recognizes that the memory of this quickly fades (cf. 2:16) and can therefore offer no consolation to the dead.

6. The enumeration of **love, hate** and **envy** (or, more probably, rivalry or striving for success in life—cf. 4:4) is not intended to be a catalogue of all that is best in the human character! Qoheleth sees these rather as the strong passions which, whether admirable or not, form the mainspring of human activities. Better to participate in the stimulating ferment of life than to be dead, with no passions and no activities at all!

7–10. In both contents and context these verses resemble the positive statements made earlier in the book about what is best for man (see on v. 5 above); but they differ in form and content in that they are expressed in the imperative mood as positive recommendations from teacher to pupil and are more specific in giving details of the way in which life is to be enjoyed—details which incidentally give a clear indication of the social and economic status of the reader, and probably also of the author.

It has frequently been observed that these verses bear a close resemblance to the advice given by Siduri to Gilgamesh in connection with his search, which was to prove fruitless, for immortality (the Old Babylonian *Epic of Gilgamesh*, Tablet x, iii; English translation in *ANET*, p. 90). Other texts from Egypt, Greece and elsewhere similarly advocate the enjoyment of life in the face of the inevitability of death. It is generally agreed that a direct borrowing by Qoheleth from any of these texts is out of the question. Although the theme in general was probably known to him, Ranston's comment (1925, p. 146, quoted by Hertzberg) about the supposed relationship with *Gilgamesh* is valid for all the texts in question: Ec.

9:7–10 contains 'nothing which could not just as naturally have been written by one knowing nothing of the Babylonian poem'. Moreover, the extra-biblical texts cannot properly be used to interpret the *intention* of the passage. There is nothing in this book which lends colour to the purely hedonistic interpretation of these verses which has sometimes been put forward on the basis of some of the suggested parallels.

7. eat . . . drink: see on 2:24. **what you do:** literally, 'your deeds' (*ma'aśe(y)kā*). If this refers to *past* actions, it implies that only those whose past conduct has been acceptable to God are able to enjoy his gifts: in other words, that those gifts are a reward for virtuous conduct (cf. 2:26). However, *ma'aśeh* does not necessarily refer to the past: it can, for example, refer to *future* behaviour, as in Exod. 18:20 ('what they must do'). Here it may refer to the *present* enjoyment of life—'what you are doing (in following this advice)'. God delights in man's enjoyment of the good gifts which he has provided for him. The same idea is found in 12:1.

has . . . approved: the verb *rāṣāh* and the cognate noun *rāṣôn* have the connotation of 'delight' regularly in Proverbs. **already**: this may mean that the enjoyment of God's gifts is something which God has decreed from the beginning (cf. 5:18 [MT 17], 'for this is his lot').

8. Both the wearing of **white** clothing and the anointing of the **head** with fragrant **oil** were signs of joy and were practised on festive occasions. The former, which may have been adopted relatively late among the Jews, is attested elsewhere in the Old Testament only in Est. 8:15 (blue and white combined); for other references to its practice by Jews, see Brenner, 1982, pp. 90–1, and p. 244, note 10. For the latter, compare among other passages Ps. 23:5; 45:7 [MT 8]; 104:15; Prov. 27:9. Qoheleth here recommends the wearing of white **always:** that is, the enjoyment of life whenever possible.

9. Enjoy life: literally, 'see life'. But *rā'āh*, 'see' is sometimes used in the sense of 'experience'—e.g. 'see famine' (Jer. 5:12), 'see good' (Job 7:7); and, in this book, 'see sleep' (8:16). In 2:1 *rā'āh beṭôb* appears to mean 'enjoy yourself'. *RSV*'s rendering is probably correct.

the wife whom you love: the word *'iššāh* does not necessarily refer to a wife (it has no article here), but is also the regular word for 'woman'. Qoheleth nowhere else refers to marriage, and there is no way of telling whether he is here referring specifically to married life. It is perhaps significant that neither here nor anywhere else does he refer to children, despite the great importance attached generally by the Jews to the joys of family life and to the father-son relationship. Some commentators have seen irony here, arguing partly on the basis of Qoheleth's supposed low opinion of women (7:26–28) that he is subtly suggesting that living with a woman is hardly a pleasure: it is one of the things which make up a man's **vain** (or frustrating) **life**. In fact this latter phrase (*ḥayyê hebel*) may refer to the brevity of life rather than to its futility (see on 1:2 and compare 6:12). Moreover, as has been noted above, the meaning of the references to woman in 7:26–28 is not clear; they do not necessarily express disparagement.

The remainder of the verse does not add to what Qoheleth says in the similar passages which have been discussed above, especially 3:22; 5:18 [MT 17]; 8:15.

10. Whatever . . . your might: the accentuation in MT divides the words somewhat differently: 'Whatever your hand finds to do in your might, do'—that is, 'do whatever lies within your strength'. *RSV* here follows the Versions, a few Hebrew MSS and a number of modern commentaries in giving what seems to be a more natural rendering. **Whatever your hand finds:** whatever occasion presents itself (cf. Jg. 9:33; 1 Sam. 10:7). Qoheleth is not here recommending the pursuit of sensual pleasures alone, but also all useful and intellectual activity, as the series of nouns which follows (**work . . . wisdom**) makes clear. This recommendation is fully in line with the positive attitude to life found throughout the Old Testament. It is, however, characteristic of Qoheleth that three of the four words which he chooses to sum up the pleasurable aspects of life which will cease after death refer to intellectual activity, in spite of his comments elsewhere on its relative and limited value. *ḥešbôn* here probably means 'inductive thought' (see on 7:27).

Sheol: Qoheleth uses the traditional term for the abode of the dead. His negative portrayal of it corresponds to what is said about it elsewhere in the Old Testament, especially in Isa. 14:9–11; Ezek. 32:18–32.

TIME AND CHANCE

9:11–12

This appears to be an independent piece (on the first words, **Again I saw**, see above on 9:1–10; on the use of the infinite absolute see GK § 113z). The theme is one which occurs frequently in the book but especially in 3:1–11, and is succinctly expressed here in the words **man does not know his time**. Although God is not specifically mentioned, other passages in the book make it clear that Qoheleth means that it is he who has determined the 'proper time' for everything that happens, but has concealed this knowledge from men, who are thus **snared** when the unforeseen occurs.

11. As Zimmerli remarks, Qoheleth here as elsewhere does not intend to assert that the principle of cause and effect *never* operates (cf. 8:14). This is clear from some of the illustrations which he employs, for in fact races *are* usually won by the swiftest and battles by the strongest. The point which he is making is that there is always the possibility—of which he himself has noted examples—that this may not happen, because ultimately everything is determined by **time and chance**. This expression (*'ēt wāpega'*) is probably a hendiadys, expressing a single idea. On what Qoheleth means by *'ēt* see on 3:1, 16–22; 8:6. *pega'*, like *miqreh* (see on 2:14) does not mean 'chance' in an impersonal sense, but simply what happens. What will happen, and when it will happen, are beyond human ability to foresee.

bread (i.e. a good livelihood) **to the wise:** this is an interesting sidelight on the status of the 'wise man' in Qoheleth's time. **intelligent:** again an interesting sidelight on the financiers and entrepreneurs of the time, who could make large fortunes simply by using their brains. **favor** (*ḥēn*): this may refer not to recognition of skill but to the attractiveness of the product (see Willi-Plein, 1973, pp. 92–3). **men of skill** (*yōdᵉ'îm*) are, literally, those who know (how to do or make something). So eminence in whatever sphere of activity is no guarantee of success. It is improbable that it was Qoheleth's intention here to single out the inadequacy of wisdom as some commentators have supposed. 9:13 begins a quite separate section of the book.

12. For (*kî gam*): elsewhere in the book (8:12) this expression has an adversative sense: 'yet', 'even though'. Here, however, the general sense of the passage requires the meaning 'for also', introducing an additional reason for man's predicament: he does not know *when* in his case the normal operation of cause and effect will be suspended. The **evil time** is thus probably not death, but unexpected misfortune. The analogies of the netted **fish** and snared **birds** emphasize the fact that men, for all their superior abilities, are as helpless as the rest of creation.

are snared (*yûqāšîm*): this may be an unusual form of the Pual participle (see GK § 52s); or the initial *mēm* which normally forms part of that participle may have been lost by haplography or through wrong word-division.

THE LIMITED VALUE OF WISDOM

9:13–18

These verses begin a section of the book—9:13–10:20, or 9:13–11:6—on which there is a very wide difference of opinion about how it should be divided. The little parable of 9:13–16 is followed by a series of sayings mainly in poetical form reminiscent of material in the Book of Proverbs. They are loosely strung together (though see Ogden, 1980, pp. 27–37); but the predominating theme is that of the value, absolute or relative, of wisdom. Without pronouncing judgement on the question of their literary unity, it seems best to look for small-scale inner coherences and to divide the material in accordance with these.

The parable in 9:13–16 is complete in itself; but the two sayings in vv. 17 and 18 are closely connected with it in theme; and in view of Qoheleth's habit of using such short sayings to emphasize his points, they will be treated here as integral with it.

13–16. Despite various attempts to find here a reference to a particular historical event, it is now generally agreed that this is not what Qoheleth had in mind: this is an example of wisdom teaching in narrative form (see on 4:13–16). With regard to the details of the story, it is not certain that **delivered the city** in v. 15 is a correct translation. Many recent commentators, including Hertzberg, Galling and Loader, are of the opinion that the Hebrew phrase means '*could have* delivered the city'—that is, the poor wise man would have been able to do so by the exercise of his wisdom, but did not in fact do so because no one thought of him (on the phrase, and on **remembered**, see below, on v. 15).

13. this example of wisdom: the word **example** has no equivalent in the Hebrew, which has simply 'This also I have seen—wisdom'. This may be a case of apposition, a construction rather loosely used in Hebrew: see GK §131, especially paragraphs a, k, l. *BHS* proposes the deletion of **wisdom**, without giving a reason; this would make sense, but is unnecessary.

great: that is, important or significant, referring to what Qoheleth has 'seen'; for this meaning of *gādôl*, see Exod. 18:22; Dt. 4:32; 1 Sam. 12:16, and similar passages. Some commentators take the word as qualifying **wisdom** and interpret it as ironical: the story illustrates how *un*important or ineffectual wisdom actually is. But this is unnecessarily speculative.

14. siegeworks (*m*ᵉ*ṣôdîm*): in 7:26 this word clearly means 'nets'; and similarly in 9:12 the singular noun *m*ᵉ*ṣôdāh* means 'net'. There is, however, a word *m*ᵉ*ṣûdāh*, meaning a fortified place or stronghold, and it is possible that this meaning could have been extended to cover earthworks thrown up round a city by its besiegers. Two MSS read *m^e^ṣûrîm*, derived from *ṣûr*, 'besiege'; but this form is not precisely attested elsewhere (Gordis).

15. And there was found (*ûmāṣā'*): literally, 'and (someone) found'. On this indefinite construction, see GK § 144d. **poor:** on this word (*miskēn*), see on 4:13.

and he delivered (*ûmillaṭ-hû'*): grammatically there is no objection to this translation. The use of the simple *waw* with the perfect to refer to past time is frequent in late Hebrew, and a normal feature of Qoheleth's style. It has, however, been argued that 'he could/would have delivered' is an equally possible translation (see Gordis and Hertzberg for opposite views on this point), and one which is demanded by the next verse: if the poor man's wisdom was **despised** and **his words . . . not heeded**, presumably he had no opportunity to save the city. In that case *zākar* (**remembered**) must mean 'called to mind', 'thought of' (for this meaning see *TDOT* IV, pp. 64–82; Childs, 1962, pp. 17–30).

It was a commonplace of the wisdom tradition that the **poor** in general were treated with contempt (e.g. Prov. 14:20; 18:23; 19:7); and Ben Sira (Sir. 13:22–23) specifically refers to the fact that no one listens to their opinions. But this is not Qoheleth's main point here. He is primarily concerned to point out, as elsewhere, the limitations of the achievements of wisdom: *either*—if the poor wise man *did* save the city—it receives no proper reward, *or*—if he *could* have saved it but was not allowed to—it is ineffective because it is not put to use.

It is not stated *how* the poor wise man could have saved the city. But—although for Qoheleth it also had a more abstract connotation—wisdom was regarded as essentially a *practical* attribute which was essential to all human enterprises including politics and even military operations: 'A wise man scales the city of the mighty and brings down the stronghold in which they trust' (Prov. 21:22). It is assumed here that the poor wise man—perhaps like Archimedes with his machine which destroyed the Roman ships, or by some other subtle strategy—would have been able to devise a scheme which would have outwitted the besiegers of the little city.

16. But I say: Qoheleth now formally draws his personal conclusion. In fact he says nothing new here, but the verse is a characteristic example of his technique of the 'broken aphorism'. First, he quotes what was presumably a well-known three-word saying: **wisdom is better than strength**—that is, more effective (in principle) than physical force. This is a saying of very wide application, similar to 'brains are better than brawn'. He does not disagree with it (cf. 7:19). And yet (this may be the meaning of *w*[e]—*RSV*, **though**), the story which has just been told shows that wisdom will go for nothing, if (it is implied that this is often the case) it does not succeed in making its voice heard.

17. This verse, which is a quotation of an older saying (see Whybray, 1981, pp. 443, 449) is connected with v. 16 both by its theme and by the repetition of the word *nišmā'îm* (*RSV*, **heard**; v. 16, **heeded**). It belongs to the type of the so-called 'Better-saying' of which there are many examples in Proverbs and in this book (e.g. vv. 16, 18); but the words **are better** (normally *ṭôbîm*) are lacking in the Hebrew. *RSV*, following many commentators, assumes that this is an example of a comparative statement in which the relationship between the things compared is to be assumed from the context, as in 5:1 [MT 4:17] (GK § 133e). But here this explanation is unnecessary and improbable. As Kroeber and Lauha have pointed out, *nišmā'im* may mean not **heard** but 'are (more) worth hearing': cf. the corresponding use of the Niphal participle *neḥmād*, 'desirable', in Gen. 3:6, and see GK § 116e. If this is so the phrase should be translated: 'Wise men's words (spoken) in calm are worth hearing rather than . . .'. This avoids the otherwise curious emphasis on the *hearing* of their words rather than on their being *spoken*.

the shouting of a ruler among fools: Gordis's 'the ranting of the king of fools' may be a truer interpretation.

18. Each half of this verse is probably a quotation of an originally separate older saying, though the language employed (the late words *q*[e]*rāb*, **war**, and *harbēh*, **much**) is identical with that of Qoheleth himself. Each makes a complete statement. The first part recalls v. 16*a* and is an unqualified appreciation of the superior power of wisdom over brute force. The second was originally not necessarily concerned with wisdom at all. It states an obvious truth of a very general kind. In its present position, however, it picks up and repeats the word *ṭôbāh* (*RSV*, **better**, **good**) from the first half. Its present function is thus to qualify, though not to contradict, the first saying. Once again, wisdom is characterized as powerful and yet liable to be rendered ineffective by external accidents: **one sinner** can destroy its achievements. The meaning of the word *ḥôṭe'* (**sinner**) here is disputed. Elsewhere in the book (2:26; 7:20, 26; 8:12; 9:2) it is certainly or probably used in its moral or religious sense, which may well have been its original meaning here; but in its present context, in which it is contrasted with wisdom, it probably means one who misses, or is lacking: in this case, lacking in sense (for this meaning, cf. Prov. 8:36).

MISCELLANEOUS SAYINGS

10:1–11:6

This section consists of short apparently independent pieces, of which the majority are similar in form to the sayings in the Book of Proverbs (cf. 7:1–14). Although some of them appear to have been arranged roughly according to theme, it is not possible, despite various attempts which have been made, to find any overall structure in the section as a whole. Some of the sayings are probably quotations, though Qoheleth's ability to compose his own aphorisms in traditional style should be borne in mind. He appears here as a wisdom teacher. Some of the sayings would occasion no surprise if they occurred in the Book of Proverbs. In others, Qoheleth's characteristically critical attitude towards conventional wisdom shows itself clearly.

1. At first sight this verse seems to make the same point as the immediately preceding 9:18*b*, and some commentators consider it to be the concluding verse of the previous section. But it may be taken in a somewhat different sense: as referring not to the frustration of wisdom by *outside* forces, but—especially if vv. 2–3 are connected with it—to the corruption which takes place *within* a person's **heart** (*lēb*, v. 2) when he gives way, even for a moment, to **a little folly**.

Unfortunately this verse, which puzzled the early translators, has almost certainly suffered some textual corruption; it also contains some grammatical irregularities. Nevertheless the general sense is fairly clear. **Dead flies:** literally, 'flies of death'. This unusual expression might also mean 'poisonous (lethal) flies' or 'dying flies'; but *RSV*'s translation is equally possible and makes better sense. The oil or **ointment** (*šemen*) goes bad because of the dead flies which have fallen into it. **give off an evil odour:** the verb is singular although the subject is plural. It is followed by another singular verb *yabbîa'*, possibly meaning 'ferments', which is not represented in *RSV*. This may be a gloss, as also may be **and honor** (*mikkābôd*). **outweighs** (*yāqār*) is a masculine adjective although it qualifies a feminine noun (though see GK § 145or). This is a most unusual meaning of the word, which usually means 'precious', though it may have a somewhat similar sense in Ps. 116:15—'costly', and so 'grievous' (Gordis).

2–3. These two verses are closely connected (for a possible connection with v. 1, see above). Verse 2 is a quotation of an earlier saying which in form, language and thought is identical with sayings in the Book of Proverbs (see Whybray, 1981, pp. 444, 445–6). Verse

3 is a comment on it by Qoheleth, who picks up and elaborates the second half.

2. inclines him: there is no verb here in the Hebrew but simply 'to his right (hand)' and 'to his left (hand)'. There are no other examples in the Old Testament of precisely this figure, but the two sides, **right** and **left**, were generally regarded in antiquity as indicating good and bad fortune respectively (cf. the English word 'sinister'). The thought is similar to that of 2:14*a*, and the contrast between the fates of the **wise man** and the **fool** is a commonplace of the Book of Proverbs. The **heart** was the seat of the intelligence and the will in Hebrew thought.

3. when the fool: *Kethib* has the article here; *Qere* lacks it. There is no difference in meaning. **walks on the road:** this is probably to be taken literally in the sense of 'goes out and about', though it may have been the metaphorical **right** and **left** of v. 2 which suggested the example of walking. **lacks sense:** literally, 'his heart (that is, his intelligence) is lacking'—a phrase typical of the wisdom literature. **that he is a fool:** *RSV* is ambiguous; but the Hebrew is equally so. The phrase means either that the fool calls **every one** else a fool, or that by his words and actions he proclaims (**says**) that he himself is a fool (cf. Prov. 13:16). In either case Qoheleth is stressing that folly is incurable: it is due to an innate mental handicap which makes the fool incapable of sensible behaviour in any circumstances. So he inevitably 'walks to the left' and comes to a bad end. The word used for 'fool' here (*sākāl*) is virtually peculiar to Qoheleth and never occurs in Proverbs.

4. Qoheleth here reverts to the admonition form in which direct advice is given by a teacher to his pupil. But as in 8:2–5 he is perhaps not envisaging an actual situation which might confront his readers (see on 8:2). Rather he may be citing—though in his own words—a common theme of the wisdom literature in order to illustrate the point which he wishes to make in the second half of the verse.

deference: *marpē'* generally elsewhere means 'healing' (from *rāpā'*, 'heal'). The verb is used metaphorically in Jg. 8:3 of the abatement of anger. The meaning could thus be similar to that of Prov. 16:14: a wise man will appease (though a different verb is used) the king's anger, that is, show deference or submission to him (cf. also 8:2–5). But some commentators believe that the word is derived (by a confusion of spelling) not from *rāpā'* but from *rāpāh*, to sink or relax, and thus denotes calmness or composure, an attitude frequently advocated in the wisdom literature. This may be its meaning in Prov. 14:30 (*RSV*, 'tranquil'); 15:4 (*RSV*, 'gentle').

5–6. These verses form a single unit, probably together with v. 7.

It has also been argued that they are a continuation of v. 4: Qoheleth is thought to be qualifying the statement in v. 4*b*, pointing out that in fact rulers do not always overlook the faults of their ministers or advisers, but sometimes depose them and appoint less fit persons to succeed them. But this connection is improbable, especially in view of the fact that the word **ruler** here (*šallîṭ*) is different from that used in v. 4 (*môšēl*), although both verses are clearly the work of Qoheleth himself.

5. as it were an error: or, perhaps better, 'entirely an error'—see GK § 118x. The word may be intended ironically. **proceeding** (*yōṣā'*): the Qal participle feminine of the Lamedh Aleph verb *yāṣā'* has here been written as though it was a Lamedh He. This confusion between two similar types of verb is not uncommon: see GK § 75 o o.

6. folly (*hassekel*): that is, fools in general. The abstract stands for the concrete. It is not necessary to repoint the word as *hassākāl*, 'the fool'. **many:** Gordis takes *rabbîm* as meaning 'great', and translates the phrase by 'the great heights'. The reference is certainly to high rank or office; but 'great' is as strange as 'many' in the context. Possibly the word should be taken with the second half of the verse which it immediately precedes: 'the great ones and the rich . . .', although this would involve the moving of the accent in MT. Whitley's suggestion (pp. 85–6, following Dahood) that the word means 'the aged' is less probable.

The theme is a familiar one in ancient Near Eastern literature, where such an unaccustomed reversal of roles was regarded as a sign of the collapse of society (cf. especially *The Admonitions of Ipu-Wer*, *ANET*, pp. 441–4; and, in the Old Testament, Prov. 19:10; 30:21–23).

7. I have seen: Qoheleth confirms the general statement of v. 6 with his personal observation. **princes:** this word (*śārîm*) can denote any highly placed person or leader, but here—as often elsewhere in the Old Testament—it means a highly placed but nevertheless subordinate official (cf. its use in vv. 16, 17). **walking on foot:** literally, 'walking on the ground'. Some commentators have expressed surprise that the verse does not conclude with a comment that all this is 'vanity'; but these comments are in fact used sporadically rather than systematically throughout the book.

8–11. These sayings have in common the fact that they are all concerned with pitfalls and frustrations which may beset various activities of everyday life, though they do not all make the same point. Verses 8–9 are connected both by their theme, and also by their form: they each begin with a participle. Verses 10–11 also have the same form: a conditional sentence beginning with 'if'. But there is also a thematic correspondence between verse 9*b* and 10. These links do not, however, necessarily indicate an original literary unity.

8. This saying has nothing to do with those passages in the Old Testament (Ps. 7:15 [MT 16]; 9:15 [MT 16]; possibly Prov. 26:27) which speak of the wicked or malicious who themselves fall into pits which they have dug to encompass the destruction of others. No idea of retribution is entertained here. Qoheleth is speaking of the agricultural worker who *may* (not **will**: on this use of the imperfect, see GK § 107r) have an unforeseen accident at work. The point of the saying may be simply that one should take care over one's work (cf. the comment in v. 10 about the importance of the exercise of 'wisdom'), or—more characteristic of Qoheleth—that no one can be certain of what will happen to him at any time (cf. vv. 6–7).

9. The situations envisaged in this verse are similar to those in v. 8, though with the addition of the notion—perhaps already partly present in v. 8—that the worker may be (*RSV*, **is**; see above) hurt or endangered by the very material with which he is working. It would be possible to see the verse in terms of 'poetic justice'—the idea frequently found in the Old and New Testaments and elsewhere in antiquity that evildoers are punished in strict accordance with their deeds; but in this context it is very unlikely that this is what Qoheleth had in mind.

is hurt: in the Old Testament this verb (*'ṣb*) refers to mental distress rather than to physical injury; but the cognate noun *'eṣeb* appears to mean physical pain in Gen. 3:16, and a somewhat similar meaning is attested in later Hebrew. **is endangered:** this verb *skn*, here in the Niphal, occurs only here in the Old Testament, but again this meaning is attested in late Hebrew. The suggestion that this is the same verb as another, better attested, *skn*, 'to be useful, to benefit', but in the derived sense of 'have to be careful' (*KBL* p. 658), is improbable.

10. This verse has been described as linguistically the most difficult in the book, and both ancient and modern translations have rendered it very differently. However, the general meaning of the first part (to **more strength**) is reasonably clear, although there are some textual and linguistic problems here. The last part (from **but wisdom**) has been described as 'untranslatable', and its meaning is conjectural.

iron: here meaning an axe (cf. 2 Kg. 6:5). **one:** this would be a unique meaning for *hû'*: the other supposed examples cited by Gordis (Job 8:16; 13:28) are best explained in other ways. The normal meaning 'he', which would refer back to the woodcutter of v. 9*b*, is unlikely as this is clearly a separate saying. The word could, however, refer to the axe: '*it* has not been sharpened'. But this would necessitate a passive meaning for the verb **whet** (this would simply require a repointing of the consonants), and some emendation of *pānîm* (**edge**). *NEB*, by repointing the verb and emending *pānîm* to *lᵉpānîm*, 'beforehand', translates: 'and has not first been sharpened'. This is partly supported by Vulg. and is perhaps the best solution to the problem. The meaning of 'edge' for *pānîm* (a plural form) is, however, not impossible: it appears to have that meaning in Ezek. 21:16 [MT 21]. **he must put forth more strength:** compare a similar phrase in Job 21:7.

but wisdom helps one to succeed: this sentence consists of three words. The meanings of the first, *(wᵉ)yitrôn*, 'advantage', and the third, *ḥokmāh*, 'wisdom', are not in doubt. It is the second word, *hakšêr*, which causes difficulty and puts in doubt the meaning of the whole. Its form is that of the Hiphil infinitive construct (see GK § 53k) of *kāšar*. In the Old Testament it would normally mean 'to cause to succeed, give an advantage'; but in late Hebrew it can mean 'to make fit or to prepare'. The sentence has been variously interpreted. Among these interpretations are that represented in *RSV* and, alternatively, 'It is an advantage to prepare one's skill in advance' (Gordis). But the syntax is very strange; and some commentators (Hertzberg, Galling) emend *wᵉyitrôn hakšêr* to *hᵃkišrôn wᵉyitrôn* and take it as a question implying a negative: 'Is there a profit or advantage in wisdom?' This emendation, however, has no support in the MSS or the Versions. In the absence of certainty, *RSV*'s translation seems as probable as any. The meaning may be that 'wisdom', or skill, is necessary to any successful undertaking (cf. v. 11).

The clause **he must put forth more strength** begins with the copula *wᵉ* (here *wa*). This is to be understood not as meaning 'and' or 'but' but as the apodosis of a conditional sentence, i.e. 'then' (see Brockelmann, § 166).

11. This saying is quite straightforward: it illustrates the truth that success in any undertaking depends on skill or competence ('wisdom'). Snake-charming was evidently a common occupation (cf. Jer. 8:17; Ps. 58:4–5[MT 5–6]; Sir. 12:13). **advantage** (*yitrôn*): if it is meant that it is the snake-charmer who is bitten, this is a humorous understatement, as the bite was likely to be fatal. **charmer:** literally, 'master (or controller) of the tongue'. This could mean the snake's tongue, thought to be the source of its venom (Job 20:16; Ps. 140:3 [MT 4]), or that of the charmer, whose power over the snake lay in the use of his voice (cf. Ps. 58:4–5[MT 5–6]). *wᵉʾên* (**there is no**): the *waw* here, as in v. 10, introduces the apodosis.

12–15. These verses comprise three sayings (12–13, 14, 15) about the wise and foolish use of speech. Each expresses the teaching of conventional wisdom, though it is characteristic of Qoheleth that in their arrangement the emphasis is placed on folly rather than wisdom, which is only referred to once at the beginning of the series (see Whybray, 1981, pp. 446–7).

12. win him favor: literally, '(are) *ḥēn*'. This word signifies that which attracts others or impresses them favourably: cf. Prov. 28:23, and see on 9:11 above. The theme of the verse is a frequent one in the wisdom literature: see, e.g., Prov. 10:13; 12:18; 14:3. **consume:** literally, 'swallow up'—that is, the fool's utterances ruin his reputation or his career: cf. Prov. 18:7.

13. This appears to be Qoheleth's own comment on the older saying which he has quoted in v. 12 (see Whybray, 1981, pp. 444, 446). It is presumably intended in some way to expand or elucidate the older saying, but its precise meaning is not clear. It has been suggested that the word-pair **beginning—end** is an example of merismus (see on 9:1), meaning that the *whole* of the fool's talk 'from beginning to end' is foolish or mad (Loader). But this view does not take account of the evident difference between **foolishness** (*kislût*) and **madness** (*hôlēlût*). Although the two are linked in 2:12 they are probably not intended to be synonymous; and in any case the addition of the adjective *rā'āh* (*RSV*, **wicked**) qualifying madness shows that Qoheleth is speaking of a *progression* in the state of the foolish talker. *ra'*, however, does not necessarily mean 'wicked'; it can equally mean 'disagreeable', 'harmful' or (of a physical or mental state) 'serious'. If this is a comment on v. 12, its most probable meaning is that the progressive insanity observable in the fool's babbling is injurious to himself (rather than to others).

14. The connection between the first part (to **words**) and the rest of this verse is not clear (**though** is not represented in the Hebrew). The first part strongly resembles part of a typical wisdom saying of the kind found in Proverbs, of which the second half is missing. The theme of the folly of speaking too much is a frequent one in the wisdom literature, but also occurs in this book (5:2–3, 7 [MT 1–2, 6]; 6:11). The second part of the verse (from **and who can tell**) is strikingly similar to 6:12; 7:14 and 8:7, and is entirely in Qoheleth's own style. Although a kind of logic can be made out for the two parts together—e.g., it is characteristic of a fool to think that by endless talk he will be able to solve the hidden mysteries of life—it is a very doubtful connection, probably the work of a glossator attempting to throw light on a truncated saying by a near-quotation of one of Qoheleth's own aphorisms.

what is to be; what will be: the Versions and a few MSS read 'what has been' in place of the first of these phrases. This avoids the apparently meaningless repetition of a reference to the future. But MT is almost certainly correct. **what is to be** refers to future events in this life, while **what will be after him** refers to the future after this life, as in 3:22.

15. The first half of this verse (to **wearies him**) contains two grammatical peculiarities which have led to suggestions for emending the text; but this is unnecessary. **toil** (*'āmāl*) is here construed with a feminine verb although elsewhere it is always masculine; but such exceptions sometimes occur with other nouns. **fool** is plural in the Hebrew, but the verbal suffix (**him**) is singular; however, this phenomenon, the so-called distributive singular used of a class or group, is attested elsewhere in the Old Testament (see GK § 145m).

so that: the particle *'ašer* is here best taken as a relative—'(him) who' (GK § 138e). The fool's efforts are bound to come to nothing: he remains as before one who cannot even find his way home. The second half of the verse is probably a popular saying about people who 'do not know enough to come in out of the rain' (Gordis).

16–17. Woe to . . .; Happy are . . .: the former of these modes of speech—the spelling is slightly different from that of classical Hebrew—was used earlier in prophetic denunciations (on its original function, see Wanke, 1966). The latter expression occurs several times in Proverbs: see Westermann (1974).

16. a child: this word (*na'ar*) covers a wide age-range. Here it refers to a king who is too young to control his ministers (*śārîm*, **princes**). Alternatively it could mean 'slave' (which would provide a better contrast with **free men**); but see below.

to feast in the morning was regarded both in Israel and in antiquity generally as a sign of dissoluteness and, in the case of persons of responsibility, of neglect of duty (cf. Isa. 5:11–12, 22–23).

17. the son of free men: or, of men of high rank. The term *ḥôrîm* has the latter meaning in the later books of the Old Testament, especially in Nehemiah (e.g. 2:16; 5:6; 6:17). Although this phrase does not appear to make the expected contrast with **child** in the first half of the verse, the point may be that a king who comes from the higher ranks of society—as some in the Hellenistic period did not: cf. 4:14—could control his ministers by setting a good example; but a child-king, whatever his origins, could not. The saying no doubt reflects the times in which Qoheleth lived, although it is not possible to identify the particular situations—if any—to which he was referring.

for strength and not for drunkenness: the parallelism is spoiled by the addition of this final sentence, which may be a gloss. **for strength:** for physical nourishment. Other interpretations such as 'as men' (that is, in a manly fashion) or 'in moderation, with self-control' are not well founded. **for drunkenness:** or, 'for the sake of drinking'. This word (*šᵉtî*) from *šātāh* 'to drink', occurs only here, but the cognate form *šᵉtiyyāh*, 'drinking', is found in Est. 1:8.

18. This verse has many parallels with sayings in the Book of Proverbs both in form and theme, but consists almost entirely of rare or unique words which betray a late date of composition. There is no reason to deny its authorship to Qoheleth, though it could be a quotation. The general theme is very common in Proverbs (e.g. 6:6–11; 12:11; 28:19), though it is not expressed elsewhere in terms of neglected repairs to a house.

sloth: the dual form *ʿᵃṣaltayim* is strange. Some commentators and BDB think it to be a 'dual of intensity', of which the proper name Cushan-rishathaim, supposedly 'Cushan of double wickedness' (Jg. 3:8, 10) may be another example. But there are alternative explanations: see GK § 88b and Whitley, p. 89. **indolence:** literally, 'lowering of hands'. The word *šiplût* occurs only here, but its meaning is not in doubt. Cf. the 'slack hand' of Prov. 10:4. **leaks:** the verb *dālap* is rare, but appears to refer to the dropping of tears in Job 16:20. In Prov. 19:13; 27:15 the noun *delep* means the dripping of rain.

Some commentators connect this verse with vv. 16–17, seeing it as a comment on the effect of inattention to public duty.

19. This saying is not about **bread** and **wine** as such but about dinner-parties. *RSV*'s **Bread is made** misses the point. The Hebrew means 'one (literally, 'they') prepares a meal' (cf. Ezek. 4:15). **laughter** (*śᵉḥōq*) here probably has the wider meaning of pleasure or enjoyment (as apparently in 3:4). The key word of the verse, however, is **money** (written with the article, probably to emphasize its importance), which **answers everything**. This probably means that it *provides* everything: it is the *sine qua non* for the enjoyment of life (*NEB*, 'money is behind everything'). This precise meaning of *ʿānāh*, normally 'to answer', is not found elsewhere, but is probably an extension of the notion of answering a request or demand (cf. Isa. 30:19; Ps. 118:5).

The saying, like many in the Book of Proverbs, makes a statement without explicitly drawing a moral. Galling and Lauha suggest that it may be a quotation from a drinking song. If so, it would reflect the prevailing mood of the times, in which money was all-important and something to be openly flaunted and boasted about. On the other hand, it may be a cynical comment of Qoheleth, who elsewhere appears to despise 'laughter' (2:2; 7:3, 6) and warns his readers against thinking that wealth can provide happiness (4:7–8; 5:10–17 [MT 9–16]). Yet on the other hand he recommends the enjoyment of the 'good life', and specifically eating and drinking (2:24; 3:12–13; 5:18–20 [MT 17–19]; 8:15; 9:7–9). It is this ambivalence which makes it difficult to know what lesson, if any, he wished to teach in this verse. The suggestion that the verse is intended to be a comment on vv. 16–17 is improbable.

20. The advice given in this verse corresponds to Qoheleth's warning about the sovereign power of kings in 8:2–4. To speak ill of **the king** (see on 8:2) is dangerous because 'walls have ears'. The notion that birds picked up secrets and spread them abroad was a frequent motif in antiquity; but Qoheleth is here almost certainly referring to spies or informers. The person who kept domestic slaves (cf. 7:21) was not safe from eavesdropping even in his **bedchamber**.

in your thought: this late and rare word (*maddāʿ*), derived from *yādaʿ*, 'to know', elsewhere means 'knowledge'. While it is possible that here it may have the extended meaning of 'thought' or 'mind', this is purely conjectural. It is also difficult to understand how an unspoken thought can be overheard. Various interpretations and emendations have been suggested (see Whitley, pp. 90–1). Possibly the most plausible of these is the proposal to emend *bᵉmaddāʿᵃkā* to *bᵉmaṣṣāʿᵃkā*, 'in your bed'. This gives a good parallel to **in your bedchamber**; but *maṣṣāʿ* is a very rare word which is found only once (Isa. 28:20). The problem remains unsolved.

the rich: this seems at first sight to be rather an anticlimax; but, as v. 19 points out, money is power. **will carry:** better, '*may* carry'. **some winged creature:** literally, 'a possessor of wings', i.e. a bird. A similar expression occurs in Prov. 1:17. The poetical form of the verse required a parallel phrase to **a bird of the air**.

11:1–2. It is generally agreed that these two verses, both of which are in the imperative form in which Qoheleth gives advice to his readers, belong together. Grammatically and linguistically they present few problems. Yet they have been interpreted in quite different ways. Traditionally, they were taken metaphorically as a recommendation to almsgiving: those who distribute their wealth widely to the needy may find unexpected help when they themselves are in need. Hertzberg and Galling correctly recognize that the final line of v. 2 (**for you know not what evil may happen on earth**) is the key to the passage. They interpret it as meaning that since the future is hidden even the most senseless actions may turn out well, and equally the most prudent ones may lead to disaster (taking *kî*, **for**, in v. 2 as meaning 'yet' or 'however'). Other modern commentators (e.g. Gordis, Zimmerli) understand the passage literally rather than metaphorically, as straightforward advice to merchants. So also *NEB*: 'Send your grain across the seas, and in time you will get a return. Divide your merchandise among seven ventures, eight maybe, since you do not know what disasters may occur on earth' (margin: 'on land'). It should be noted in support of this translation that *leḥem* (v. 1; *RSV*, **bread**) also means grain (or corn): e.g. Prov. 28:3 ('food'); Isa. 28:28 ('bread grain'); 30:23 ('grain'). Whether **find it** can mean 'make a profit' is more doubtful, although there is some evidence that the verb *māṣā'* can mean 'acquire wealth' (Hos. 12:8 [MT 9]; Job 31:25). This is the most probable meaning of the passage: Qoheleth advises his readers to take the risk involved in sea-trade (v. 1), but also to spread the risk by sending the goods in separate consignments (v. 2). As elsewhere (e.g. 9:10) he takes the uncertainty of life as a reason not for apathy or despair but for making the most of whatever opportunities present themselves.

seven, or even to eight: on this mode of speech, found frequently in the Old Testament (e.g. Prov. 30:15–31; Am. 1–2) and in ancient Near Eastern literature, see Roth, 1965.

3–6. This series of sayings may be related to the foregoing. The repeated refrain **you do not know** (vv. 2, 5 [twice], 6, with slight variations in the grammatical form) stresses man's ignorance and so helplessness (with regard to the future, the workings of natural forces, and the mystery of human birth). The fact that the imperative form of v. 1 is repeated in v. 6 may also indicate a deliberate arrangement.

3. The first of these two sayings points to the *inevitability* of the natural process which produces rain; the second to the apparent *randomness* of nature: whether (*RSV*, **if**) **a tree** uprooted by natural causes will fall in one direction or another is unpredictable. In neither case, it is implied, can man control what happens.

there it will lie: the Hebrew has either 'there it will be' or 'there it (is)'. The anomalous form *yᵉhû'* has been variously explained as a mistake for *hû'*, 'it' (a reading found in four MSS), as a shortened form of the imperfect of *hāwāh* (a variant of *hāyāh* 'to be', also found in 2:22) with an additional aleph (see GK § 23i:, 75s) or of the Aramaic verb *hᵃwā'*, or as a conflation of two readings, *hû'* and *yihyeh*, ('(it) will be'). The meaning is unaffected.

4. By itself this saying could mean either that because both wind and rain are unpredictable, farming is yet another example of futility, or that it is best to get on with one's sowing and harvesting without worrying too much about ideal weather conditions. If vv. 3–6 (or 1–6) form a connected series of sayings, v. 6 suggests that the latter interpretation is correct.

5. A further specific example (or, alternatively, two examples—see below) of human ignorance is now followed by a comprehensive statement on that subject similar to those of 3:11; 8:17. Modern commentators are divided on the question whether the first part of the verse (to **woman with child**) comprises a single example or two. MT seems to imply the latter: it reads, literally, 'As you do not know the way of the wind (*hārûaḥ*), like the bones (*ka'aṣāmîm*) in the womb . . .', presumably meaning the *formation* of the bones in the womb. In other words, man is *as* ignorant of the process of the development of the embryo in the womb as he is of the causes of changes in the wind (so Barton, Hertzberg, Zimmerli, Lauha, Lohfink). However, other commentators (Gordis, Kroeber) and modern translations (*RSV*, *NEB*) follow the reading of a large number of MSS (cf. Targ.) which have *ba'aṣāmîm*, 'into the bones', that is, into the embryo. According to this reading, Qoheleth is giving only one example: that of man's ignorance of the mystery of the life-breath which animates the new-born child (another meaning of *rûaḥ*). Syntactically the second of these interpretations presents fewer difficulties than the first. Moreover, there is an analogy for the association between *rûaḥ* (breath) and bones in Ezek. 37:1–10. The fact that *rûaḥ* is used in a different sense in v. 4 is not an impediment to this interpretation, especially if v. 4 is a quotation of an originally separate saying.

woman with child: the word *melē'āh*, literally, 'full', is used of a pregnant woman only here in the Old Testament, but it occurs once in the Mishnah; and the idiom is also found in Akkadian and Latin.

6. This concluding verse is similar both in form and sense to vv. 1–2. Gordis regards it as a warning against idleness; but, although it is certainly, like vv. 1–2, 4, an encouragement to activity, it is more than that: Qoheleth here gives the reason why one should work hard: it is precisely because the result is uncertain that one should work hopefully and without anxiety. See the comments on the earlier verses mentioned above.

sow your seed: the agricultural theme of vv. 3–4 is resumed. The literal sense—advice to the farmer—is not excluded, but the advice is intended to refer to all kinds of work or activity. (The ancient Jewish view—influenced by the theme of v. 5—that 'sowing seed' here means the procreation of children is fanciful.)

In the morning . . . at evening: there is no need to suppose, with Barton and others, that these expressions are intended to refer to the human life-span—an anticipation of the theme of 11:7–12:7. They refer simply to a full day's work from morning to evening. **at evening withhold not your hand:** *NEB*'s 'do not stop work until evening' expresses the sense correctly. The verb *nûaḥ* in the Hiphil (*RSV*, **withhold**) here as elsewhere means 'cause to rest'. **for:** see on v. 2. **alike:** literally, 'as one'—a late expression.

REJOICE IN THE LIGHT

11:7–8

Some commentators regard these verses as the first part of the section which ends with 12:7 (see also Ogden, *VT* 34, 1984). Their theme is certainly similar to what follows. But they are stylistically different from 11:9–12:7, which is specifically addressed to young men (11:9) and takes the form of a series of imperatives (11:9, 10; 12:1). The key words are **light** and **darkness**.

7. Despite occasional reservations (e.g. 4:2) Qoheleth consistently maintains that life is essentially good because 'where there's life there's hope' (cf. 9:4). **sweet:** the same metaphorical sense is found in 5:12 [MT 11]. **see the sun:** that is, to be alive, as in 6:5; 7:11. Here, however, the phrase is used in more than a conventional sense.

In the Hebrew the first word of this verse is preceded by the connecting particle 'and'. But Qoheleth often begins a new thought or saying in this way (cf. 3:16; 4:4; 8:10; 12:1).

8. Qoheleth's intention here is not to introduce a note of gloom to negate or qualify the cheerful note struck in v. 7, but to use the backdrop of inevitable death to highlight the positive opportunities for joy in this life. **let him rejoice:** better, 'he can have enjoyment'. As long as one lives, the possibility of joyous living remains. **remember:** rather, 'consider' or 'bear in mind', as in 5:20 [MT 19]; 9:15 and 12:1. **the days of darkness:** darkness is a metaphor for death (as light is for life in v. 7) also in 6:4 and frequently in the Old Testament. **All that comes** (*kol-šebbā'*): *(hab)bā'* here means 'that which will happen afterwards': that is, the future (after death). It is then that there will be nothingness or futility. Qoheleth does not mean that because death is certain, *life* is 'vanity'.

MAKE THE MOST OF YOUTH

11:9–12:7

In its present position this passage constitutes Qoheleth's final words to his readers. From a literary point of view it differs from the rest of the book in several respects—sustained poetical form, wealth of imagery, the use of allegory; and this may partly account for its present climactic position (though see on 12:7). But its message—it is a direct address to the **young man** (11:9)—is not essentially different from what Qoheleth says elsewhere.

As in 11:7–8, the thought of the inevitability of death at the end of the poem (12:7) is used as an incentive to make the most of present opportunities. The only important difference between this and other passages with the same theme is that Qoheleth here extends the thought by pointing out that inability to enjoy one's life may in fact begin already in old age, when physical and mental powers begin to fail. This extension of the thought is neither new nor surprising: for the Israelite 'the life of a sick person has become so weak that it no longer deserves the name, and can now only be termed darkness. The power of death has already gained the upper hand over him' (Barth, 1947, p. 101). The detailed allegorical description of failing health (12:1*b*–6) is intended to reinforce the positive advice given in 11:9–12:1*a*. The description of death itself in 12:7 is expressed in completely conventional and orthodox terms with no negative overtones: death is a normal event, simply the withdrawal, after a period, of a gift of God (cf. Job 1:21, and see Martin-Achard, 1956, pp. 23–7).

9. **walk in the ways of your heart and the sight of your eyes:** that is, do whatever seems good to you. This sounds like pure hedonism; but in view of such passages as 2:24–26; 3:12–13, 22; 5:18–20 [MT 17–19]; 9:7, 10, and Qoheleth's frequent castigation of foolish conduct, this is improbable. Rather this is an elaboration of the immediately preceding recommendation to make the most of life. **let your heart cheer you:** compare the use of this phrase in 7:3. **the sight of your eyes:** see on the same phrase in 6:9 (read the singular *mar'ēh* with *Qere* and a large number of MSS).

But know . . . judgment: most commentators including Zimmerli, Galling and Lauha regard this as an addition made by the editor who made a similar statement in 12:14. They suppose that it was added to correct or prevent a misunderstanding of the first part of the verse. However, Gordis (who translates *wᵉdā'* as '*And* know') argues that what God will judge is *failure* to take full advantage of **all these things** which he has given to man to enjoy. This interpretation is supported by other passages (e.g. 9:7) in which Qoheleth asserts that God regards man's enjoyment of his life as his 'lot', that is, his proper function (e.g. 5:18–19 [MT 17–18]; 9:9). Hertzberg also accepts the authenticity of these words, but regards them as intended to modify the preceding advice with a warning not to exceed the bounds of what God will approve, for God *does* make judgements on the living (3:17), and the wise man will know his limitations and not act on impulse but 'will know the time and way' (8:5). The view that **judgment** here means death (Loader) is improbable.

10. **pain** (*rā'āh*): better, 'misery'. This advice is basically the same

as in v. 9, but expressed negatively. **from your body:** literally, 'from your flesh'. The phrase means little more than 'from yourself' (see on 5:6). **the dawn of life:** in Hebrew this is a single word, *haššaḥᵃrût*. It occurs only here. It is not certain whether it is derived from a root meaning 'dawn' or from another meaning 'black'. If the latter, it refers to the black hair of youth (cf. *śêbāh*, 'old age', literally 'grey hair').

vanity: as many commentators agree, *hebel* here means what is fleeting or ephemeral rather than 'vanity' (see on 1:2–3, and cf. 6:12; 9:9).

12:1. Remember: rather, 'consider', as in 11:8, or, perhaps better, 'obey' (see Childs, 1962, pp. 45–65). **your Creator:** the apparently plural form *bôrᵉ'e(y)kā* has been variously explained as the so-called 'plural of majesty' (GK § 124k) or as the consequence of a confusion between Lamedh Aleph and Lamedh He verbs (GK § 93ss; 75nn-rr). This reference to the Creator—the only occurrence of *bārā'*, 'to create', in the book—has been thought by some commentators to be improbable in the context; and various emendations and alternative explanations have been proposed, among them emendation to *bôrᵉkā*, 'your cistern', thought to mean 'your wife' in view of the use of this word as a metaphor for 'wife' in Prov. 5:15 (cf. 18). The sentence would then be a recommendation of the enjoyment of marital relations (cf. 9:9). But in fact 'Creator' is extremely appropriate in view of Qoheleth's teaching elsewhere that the enjoyment of life is God's will (cf. Gordis's interpretation of 11:9). To enjoy life is to obey God, who created the world in this particular way, and indeed actually requires such an attitude.

evil days: that is, days of misery such as are described in vv. 2–6. **I have no pleasure in them:** compare the words of the aged Barzillai in 2 Sam. 19:34–35 [MT 35–36].

2–6. These verses have been regarded since ancient times as an 'allegory of old age'; but there has been no agreement about the precise nature of the allegory. The series of images of which it consists has been variously taken to be a series of metaphors describing the increasing decrepitude of old age in terms of the loss of physical and mental faculties, or of the coming of night, or of the gradual falling into ruin of an old house; and in other ways. None of these hypotheses, however, can be wholly sustained without straining the sense of some of the items in the list. A number of recent studies of the passage (notably Sawyer, 1975; Witzenrath, 1979; Gilbert, 1981) have recognized that since the essence of an allegory is that it consists of a *coherent* series of metaphors forming a consistent whole, this is not an allegory. Rather the imagery, though creating an impressive effect, is varied and derived from different sources. It is therefore necessary to take each image separately and to attempt to decide its particular reference. That they all refer in some way to old age, however, can hardly be doubted: Sawyer's theory that vv. 2–5 have nothing to do with old age, but are an independent 'parable on the fate of human efforts in a topsy-turvy world' (p. 531) using the imagery of a house fallen into ruin is ingenious but unduly speculative.

2. The imagery here is taken from the Palestinian winter. Usually the winter rainstorms were followed by blue skies. The unexpected **return** of **the clouds** soon after a storm, once more shutting out the light, is a bad sign and brings gloom, both literally and psychologically (see Hertzberg, 1957, p. 115 on this phenomenon). The imagery of unrelieved darkness may stand for the gloom into which the elderly may fall (cf. the loss of 'pleasure' in v. 1), or a failure of eyesight—though this is expressed through a different metaphor in v. 3.

The occurrence of **light** in the list of heavenly bodies is strange. This may be a hendiadys meaning 'the bright stars'.

3. There can be no doubt that these metaphors refer to a **house** or palace and its inhabitants. The imagery is continued in v. 4. It is not clear whether this is a household falling into decay or a house struck by a violent storm. The latter interpretation would preserve a continuity with v. 2, but some of the imagery is difficult to interpret in that sense. Most commentators see in each metaphor a reference to a part of the body: **the keepers of the house** are the trembling hands of the old man, **the strong men** are the bones, **the grinders** are the teeth, and **those that look through the windows** are the eyes. It has been argued, however, that this is a generalized description, and that no such detailed identifications are intended.

In their literal meaning **the keepers of the house** are the servants who guard it; **the strong men** may be the masters, but are probably the stalwart men-servants; **the grinders** (feminine) are the women making the flour for the household's bread; **those** (feminine) **that look through the windows** are probably the ladies of the house who peer through lattices to avoid being seen by men in the street. The verbs, however, do not entirely fit the imagery of the threatened house: it is not clear why the strong men should, under those circumstances, be **bent**, why it should be said that the mill-girls should **cease because they are few**, or what is meant by saying that the ladies of the house **are dimmed** or darkened. There seems to be a confusion or alternation in the verse between the metaphors and the realities which they represent.

4. and the doors . . . shut: the metaphor of the house is continued. The **doors** would be shut either against a storm or because the normal activity of the household has ceased. In view of the supposed reference in the last part of v. 3 to the teeth and the eyes, and the allusion to **sound** in the phrase which follows, it may be—if the theory of the parts of the body is correct—that the doors are the ears. To close the ear (a different verb is used) means not to hear in Prov. 21:13; and to uncover (*gālāh*), that is, open the ears of others, frequently means to cause them to hear. **doors** (on the dual form see GK § 93n): literally, 'double doors', only found at the entrance to cities, temples and exceptionally grand houses.

when the sound of the grinding is low: the word *ṭaḥ*ᵃ*nāh* (**grinding**) occurs only here. It is cognate with *ṭōḥ*ᵃ*nôt*, 'grinders', in v. 3 and probably means 'mill'. This phrase appears to be misplaced from v. 3, unless the meaning is that imperfect hearing fails to pick up the now reduced noise from the mill.

At this point the metaphor of the house is abandoned, and there begins what appears to be a series of allusions to general signs of old age. The interpretations which have been offered of this passage (up to **desire fails** in v. 5) are very speculative, as most of the modern commentators agree. Various emendations have been made, but none of these carries great conviction.

one rises up at (or, 'to') **the voice of a bird** (or, in view of the article, '*the* bird'): among other interpretations this has been taken to mean either that the elderly get up early in the morning (*qûm*, 'rise up' is frequently used in this sense) as soon as the birds begin to sing because they cannot sleep, or that their voice becomes high like that of a bird. *NEB*, emending *w*ᵉ*yāqûm l*ᵉ*qôl* to *w*ᵉ*yiqmôl qôl*, has 'the chirping of the sparrow grows faint'.

daughters of song: this may be a poetical way of referring to female singers, whom the aged Barzillai stated that he was no longer able to hear (2 Sam. 19:35 [MT 36]), or to song-birds (cf. a similar circumlocution in 10:20), or to musical notes. The use of the verb *šḥḥ* (Niphal) (**are brought low**) here may suggest that the reference is to the loss of the ability to sing: the Niphal of this verb occurs in Isa. 29:4, where it is predicted that 'Ariel' (Jerusalem) will be so weakened that its voice will come feebly out of the ground (Gilbert, p. 104 and note 11). The phrase ought therefore perhaps to be rendered 'and all the singing notes are enfeebled'.

5. As all the modern commentators agree, the first part of this verse (to **way**) is a straightforward description and presents no difficulties. The elderly are afraid of heights, or of walking up slopes or stairs, and are also easily frightened by real or imaginary obstacles met with when they are out walking along the road (**in the way**). The word *ḥatḥattîm*, **terrors**, found only here but cognate with the verb *ḥtt*, 'to be terrified', was probably chosen because its redupli-

cated form suggests *extreme* fear. **they are afraid:** the plural of the verb is strange. The plural ending may be a case of dittography: the next word begins with the same letter.

The middle section of this verse (from **the almond tree** to **desire fails**) is among the most difficult passages in the book. **the almond tree blossoms** (*yānē'ṣ*): most modern commentators, following the almost complete consensus of the Versions, derive this verbal form from *nṣṣ*, 'to blossom', with an additional vocalic aleph characteristic of some late Hebrew orthography (cf. GK § 73g). It is, however, possible that the consonantal text was intended to be read as a form of *n'ṣ*, 'to despise', and that the *Qere* represents an alternative reading *yānēṣ* (without the aleph). This possibility was pointed out by Ibn Ezra, and was accepted by many early commentators and by some more recent ones (e.g. Ginsburg). It has recently been revived by Gilbert. 'He despises the almond tree' or 'the almond tree is despised' would mean that the loss of the sense of taste in old age makes even the almond, a particularly delicious dish, unattractive. The more common interpretation is that the almond blossom stands for the coming of white hair in old age. It has been further suggested that there is a certain irony here in that the almond tree is the first to blossom, in early spring.

the grasshopper (or 'locust') **drags itself along:** if this is the correct meaning, the phrase is most likely to refer to the awkwardness or painfulness of the bodily movement of the aged. The verb *sbl* means to bear a burden or be weighed down; the Hithpael, which only occurs here, could signify 'makes itself a burden'. Some commentators have seen here a reference to the enormous appetite of the locust, which becomes weighed down by its full stomach and moves as if weighed down by a heavy burden (LXX and some other Versions render the verb by 'swell, grow fat'). The Talmud saw here a reference to the failure of arousal of the male sexual organ in old age.

and desire fails: *RSV*'s rendering of these two words is an interpretation rather than a translation. The word *'abiyyônāh* (**desire**) occurs in the Old Testament only here; but its occurrence in later Hebrew and its rendering in the Versions confirm that it means 'caper', that is, the plant *capparis spinosa* (the word 'caper-berry', found in some English commentaries, does not appear in the English dictionaries). The fruit of this bush ('capers') is used as a flavouring, to stimulate the appetite. It has been suggested that Qoheleth is referring here, however, to its supposed aphrodisiac qualities (hence *RSV*'s 'desire'). The word is often taken to be derived from the verb *'ābāh*, which supposedly means 'to desire', from its frequent use with the negative in the sense of being unwilling to do something (it never means 'desire' when it appears in other contexts); but this derivation is uncertain (so *KBL*). In fact the idea that the caper has aphrodisiac qualities does not appear in extant literature earlier than the mediaeval Jewish commentaries (see Ginsburg, pp. 463–4). It is probably best, therefore, to take the phrase simply as referring to lack of appetite (Gilbert, pp. 105–6).

An alternative but less probable interpretation of the central part of the verse is to take the imagery as descriptive of the renewal of nature each year: the almond tree blossoms again, the grasshopper gorges itself, and finally the caper bears its fruit (deriving the verb *tpr* [*RSV*, **fails**] not from *prr* but taking it as an anomalous shortened form from *prh* 'to bear fruit'). The verse then continues: but (*kî*, *RSV*, **because**) *man* experiences no such revival: his death is the end of him.

The last part of the verse is again straightforward. **eternal home:** that is, the grave. This expression occurs only here in the Old Testament, but the Greek Book of Tobit similarly speaks of the 'eternal place' (3:6), and corresponding expressions are found in Egyptian literature and also in the Talmud, the Quran and in some non-Hebraic Semitic inscriptions. **mourners:** that is, hired mourners; cf. Am. 5:16; Jer. 22:18; 34:5. **go about the streets** (singular 'street' in Hebrew): this may mean that they gather and walk up and down in front of the house of the dying man in the hope of employment.

6. before: this word, which has already recurred twice (vv. 1, 2) in this extremely lengthy sentence, resumes the main line of thought which had been somewhat obscured by the series of images which began with **in the day when** (i.e. vv. 3–5). The whole passage from **Remember also your Creator** in v. 1 is a single sentence which, after the original admonition, consists entirely of a long series of temporal adverbial clauses which give reasons for it.

These four metaphors signifying death probably divide into two pairs which refer respectively to the cutting off of two necessities of life, light and water. All the verbs denote irreversible destruction.

The **silver cord** and the **golden bowl** should probably be taken together as referring to an oil lamp suspended on a cord. **is snapped:** this rendering is based on a widely accepted emendation. The *Kethibh* reads *yērāḥēq*, 'is removed'; and the *Qere yrtq*, despite ingenious attempts to connect it in some way with *rātaq*, 'bind' or *rattôq*, 'chain' (Gordis), hardly yields a meaning appropriate to the context. *RSV* follows commentators who, on the evidence of Vulg. and Pesh., emend the word to *yinnātēq*. **is broken** (of the **golden bowl**): better, 'is crushed'. This may be the imperfect Qal of *rāṣaṣ* (see GK § 67q); but this verb is not elsewhere intransitive, and the word should perhaps be repointed as the Niphal *tērōṣ* (see GK § 67t). The meaning is unchanged.

A golden lamp with a silver cord would obviously be found only in the most luxurious houses. This emphasis on luxury is perhaps intended to make the point that even great wealth cannot protect its possessor from the common fate.

The second pair of metaphors refers to accidents which prevent the drawing of water. **fountain:** better, 'spring' as in Isa. 35:7; 49:10, the only two other occurrences of the word in the Old Testament. **broken** (of the **wheel**): on this form see GK § 67t. **wheel:** used for raising water from a well, or from a **cistern** in which rainwater was stored (the word may mean either).

7. Qoheleth now abandons metaphor and states plainly the traditional view about what happens at death. It is generally agreed that this verse was written with Gen. 2:7 and 3:19 in mind. On the meaning of **the spirit**, see on 3:21. There is no question of an entity called 'the spirit' which survives death: the two components of all living creatures, the body, which was fundamentally only **dust**, and the breath, which God had breathed into it giving it life, part company and cease to have separate identities. Contrary to the opinion of Lauha, there is here no contradiction with 3:21, where also the traditional view holds good. **returns:** on the jussive form standing for the imperfect see GK § 109k.

to God who gave it: whether the present arrangement of the book is the work of an editor or of Qoheleth himself, it is not an accident that these are the final words of Qoheleth in the book. This long sentence begins with a reminder that life should be lived in the awareness of dependence on the Creator (v. 1), and ends with a further reminder that creatureliness implies mortality. To the Israelite death 'in a good old age . . . and full of years' (Gen. 25:8) was not a matter for regret, even though it was mourned by the survivors. Life was a gift from God for which one should be thankful; but it was in the nature of human existence that it should be a temporary gift which God would one day withdraw. Qoheleth never reproaches God for ordaining things in this way. It is characteristic that these should be his final words, echoing the theme of God's gift which recurs again and again throughout the book.

EDITORIAL CONCLUSION

12:8

This verse is virtually identical with 1:2: the only differences are that 'Qoheleth' has the article and that **vanity of vanities** occurs only once (a few MSS and Pesh. have it twice, but MT is certainly correct). On the function of these two verses as a framework to the words of Qoheleth see on 1:2. On the form *haqqōhelet*, see the Introduction, p. 2, and the comment on 7:27.

EPILOGUE

12:9–14

It is universally agreed that this final section of the book is the work not of Qoheleth but of one or more persons who were familiar either with the book in its present form or at least with its contents. A further step was taken by some commentators, who suggested that the epilogue is the work of an editor or editors who gave the work its present shape. (On the view that the epilogue, or part of it, is in fact a colophon, see Fishbane, 1985, pp. 27–32.)

There is good reason to suppose that there are in fact not one but two separate 'epilogues' here: vv. 9–11 and 12–14 respectively. The first of these praises Qoheleth uncritically, while the second appears to be attempting to soften the effect of his teaching on the readers by emphasizing what it regards as its more edifying features. Some commentators (e.g. Galling, Lauha) go further in suggesting that it was this epiloguist who himself inserted these features, often thought to be inconsistent with the rest, into the book, in order to present Qoheleth in a more 'orthodox' light.

There can be no proof of the correctness of these theories about the editorial work of the second epiloguist. In this commentary the view has been taken that virtually the whole book from 1:4 to 12:7 is the work of Qoheleth, and that the supposed inconsistencies can be explained in other ways (see the commentary on 2:26; 3:17; 8:10–15; 11:9). In some cases these passages are quotations made by Qoheleth with which he did not himself agree, while others represent hesitations or even inconsistencies within his own mind (see the Introduction, pp. 5–6, 17–19, 21). It cannot be too strongly emphasized that complete consistency in a work of this kind is hardly to be expected.

9–10. These verses contain the only direct information about

Qoheleth's life and activities. It is most natural to suppose that they were written by a personal acquaintance, for example a former student or admiring colleague.

9. **Besides being** (*wᵉyōtēr še-*): the root *ytr* signifies 'to remain over' (see on 1:3), and *yōtēr* is used elsewhere in this book in the sense of 'advantage' (6:8; 7:11) and as an adverb meaning 'very' (2:15; 7:16). Here it is used with *še-* ('that') as a conjunction meaning **Besides** or 'in addition to' (so Gordis and many earlier commentators). This interpretation is more probable than 'moreover' (Hertzberg, Galling, Lauha), an interpretation which does not adequately account for the particle *še*. There are thus two distinct statements about Qoheleth here: first, he was **wise** (*ḥākām*); secondly, he **taught the people knowledge**. What is meant by his **being wise** is clear from many passages in the book (e.g. 1:13; 2:15, 19; 7:23). Qoheleth himself never uses the word *ḥākām* to mean a professional teacher but employs it in a quite general sense as in the Book of Proverbs, often in contrast with the 'fool' (2:14, 16; 6:8; 7:4, 5; 10:2, 12), and there is no reason to suppose that the epiloguist is using it in a different sense (see Whybray, 1974, pp. 47–8).

also: this word (*'ôd*) has several meanings. Some commentators take it as meaning 'always' or 'regularly, continuously' here; but *RSV*'s translation is correct (see on 3:16). **taught the people knowledge:** like Ben Sira (Sir. 37:22–26) the epiloguist has a high regard for a wise man who does not keep his wisdom to himself but instructs others.

The three verbs which follow constitute a third statement about Qoheleth's activities. There is no justification for translating them as participles (**weighing, studying** and **arranging**): in the Hebrew all the verbs are in the perfect tense and are joined to the preceding clause by 'and'—so 'and he weighed' etc. This is a statement about Qoheleth's purely literary activity.

weighing: this verb, *'zn*, occurs only here, but is almost certainly cognate with *mô'zᵉnaim*, 'scales, balances' (rather than with *'ōzen*, 'ear', as supposed by the Versions). It here means 'weighed' in the sense of 'assessed' or 'tried out'. **studying:** this verb, *ḥqr* (only here in the Piel) means, in the Qal, to search, explore or examine. Here it could therefore mean that Qoheleth searched for proverbs in order to form a collection of them: but since in the Hebrew text of Sir. 44:5 it appears to refer to (musical) composition, it may mean here that Qoheleth actually composed proverbs after diligent study. (The Piel form in all three verbs probably implies intense concentration on the work.) **arranging:** *tqn*, the third verb in the series, lacks the conjunction 'and'; but there is no reason, with some commentators, to suppose that it is a subsequent addition to the series. It may mean 'arrange' (see on 1:15); but in rabbinic Hebrew it can mean 'set in order' or 'establish, ordain'. In Sir. 47:9 (Hebrew text) it may mean 'compose (music)'. Taken together, these three verbs may refer to the stages in the process of literary composition: experimenting with, working on, and shaping proverbs. (For a somewhat different interpretation, see M. Fishbane, 1985, pp. 29–32.)

The meaning of *mᵉšālîm* (**proverbs**) is not restricted to brief sayings but also comprises longer compositions of various kinds as well: cf. Ps. 49:4[5]; 78:2 (*RSV*, 'parable'). **with great care:** this is presumably a rendering of *harbēh*, which in other passages in the book means 'much' or (as in 5:7 [MT 6]; 11:8) 'many'. There is no reason to doubt that it means 'many' here.

10. The repetition of *qōhelet* (**The Preacher**) may suggest that this verse and v. 9 were written by different persons. However this may be, this verse expands the thought of v. 9 with regard to Qoheleth's literary work, and perhaps also to his oral teaching. It is an extremely favourable comment on his care for elegance of expression and on the honesty and truth of his writings.

pleasing words (*dibᵉrê ḥēpeṣ*): literally, 'words of delight'. Qoheleth uses *ḥēpeṣ* in this sense in 5:4 [MT 3]; 12:1, and it frequently has this meaning elsewhere in the Old Testament. Compare the phrases 'stones of delight' (i.e. precious stones) in Isa. 54:12, and 'land of delight' in Mal. 3:12. These analogies show (*pace* Galling) that the writer is referring to the aesthetic quality of Qoheleth's literary style.

uprightly: the noun *yōšer*, 'uprightness, honesty', is here used as an adverb: see GK § 118m, q. **he wrote:** this is clearly the meaning, but MT has the Qal passive participle *kātûb*, 'written'. Some MSS have *kātab*, 'he wrote'. Alternatively it has been suggested that the word should be pointed as the infinitive absolute *kātôb*, standing for the perfect tense (GK § 113y, z). The meaning 'he wrote' is supported by several of the Versions.

11. The first part of this verse (to **collected sayings**) is probably a current wisdom saying about the value of wisdom teaching in general, quoted here to confirm the appreciative statements in vv. 9–10 about the merits of the teaching of Qoheleth: he was himself a worthy example of such 'wise men'. On the meaning of **the wise** (or rather, of 'wise men'—there is no article here: cf. the same phrase *dibᵉrê ḥᵃkāmîm* in Prov. 22:17; 24:23), see on v. 9.

This saying is in chiastic parallelism. In the first half the wise men's words are compared with ox-**goads** (the word occurs only once elsewhere in the Old Testament—1 Sam. 13:21, if the text is correct—and in a slightly different form, but the meaning is clear from rabbinic usage) which were used to drive cattle in the same way that spurs are used in riding. Their function is thus through persuasion to spur their audience or readers to action: that is, to base their conduct on their advice. Comparable imagery about the words of wise men is found also in Proverbs, e.g. in Prov. 13:14, where 'the teaching of a wise man is a fountain of life'.

collected sayings forms a good parallel with **The sayings of the wise** and may be correct, but the phrase (*ba'alê 'asuppôt*) is not without difficulties and has been interpreted quite differently by some commentators. *'asuppôt* occurs only here in the Old Testament, although a masculine form *'asuppîm* is found in 1 Chr. 26:15, 17; Neh. 12:25 in the sense of 'stores' or 'storehouse'. The verb *'āsap* means to gather or collect, and is used with regard both to objects and persons. The whole phrase occurs in the Talmud in the sense of 'assemblies of scholars'; and this has led some commentators (e.g. Galling) to take it here as meaning 'leaders of learned assemblies' who might be the editors of wisdom sayings. The question turns on the meaning of *ba'alê* here. The translation **collected sayings** assumes that *ba'al*, which has a wide range of meanings, can refer to the individual items in a collection of sayings (cf. 'participants in—or, 'members of'—a covenant', Gen. 14:13). If so, *RSV* may be correct; but there is some doubt whether the word can be used in this sense of inanimate objects. **firmly fixed:** literally, 'planted'. This second simile complements the first: the teaching of the wise or learned such as that of Qoheleth may be said both to spur its recipients to action and to constitute a reliable basis for life.

which are given: there is no relative particle in the Hebrew. This seems to be a new sentence: 'They were given . . .'. It is appended to the previous saying and may be a subsequent addition. **Shepherd:** the capital letter in *RSV* shows that the translators understood the 'shepherd' to be God. This is the opinion of the majority of commentators and translators. If it is correct, the meaning of the sentence is that the ultimate source of the teaching of wise men is God himself, who is called a shepherd elsewhere in the Old Testament. However, there seems to be no good reason why this epithet should be used of him in this context, whether this sentence is an original continuation of the first part of the verse or not. **one:** this apparent assertion of the oneness of God also seems to be made with no obvious reason. However, no plausible alternative interpretation of the sentence has been offered. Galling's proposal that *rō'eh*, 'shepherd', should be repointed as *rē'eh*, 'friend' and the whole translated by 'They were transmitted by a certain friend', meaning the writer himself, lacks plausibility and has not found favour.

12. This verse, probably the work of a different writer (see above on 12:9–14), makes no reference to Qoheleth but warns the reader against an increasing spate of literature which the author regards as harmful. These books cannot be identified; whether this is a warning against Qoheleth's own book among others cannot be determined.

beyond these: literally, 'in addition to these things' (see on v. 9 for the meaning of *weyōtēr*). The phrase, which stands at the beginning of the verse, is simply an announcement of a further piece of advice. It does not refer to the teachings of the wise mentioned in v. 11. **My son:** this form of address by a teacher to a pupil is a standard expression in Proverbs, especially in chapters 1–9. It is never used by Qoheleth himself. The author of this verse clearly regards himself as a wisdom teacher.

The remainder of the verse (from **Of making**) has the form of a wisdom saying. On the syntax of the sentence **Of . . . end**, see GK § 143a. **study:** this word (*lahag*) occurs only here in the Old Testament. Its etymology is uncertain. It may be cognate with Arabic *lahija*, 'to apply oneself assiduously' (Gordis). Others take it to be an anomalous or defective form of the infinitive construct of *hāgāh*, 'to study, meditate'. The reader is warned against poring over unsuitable literature, which will only weary him and do him harm.

13. The first half of this verse (**The end . . . heard**) may have marked the conclusion of the book, the remainder of the verse and v. 14 being a still later addition. There is, however, an alternative rendering of **all has been heard** which would connect the two halves of the verse: *nišmā'* may be not the Niphal (**has been heard**) but, as Vulg. took it, the cohortative Qal, 'Let us hear' (or, 'obey'). The second half of the verse would then have been intended as a summary of Qoheleth's teaching.

Fear God, and keep his commandments: Qoheleth himself frequently advocates the fear of God (3:14; 5:7 [MT 6]; 7:18; 8:12; see the commentary on 3:14), but nowhere makes any reference to keeping his commandments. In associating the two the epiloguist is deliberately interpreting Qoheleth's teaching in terms of the keeping of the Law and thus attempting to represent him as an 'orthodox' wisdom teacher like Ben Sira, who virtually identifies the fear of God and the Law (e.g. Sir. 1:26–28; 2:15–16).

for this is the whole duty of man: the Hebrew has simply 'for this is all men' (cf. the expression *kol-hā'ādām*, 'all men, every one', in 3:13; 5:18 [MT 17]; 7:2). The meaning is that these admonitions *apply* to all men. On the idiom, see GK § 141d, and compare similar expressions in Ps. 120:7 (literally, 'I am peace') and Job 8:9 (literally, 'we are yesterday').

14. will bring every deed into judgment: this phrase is a clear reference to 11:9, which has almost identical words. If the sentence in question in 11:9 is Qoheleth's own work, the epiloguist has here selected another element of his teaching (in addition to the fear of God) for especial emphasis as particularly memorable and important (on the alternative view that the sentence in 11:9 is the work of the epiloguist himself, see above on vv. 9–14). The context shows, however, that he has given the doctrine of judgement a somewhat different nuance: judgement is now to be pronounced on the basis of the criterion of obedience to the Law. Whether this writer is thinking of judgement *after death* (Lauha) is uncertain.

with (*'al*): the parallel with 11:9 suggests that *'al* here also means 'on' or 'concerning'. **every secret thing:** literally, 'everything (which is) hidden'. The epiloguist here picks up (though Qoheleth himself does not use this word) Qoheleth's frequent insistence on man's ignorance. Qoheleth knows that there is no one who does not sin (7:20), but also that the relationship between human behaviour and divine justice is hidden from human knowledge (e.g. 3:11; 8:17). The epiloguist points out here that nothing is hidden from God, who will eventually and inevitably pronounce his judgement.

As with Isaiah, the Minor Prophets and Lamentations, the Masoretes thought this last verse of the book, and perhaps especially the last word, **evil**, too harsh as the conclusion to the whole book, and ordered v. 13 to be repeated after v. 14 when the book was read in public.

INDEX OF AUTHORS

GENERAL INDEX